**Learni** ... ...ding new
... ... a difference to your studies and our
exciting online resources really do offer something
different to students looking for exam success.

This book comes with free MyKaplan online resources so that you can study anytime, anywhere. **This free online resource is not sold separately and is included in the price of the book.**

Having purchased this book, you have access to the following online study materials:

| CONTENT | AAT | |
|---|---|---|
| | Text | Kit |
| Electronic version of the book | ✓ | ✓ |
| Progress tests with instant answers | ✓ | |
| Mock assessments online | ✓ | ✓ |
| Material updates | ✓ | ✓ |

## How to access your online resources

Kaplan Financial students will already have a MyKaplan account and these extra resources will be available to you online. You do not need to register again, as this process was completed when you enrolled. If you are having problems accessing online materials, please ask your course administrator.

If you are not studying with Kaplan and did not purchase your book via a Kaplan website, to unlock your extra online resources please go to www.mykaplan.co.uk/addabook (even if you have set up an account and registered books previously). You will then need to enter the ISBN number (on the title page and back cover) and the unique pass key number contained in the scratch panel below to gain access. You will also be required to enter additional information during this process to set up or confirm your account details.

If you purchased through Kaplan Flexible Learning or via the Kaplan Publishing website you will automatically receive an e-mail invitation to MyKaplan. Please register your details using this email to gain access to your content. If you do not receive the e-mail or book content, please contact Kaplan Publishing.

## Your Code and Information

This code can only be used once for the registration of one book online. This registration and your online content will expire when the final sittings for the examinations covered by this book have taken place. Please allow one hour from the time you submit your book details for us to process your request.

Please scratch the film to access your MyKaplan code.

Please be aware that this code is case-sensitive and you will need to include the dashes within the passcode, but not when entering the ISBN. For further technical support, please visit www.MyKaplan.co.uk

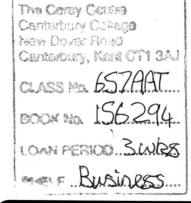

**KAPLAN**
PUBLISHING

# PROFESSIONAL DIPLOMA IN ACCOUNTING

# SYNOPTIC ASSESSMENT

# STUDY TEXT

**Qualifications and Credit Framework**

**AQ2016**

The Study Text supports study for the following AAT qualifications:

AAT Professional Diploma in Accounting – Level 4

AAT Level 4 Diploma in Business Skills

AAT Professional Diploma in Accounting at SCQF – Level 8

**British Library Cataloguing-in-Publication Data**

A catalogue record for this book is available from the British Library.

Published by
Kaplan Publishing UK
Unit 2, The Business Centre
Molly Millars Lane
Wokingham
Berkshire
RG41 2QZ

ISBN: 978-1-78740-522-6

We are grateful to the Association of Accounting Technicians for permission to reproduce past assessment materials and example tasks based on the new syllabus. The solutions to past answers and similar activities in the style of the new syllabus have been prepared by Kaplan Publishing.

This Product includes content from the International Ethics Standards Board for Accountants (IESBA), published by the International Federation of Accountants (IFAC) in 2015 and is used with permission of IFAC.

# CONTENTS

**STUDY TEXT**

**PART A – ACCOUNTING SYSTEMS AND CONTROL**

*Chapter*

**PART B – SYNOPTIC ASSESSMENT QUESTIONS**

## PART C – RECAPS OF CORE KNOWLEDGE FROM UNDERLYING UNITS THAT HAVE SEPARATE UNIT ASSESSMENTS

*Appendix*

# INTRODUCTION

## HOW TO USE THESE MATERIALS

These Kaplan Publishing learning materials have been carefully designed to make your learning experience as easy as possible and to give you the best chance of success in your AAT assessments.

They contain a number of features to help you in the study process.

The sections on the Unit Guide, the Assessment and Study Skills should be read before you commence your studies.

They are designed to familiarise you with the nature and content of the assessment and to give you tips on how best to approach your studies.

## STUDY TEXT

This study text has been specially prepared for the revised AAT qualification introduced in September 2016.

It is written in a practical and interactive style:

- key terms and concepts are clearly defined

- all topics are illustrated with practical examples with clearly worked solutions based on sample tasks provided by the AAT in the new examining style

- frequent activities throughout the chapters ensure that what you have learnt is regularly reinforced

- 'pitfalls' and 'examination tips' help you avoid commonly made mistakes and help you focus on what is required to perform well in your examination.

## ICONS

The chapters include the following icons throughout.

They are designed to assist you in your studies by identifying key definitions and the points at which you can test yourself on the knowledge gained.

 **Definition**

These sections explain important areas of Knowledge which must be understood and reproduced in an assessment.

 **Example**

The illustrative examples can be used to help develop an understanding of topics before attempting the activity exercises.

 **Test your understanding**

These are exercises which give the opportunity to assess your understanding of all the assessment areas.

Quality and accuracy are of the utmost importance to us so if you spot an error in any of our products, please send an email to mykaplanreporting@kaplan.com with full details.

Our Quality Co-ordinator will work with our technical team to verify the error and take action to ensure it is corrected in future editions.

## Progression

There are two elements of progression that we can measure: first how quickly students move through individual topics within a subject; and second how quickly they move from one course to the next. We know that there is an optimum for both, but it can vary from subject to subject and from student to student. However, using data and our experience of student performance over many years, we can make some generalisations.

A fixed period of study set out at the start of a course with key milestones is important. This can be within a subject, for example 'I will finish this topic by 30 June', or for overall achievement, such as 'I want to be qualified by the end of next year'.

Your qualification is cumulative, as earlier papers provide a foundation for your subsequent studies, so do not allow there to be too big a gap between one subject and another.

We know that exams encourage techniques that lead to some degree of short term retention, the result being that you will simply forget much of what you have already learned unless it is refreshed (look up Ebbinghaus Forgetting Curve for more details on this). This makes it more difficult as you move from one subject to another: not only will you have to learn the new subject, you will also have to relearn all the underpinning knowledge as well. This is very inefficient and slows down your overall progression which makes it more likely you may not succeed at all.

In addition, delaying your studies slows your path to qualification which can have negative impacts on your career, postponing the opportunity to apply for higher level positions and therefore higher pay.

You can use the following diagram showing the whole structure of your qualification to help you keep track of your progress.

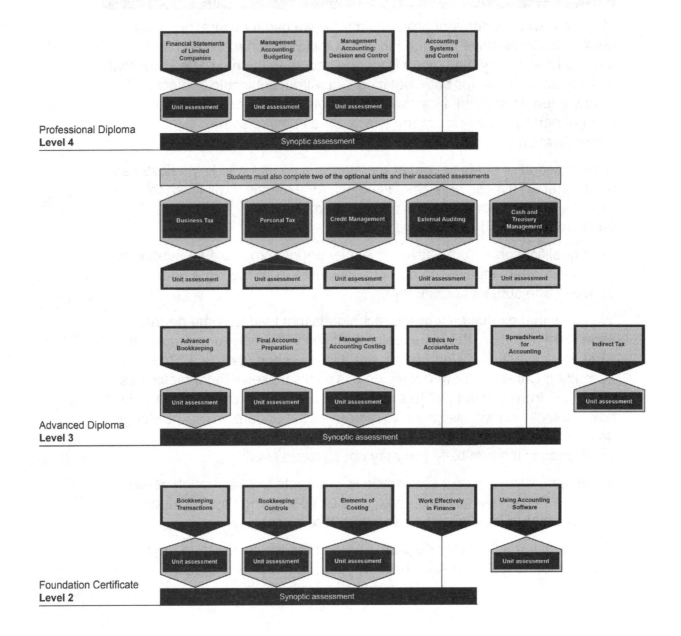

Professional Diploma
**Level 4**

Advanced Diploma
**Level 3**

Foundation Certificate
**Level 2**

# SYNOPTIC GUIDE

## Introduction

AAT AQ16 introduces a Synoptic Assessment, which students must complete if they are to achieve the appropriate qualification upon completion of a qualification. In the case of the Advanced Diploma in Accounting, students must pass all of the mandatory assessments and the Synoptic Assessment to achieve the qualification.

As a Synoptic Assessment is attempted following completion of individual units, it draws upon knowledge and understanding from those units. It may be appropriate for students to retain their study materials for individual units until they have successfully completed the Synoptic Assessment for that qualification.

Four units within the Professional Diploma in Accounting are mandatory. Of these, three are assessed individually in end of unit assessments, but this qualification also includes a synoptic assessment, sat towards the end of the qualification, which draws on and assesses knowledge and understanding from all four mandatory units:

- Financial statements of Limited Companies – end of unit assessment

- Management Accounting: Budgeting – end of unit assessment

- Management Accounting: Decision and Control – end of unit assessment

- Accounting Systems and Controls – assessed within the synoptic assessment only.

## Scope of content

To perform this synoptic test effectively you will need to know and understand the following:

| | |
|---|---|
| Assessment objective 1 | Demonstrate an understanding of the roles and responsibilities of the accounting function within an organisation and examine ways of preventing and detecting fraud and systemic weaknesses |
| Related learning objectives | **Accounting Systems and Controls**<br><br>LO1 Demonstrate an understanding of the role and responsibilities of the accounting function within an organisation<br><br>LO2 Evaluate internal control systems |
| Assessment objective 2 | Evaluate budgetary reporting; its effectiveness in controlling and improving organisational performance |
| Related learning objectives | **Accounting Systems and Controls**<br><br>LO1 Demonstrate an understanding of the role and responsibilities of the accounting function within an organisation<br><br>LO2 Evaluate internal control systems<br><br>LO3 Evaluate an organisation's accounting system and underpinning procedures<br><br>**Management Accounting: Budgeting**<br><br>LO3 Demonstrate how budgeting can improve organisational performance<br><br>**Management Accounting: Decision and Control**<br><br>LO1 Analyse a range of costing techniques to support the management accounting function of an organisation<br><br>LO2 Calculate and use standard costing to improve performance |

**KAPLAN** PUBLISHING

| Assessment objective 3 | Evaluate an organisation's accounting control systems and procedures |
|---|---|
| Related learning objectives | **Accounting Systems and Controls**<br><br>LO2 Evaluate internal control systems<br><br>LO3 Evaluate an organisation's accounting system and underpinning procedures |
| Assessment objective 4 | Analyse an organisation's decision making and control using management accounting tools |
| Related learning objectives | **Accounting Systems and Controls**<br><br>LO1 Demonstrate an understanding of the role and responsibilities of the accounting function within an organisation<br><br>LO2 Evaluate internal control systems<br><br>LO3 Evaluate an organisation's accounting system and underpinning procedures<br><br>LO4 Analyse recommendations made to improve an organisation's accounting system<br><br>**Management Accounting: Decision and Control**<br><br>LO2 Calculate and use standard costing to improve performance<br><br>LO4 Use appropriate financial and non-financial performance techniques to aid decision making<br><br>LO5 Evaluate a range of cost management techniques to enhance value and aid decision making |
| Assessment objective 5 | Analyse an organisation's decision making and control using ratio analysis |
| Related learning objectives | **Accounting Systems and Controls**<br><br>LO1 Demonstrate an understanding of the role and responsibilities of the accounting function within an organisation<br><br>LO2 Evaluate internal control systems<br><br>*(continued on next page)*<br><br>LO4 Analyse recommendations made to improve an organisation's accounting system |

| | |
|---|---|
| | **Financial Statements of Limited Companies**<br><br>LO1 Demonstrate an understanding of the reporting frameworks and ethical principles that underpin financial reporting<br><br>LO5 Interpret financial statements using ratio analysis<br><br>**Management Accounting: Decision and Control**<br><br>LO4 Use appropriate financial and non-financial performance techniques to aid decision making |
| Assessment objective 6 | Analyse the internal controls of an organisation and make recommendations |
| Related learning objectives | **Accounting Systems and Controls**<br><br>LO1 Demonstrate an understanding of the role and responsibilities of the accounting function within an organisation<br><br>LO2 Evaluate internal control systems<br><br>LO3 Evaluate an organisation's accounting system and underpinning procedures<br><br>LO4 Analyse recommendations made to improve an organisation's accounting system<br><br>**Financial Statements of Limited Companies**<br><br>LO1 Demonstrate an understanding of the reporting frameworks and ethical principles that underpin financial reporting<br><br>**Management Accounting: Budgeting**<br><br>LO3 Demonstrate how budgeting can improve organisational performance<br><br>**Management Accounting: Decision and Control**<br><br>LO4 Use appropriate financial and non-financial performance techniques to aid decision making<br><br>LO5 Evaluate a range of cost management techniques to enhance value and aid decision making |

**KAPLAN** PUBLISHING

## Summary

| Underlying paper | LOs required |
|---|---|
| Accounting Systems and Controls | LO1, LO2, LO3, LO4 |
| Financial Statements of Limited Companies | LO1, LO5 |
| Management Accounting: Budgeting | LO3 |
| Management Accounting: Decision and Control | LO1, LO2, LO4, LO5 |

# THE ASSESSMENT

**Test specification for this synoptic assessment**

**Assessment type**

Computer based
synoptic assessment

**Marking type**

Partially computer/
partially human marked

**Duration of exam**

3 hours

| Assessment objective | Weighting |
|---|---|
| **A01**<br>Demonstrate an understanding of the roles and responsibilities of the accounting function within an organisation and examine ways of preventing and detecting fraud and systemic weaknesses | 20% |
| **A02**<br>Evaluate budgetary reporting; its effectiveness in controlling and improving organisational performance | 15% |
| **A03**<br>Evaluate an organisation's accounting control systems and procedures | 15% |
| **A04**<br>Analyse an organisation's decision making and control using management accounting tools | 15% |
| **A05**<br>Analyse an organisation's decision making and control using ratio analysis | 20% |
| **A06**<br>Analyse the internal controls of an organisation and make recommendations | 15% |
| **Total** | **100%** |

# UNIT GUIDE FOR ACCOUNTING SYSTEMS AND CONTROLS

## Introduction

The purpose of the unit is to enable students to demonstrate their understanding of the role of the accounting function in an organisation and the importance of internal controls in minimising the risk of loss. Students will undertake an evaluation of an accounting system to identify weaknesses and assess the impact of those weaknesses on the operation of the organisation.

They will then make recommendations to address the weaknesses having regard for cost/benefit, sustainability and the impact of those recommendations on users of the accounting system. This unit enables students to consolidate and apply the knowledge and understanding gained from the mandatory Level 4 units of Financial Statements of Limited Companies, Management Accounting: Budgeting and Management Accounting: Decision and Control to the analysis of an accounting system.

When organisations have a planned change in policy there will be a transition period, which will present its own challenges. Students need to be able to review a planned change in policy, identify potential problem areas while one system is being changed to another and make suitable recommendations to ensure that the integrity of the accounting system is maintained.

The accounting system affects all areas of an organisation and should be capable of producing information to assist management with decision making, monitoring and control, as well as producing financial information to meet statutory obligations. In this unit, students will demonstrate analytical and problem- solving skills, exercising judgement to make informed recommendations. These are practical skills that are essential to the accounting technician.

Accounting Systems and Controls is a mandatory unit and requires students to have a sound understanding of management accounting and financial accounting information requirements, and the way that the accounting function needs to support both areas.

## Learning outcomes

On completion of these units the learner will be able to:

- Demonstrate an understanding of the role and responsibilities of the accounting function within an organisation

- Evaluate internal control systems

- Evaluate an organisation's accounting system and underpinning procedures

- Analyse recommendations made to improve an organisation's accounting system

## Scope of content

To perform this unit effectively you will need to know and understand the following:

**Chapter**

**1    Demonstrate an understanding of the role and responsibilities of the accounting function within an organisation**

**1.1  Discuss the purpose, structure and organisation of the accounting function**                1,8

Students need to know:

- the difference between financial and management accounting

- the importance of accuracy and cost-effectiveness within the accounting system

- the importance of ethics and sustainability within the accounting function

- why different types and sizes of organisation, or departments within an organisation, will require different accounting information and systems

- the different accounting team staffing structures that will be required by different types or sizes of organisation

KAPLAN PUBLISHING

**Chapter**

**1.2 Discuss the purpose of the key financial reports and their use by a range of stakeholders**      2

Students need to know:

- the purpose and content of statutory financial statements

- the purpose and content of financial information produced for internal use

- the key external stakeholders of an organisation

- how financial information is used by both internal and external stakeholders

- the importance of ethical information and sustainability practices to internal and external stakeholders

Reports

- Income statement

- Statement of financial position

- Statement of cash flows

- Budgetary control reports

**1.3 Examine the impact of relevant regulations affecting the accounting function**      1,2

Students need to be able to:

- identify the types of regulations that affect the accounting function

- explain how the structure of the accounting function supports compliance with external regulations

- assess how the existing structure of the accounting function may need to be adapted to comply with changes in external regulations

**Chapter**

**1.4 Demonstrate an understanding of the impact of management information requirements on the accounting function**                     1

Students need to know:

- how organisational requirements will inform the management information system

- how management information systems should enable the calculation of performance indicators

- why changes may be required to existing systems to meet revised organisation requirements

**2    Evaluate internal control systems**

**2.1 Discuss how internal controls can support the organisation**                     3,4,8

Students need to be able to:

- explain the purpose of internal controls

- assess how a strong system of internal controls can minimise the risk of loss to an organisation

- assess how a strong system of internal controls can ensure ethical standards in an organisation

- identify the types of internal controls used in different parts of the accounting function

- consider how different types of internal controls suit different types of organisations

**2.2 Evaluate how information from the organisation's financial statements may indicate weaknesses in its internal controls**                     5

Students need to be able to:

- use ratio analysis

- use key performance indicators

**Chapter**

**2.3 Examine ways of preventing and detecting fraud and systemic weaknesses**     6

Students need to know:

- the common types of fraud

- the common types of systemic weaknesses and their causes

- the need for segregation of duties

- the financial and non-financial implications for an organisation if fraud occurs

- the role of internal controls in preventing fraud and errors

- the role of internal controls in detecting fraud and errors

**3 Evaluate an organisation's accounting system and underpinning procedures**

**3.1 Examine an organisation's accounting system and its effectiveness**     3,4,6,7,8

Students need to be able to:

- identify the varying financial information requirements of stakeholders (payroll, sales accounting, purchases accounting, general ledger, cash-book and costing systems)

- explain how a fully integrated accounting system enables the extraction of information to meet internal and external reporting and monitoring requirements

- identify how an organisation's accounting system can support ethical standards and sustainability practices

- identify weaknesses in accounting systems that impact on cost-effectiveness, reliability and timeliness

- evaluate impact of weaknesses in an accounting system in terms of time, money and reputation

**Chapter**

**3.2 Evaluate the underpinning procedures of an accounting system, assessing the impact on the operation of the organisation**

3,4,6,7,8

Students need to be able to:

- identify how underpinning procedures in the organisation impact on the operation of the organisation (payroll, authorisation and control of sales, purchases, capital expenditure, overheads, payments and receipts)

- identify how underpinning procedures in the organisation can support ethical standards and sustainability practices

- identify weaknesses in the underpinning procedures and the impact on cost-effectiveness, reliability and timeliness

- evaluate the impact of weaknesses in the underpinning procedures in terms of time, money and reputation

**3.3 Evaluate the risk of fraud arising from weaknesses in the internal control system**

6

Students need to be able to:

- identify the impact of a poor internal control system on the exposure to risk for an organisation

- grade the risk of fraud using either 'low, medium or high' or a numerical grade where the more serious the risk the higher the number

**Chapter**

**3.4 Examine current and planned methods of operating**     3,4,6,7,8

Students need to be able to:

- explain why accounting systems should be reviewed regularly to ensure they are fit for purpose

- identify and review the methods of operating used by an organisation to ensure that they:

    - are cost-effective

    - encourage ethical standards

    - support sustainability principles and practices

- explain that appropriate controls need to be in place during the transition from one system to another

- evaluate a computerised accounting system's suitability for the specific information needs of the organisation

**4     Analyse recommendations made to improve an organisation's accounting system**

**4.1 Identify changes to the accounting system or parts of the accounting system**     7

Students need to be able to:

- identify suitable changes to the accounting system

- explain any assumptions made

- identify problems that might occur during transition

**Chapter**

**4.2 Analyse the implications of changes to the accounting system**                    7

Students need to be able to:

- quantify the costs of recommendations, stating assumptions made

- undertake a cost benefit analysis

- evaluate the implications of the changes to operating procedures and time spent

- review recommendations against ethical and sustainability principles, including social, corporate and environmental issues

- undertake a SWOT analysis

**4.3 Consider the effects of recommended changes on users of the system**                    7

Students need to be able to:

- identify the changes that users may be required to make to working practices to comply with changes to statutory and organisational requirements

- consider different methods of support that can be given to users of the accounting system to assist them in adapting to the recommended changes

**4.4 Justify recommended changes to the accounting system**                    7

Students need to be able to:

- effectively present recommendations to management

- provide a clear rational to support recommendations

# STUDY SKILLS

## Preparing to study

### Devise a study plan

Determine which times of the week you will study.

Split these times into sessions of at least one hour for study of new material. Any shorter periods could be used for revision or practice.

Put the times you plan to study onto a study plan for the weeks from now until the assessment and set yourself targets for each period of study – in your sessions make sure you cover the whole course, activities and the associated Test your knowledge activities.

If you are studying more than one unit at a time, try to vary your subjects as this can help to keep you interested and see subjects as part of wider knowledge.

When working through your course, compare your progress with your plan and, if necessary, re-plan your work (perhaps including extra sessions) or, if you are ahead, do some extra revision/practice questions.

## Effective studying

### Active reading

You are not expected to learn the text by rote, rather, you must understand what you are reading and be able to use it to pass the assessment and develop good practice.

A good technique is to use SQ3Rs – Survey, Question, Read, Recall, Review:

1   **Survey the chapter**

    Look at the headings and read the introduction, knowledge, skills and content, so as to get an overview of what the chapter deals with.

2   **Question**

    Whilst undertaking the survey ask yourself the questions you hope the chapter will answer for you.

**3      Read**

Read through the chapter thoroughly working through the activities and, at the end, making sure that you can meet the learning objectives highlighted on the first page.

**4      Recall**

At the end of each section and at the end of the chapter, try to recall the main ideas of the section/chapter without referring to the text. This is best done after short break of a couple of minutes after the reading stage.

**5      Review**

Check that your recall notes are correct.

You may also find it helpful to re-read the chapter to try and see the topic(s) it deals with as a whole.

## Note taking

Taking notes is a useful way of learning, but do not simply copy out the text.

The notes must:

- be in your own words
- be concise
- cover the key points
- be well organised
- be modified as you study further chapters in this text or in related ones.

Trying to summarise a chapter without referring to the text can be a useful way of determining which areas you know and which you don't.

## Three ways of taking notes

**1      Summarise the key points of a chapter**

**2      Make linear notes**

A list of headings, subdivided with sub-headings, listing the key points.

If you use linear notes, you can use different colours to highlight key points and keep topic areas together.

Use plenty of space to make your notes easy to use.

### 3 Try a diagrammatic form

The most common of which is a mind map.

To make a mind map, put the main heading in the centre of the paper and put a circle around it.

Draw lines radiating from this to the main sub-headings which again have circles around them.

Continue the process from the sub-headings to sub-sub-headings.

### Highlighting and underlining

You may find it useful to underline or highlight key points in your study text – but do be selective.

You may also wish to make notes in the margins.

## Revision phase

Kaplan has produced material specifically designed for your final examination preparation for this unit.

These include pocket revision notes.

Further guidance on how to approach the final stage of your studies is given in these materials.

## Further reading

In addition to this text, you should also read the 'Accounting Technician' magazine every month to keep abreast of any guidance from the examiners.

# The accounting function

## Introduction

The accounting function is an important part of any organisation. It needs to reflect the organisation's needs at all times.

| PERFORMANCE CRITERIA |
| --- |

**1.1** Discuss the purpose, structure and organisation of the accounting function

**1.3** Examine the impact of relevant regulations affecting the accounting function

**1.4** Demonstrate an understanding of the impact of management information requirements on the accounting function

**3.1** Examine an organisation's accounting system and its effectiveness

## CONTENTS

1  Introduction

2  The accounting/finance function

3  Understanding systems

# 1 Introduction

## 1.1 Organisations and the need for control

There are many different types of organisations but they all share the following key characteristics:

 **Definition**

'Organisations are social arrangements for the controlled performance of collective goals'.

The key aspects of this definition are:

- **Collective goals** – organisations are defined primarily by their goals. A school has the main goal of educating pupils and will be organised differently from a company where the main objectives are to make profits and pay dividends to shareholders.

- **Social arrangements** – someone working on his own does not constitute an organisation. Organisations have structure to enable people to work together towards common goals.

- **Controlled performance** – organisations have systems or procedures to ensure goals are achieved.

The key emphasis of the Accounting Systems and Control unit (and the Professional Diploma Synoptic Assessment) is the third of these:

- How do organisations ensure that they achieve their objectives?

- What control mechanisms can they introduce to help managers and other employees work in such a way that the organisation is successful?

## 1.2 Control mechanisms

There are a wide number of ways that control can be used within an organisation, including the following:

- Organisational **structure** – breaking the organisation down into smaller units, such as having a dedicated accounts department, with clearly defined roles, responsibilities and authority. This can be reflected in many ways, such as insisting that all capital expenditure over £1,000 must be authorised by the Finance Director, for example.

- **Target** setting and **budgeting** – so staff know what is expected of them.

- Direct **supervision** of staff by managers.

- The **culture** of the organisation – for example, where mistakes are not tolerated.

- **Self-control** where employees are encouraged to work independently and take responsibility for their own results.

- Control **systems** – for example where actual results are compared to the budget each month and variances produced. These allow managers to identify, and focus on, areas where performance is not as expected and take corrective action.

- Specific control **processes** – for example, Creditors Ledger Control Account reconciliations may identify errors in processing purchase invoices.

---

 **Test your understanding 1**

Jersey Ltd is a small business that manufactures high quality portable loudspeakers. The business is small and has only twenty members of staff, with one supervisor. The work is highly skilled and complex, with staff divided into four teams – each with very different sets of required skills.

Currently there are no control procedures or any work guidance for employees, meaning that each member of staff often works in the way they individually feel is best. The twenty employees are moderately well paid, though there are few, if any, real promotion prospects and several employees have expressed their dissatisfaction with the working conditions within Jersey.

Jersey is owned and run by one person, H. She is concerned that the level of quality of production has fallen in recent months, as evidenced by an increase in wastage and a decrease in output. H is concerned about the effect this is having on the profitability of the company. As such, H is examining the possibility of introducing control processes to ensure that all units made are of adequate quality.

**Task**

Discuss the appropriateness of each of the following possible controls for Jersey:

(a)   Direct supervision of manufacturing staff

(b)   Setting performance targets for employees based on quality of output

(c)   Relying on individual employees to control their own work.

---

In this chapter, and the chapters that follow, we shall look in particular at how some of these impact the running of the accounting function and the role of internal controls within an accounting system.

## 1.3 Organisational structure

Organisational structure is concerned with the way in which work is divided up and allocated and can involve considering the following:

- **The division of responsibility:** some organisations may be split on divisional lines based on geography (e.g. having a 'UK Division'); others will be on divisional lines based on products (e.g. having a 'motorbikes division'), some on functional lines (e.g. having a 'Marketing department') and others a mixture of these elements.

- **The degree of decentralisation:** This refers to the level at which decisions are made.

  In a centralised structure, the upper levels of an organisation's hierarchy retain the authority to make decisions. In a decentralised structure the authority to take decisions is passed down to units and people at lower levels.

  For example, a company may have a division responsible for developing a new mobile phone but the manager concerned may find that all key decisions are made not by themselves but by the main Board of Directors.

  Decentralisation can also refer to where certain functions operate – for example, within a divisional company should each division have its own accounts department (decentralised) or should there be just one at head office (centralised)?

- **The length of the scalar chain:** This is the line of authority which can be traced up or down the chain of command, from the most senior member of staff to the most junior.

  It therefore relates to the number of levels of management within an organisation.

- **The size of the span of control:** A manager's span of control is the number of people for whom he or she is directly responsible.

- **Whether organisations are 'tall' or 'flat':** A 'tall' organisation has many levels of management (a long scalar chain) and a narrow span of control. A 'flat' organisation has few levels of management (a short scalar chain) and a wide span of control.

In order to discuss these issues, it is important to distinguish between authority, responsibility and accountability:

- **Authority:** if an organisation is to function as a co-operative system of individuals, some people must have authority or power over others. Authority and power flow downwards through the formal organisation.

- **Responsibility (for):** the allocation of tasks to individuals and groups within the organisation. It means being held accountable for personal performance and achievement of the targets specified by the organisation's plans.

- **Accountability (to):** the need for individuals to explain and justify any failure to fulfil their responsibilities to their superiors in the hierarchy. It is the extent to which persons are answerable for their actions, the consequences of those actions and the measured effect on end results.

# 2 The accounting/finance function

## 2.1 The role of the accounting function

Accounting is the systematic recording, reporting and analysis of financial transactions within a business. Within this, accuracy and cost effectiveness are critical.

The accounting function affects all areas of an organisation and should be capable of producing information to assist management with decision making, monitoring and control, as well as producing financial information to meet statutory obligations.

Accountants thus have to provide information to very diverse groups, both internally and externally. The specific needs of each determine whether these can best be served by the financial accounting or the management accounting function of the business organisation.

- **Financial accounting** is concerned with the recording and processing of transactions as they occur. Accounts are kept of all receivables' and payables' transactions and of all monies paid by and to the business.

  Coupled with this will be the preparation of the annual accounts in the forms required for both shareholders and HMRC and also periodic financial statements (e.g. cash flow statements, receivable and payable balances, draft monthly profit and loss accounts and statements of financial position). For these there will be the need to incorporate adjustments such as for depreciation, asset valuation, accruals and provisions.

- **Management accounting** involves the preparation and presentation of internal accounting information in such a way as to assist management in formulating policies, planning and controlling activities.

  Based mainly on the information provided by the cost accounts, data is analysed and information is presented to management to provide a basis for decision-making.

  Associated with this will be the operating of systems of budgeting control and standard costing.

  Information requirements could thus involve anything from monitoring inventory levels to monthly variance analysis to setting and monitoring key performance indicators (KPIs).

As you will know, the preparation of cost accounts involves a separate approach from financial accounting and will thus have a separate role in the accounting function.

An **integrated** accounting system combines the needs of external and internal users of the accounts.

This type of system is increasingly common and can be:

- cheaper to operate than two or more separate systems

- provide greater consistency of data

- increase the confidence in the data.

Normally other subdivisions of the accounting function include the cashiers' department and the wages department. The cashiers are responsible for all the transactions involving cash, such as receipts from customers, payments to suppliers and payments of wages. The wages department, in addition to the calculation of remuneration due to employees, will also provide basic data for both the financial and costing systems.

The role of internal auditor ideally should be a separate function but is very often part of the accounting function.

**Note:** Larger organisations may also have a separate **treasury** function. Treasury management is the corporate handling of all financial matters, the generation of external and internal funds for business, the management of currencies and cash flows, and the complex strategies, policies and procedures of corporate finance. These are beyond the scope of your assessment.

## 2.2 Sections in the accounts department

The financial accounts department will be further divided with a supervisor or manager responsible for each section e.g. sales ledger, purchase ledger, credit control and payroll.

Management accounting work will also be divided up with accountants as supervisors of sections responsible for keeping different cost records e.g. materials, production and marketing.

Taking a section of the cost accounts department, we can outline a possible structure:

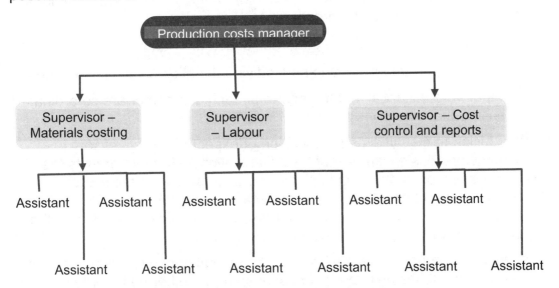

## 2.3 Location of the accounts department(s)

For organisations with different sites, the overall policy on centralisation versus decentralisation and organisational structure will have important effects on the location of the accounts departments.

In some cases the accounting function may be carried out entirely at the head office; in others each location would be responsible for all its own accounting procedures, with only interim and final financial statements being forwarded to head office.

With centralisation there is the opportunity to employ specialist accounting staff and advanced EDP systems more effectively and economically.

When staff are in one central office, supervision may be improved and there is greater flexibility of staff and easier handling of peak loads. However day-to-day control over financial control systems may be lost and there may be delays in the flow of information and documents. In addition head office staff are quite often regarded with suspicion and resentment and there may be the danger of head office becoming out of touch with the peculiar characteristics of the methods of working at each location.

Organisational structure may determine the location of departments. A divisionalised structure with different activities within the group may lend itself to separate accounts departments at each division. On the other hand a major chain of retail stores may install strong control systems at each outlet, with basic data being transmitted daily for processing and reporting by a centrally located accounts department.

## 2.4 Relationships between the accounting function and other departments/functions within the organisation

Within any organisation (when seen as an entity), departments, sections and individuals must all be organised to ensure that:

- the overall objectives of the organisation are attained

- each department, section and individual makes a valid contribution.

It is therefore essential that the efforts of each contributor are co-ordinated to ensure that objectives are met.

In addition to the initial communication of expected objectives to contributors, it is essential that the organisational structure permits the flow of required information in all directions so that the attainment and achievement may be measured or forecast at any one moment. Reporting procedures should ensure that progress is constantly monitored and that the work plan is kept to schedule.

If we briefly consider the role of the accounting/finance function, then we can see that it has an important relationship with other major areas.

Finance has three main roles:

(i)   It is a resource that can be deployed so that objectives are met.

(ii)   An organisation's objectives are often expressed in financial or semi-financial terms.

(iii)   Financial controls are often used to plan and control the implementation of strategies and financial indicators are often used for detailed performance assessment.

The accounting department can be viewed as having responsibility for handling and processing information within the organisation. This information and any control procedures are provided as a service to the other departments.

Other relationships involving the accounting function include the following:

(a)   The marketing department will rely on an analysis of sales by region, sales person, customer or town in order to formulate an advertising strategy or sales promotion effort.

(b)   There is a relationship between the personnel department and the wages department, because employee details must be updated to cover any changes. This relationship could be extended to include the industrial relations officer, who may be employed by the production department and be responsible for initiating these changes.

(c)   The IT department, whether considered part of the accounting function or not, has a very wide span of responsibility in any organisation.

Most of the department managers will expect regular reports from this department and must therefore be in constant liaison with the staff to make sure the information is relevant to their current needs. Any suggestions for changes to the system would be negotiated here.

(d)   The statistician will have responsibilities for providing information on such things as production output, variations from quality standards, comparisons of efficiency in the sales department, analysis of questionnaires for the market research staff and comparative information on wastage of materials from different suppliers.

---

### Test your understanding 2

BBO Ltd makes luxury cakes and desserts. Most of the cakes manufactured are for large food retailers who sell the cakes as their own brand. BBO packages the cakes using the brand required by each retailer. Some cakes and desserts are sold to small independent food retailers, such as hotels and coffee shops, under BBO's own brand. The smaller retailers typically take longer to pay invoices than larger retailers. Currently the Junior Accountants cover the role of credit control between them.

The board of BBO are keen to expand sales to smaller retailers under the BBO brand as margins are higher and they feel that it is important to strengthen BBO brand awareness to help in negotiations with larger retailers.

**Task**

Assess the impact of the proposed expansion on the finance function, highlighting key risks and outlining two ways risk can be mitigated.

---

# 3 Understanding systems

## 3.1 Systems

Before looking in detail at accounting control systems, it is worth considering the wider topic of what is meant by a 'system' and what are typical features of such 'systems'.

The term 'system' can be defined as a set of interacting elements responding to inputs to produce outputs.

Every system, whatever its nature and purpose (e.g. central heating system, banking system, payments system) is a way of viewing a group of components or elements and the way in which they interact.

The elements of a system are outlined in the diagram below.

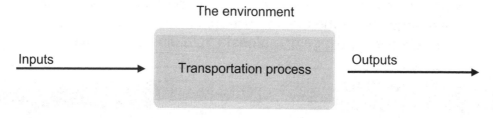

Every system exists within an environment. This is the set of elements that affect the system, but are not controlled by it. The system boundary is the limit of the system; within it is the system and outside it is the environment.

A boundary is often a matter of definition. For example, if the system under examination is 'the whole company' then within the boundary will be found the subsystems of the system, for instance, the employees and procedures contained within departments such as production, purchasing, sales and finance. The sub-systems communicate by passing messages between themselves.

Outside the boundary is the environment, which includes customers, suppliers, the labour market, shareholders, lenders, competitors and the local community as well as more abstract and indirect influences such as the law and the economy.

If we are concentrating on the finance system, then sales, production and purchasing become part of the environment, and within the system boundary will be found smaller subsystems such as product costing, financial accounting and treasury.

Financial accounting staff responsible for the preparation of the annual accounts might rely on the management accounting staff for data about inventory records so as to place a value on closing inventory in the accounts.

The receivables section relies on sales staff to send copies of sales orders or confirmation of goods delivered to customers and on the cashier to pass on information about payments received. It must also co-operate with debt collection staff by helping to prepare monthly statements and lists of aged debtors.

The payables section relies on the purchasing department to send copies of purchase orders and confirm the validity of invoices received from suppliers and also inform the purchase ledger staff about any despatches concerning goods received or purchases returned. The section also relies on the cashier to inform it of all payments of invoices.

## 3.2 The systems approach

The systems that operate within organisations can be viewed in many ways, for example:

- Social systems – composed of people and their relationships
- Information systems – relying on information to support decisions
- Accounting systems – emphasising the organisation's cash flows
- Economic systems – utilising resources to produce economic welfare.

Our focus is solely on the accounting system.

The accounting system receives inputs from other systems (production for example), it converts that data in to meaningful financial information (its output). Clearly anything outside the accounting system is its environment (the wider organisation for example).

## 3.3 Control systems

Organisations have many control systems such as quality control, stock control and budgetary control. Control is the activity that monitors changes or deviations from those originally planned. The control of an organisation is exercised by managers obtaining and using information.

To get a better understanding of control systems, it is useful to start with an example that is in everyday use – a thermostat. All central heating systems contain thermostats to regulate the temperature of the rooms they are heating. The user sets the thermostat to the required temperature on the dial. There is a thermometer in the system, which measures the temperature of the rooms. The room temperature is continually compared with the pre-set temperature on the thermostat dial. If the room temperature is above the dial temperature, the power (e.g. gas) is switched off. When room temperature falls below the dial temperature, the power is switched on.

The elements of a control system are:

- **Standard** – is what the system is aiming for. In the thermostat system it is the pre-set temperature.

- **Sensor** (or detector) – measures the output of the system. In the thermostat system it is the thermometer.

- **Comparator** – compares the information from the standard and the sensor.

- **Effector** (or activator) – initiates the control action. In the thermostat system it is the switch.

- **Feedback** – is the information that is taken from the system output and used to adjust the system. In the thermostat example the feedback is the actual room temperature.

In an organisational system, information about how the system actually performs is recorded and this information is available to the managers responsible for their achievement of the target performance. For effective and accurate control it is essential that timely and efficiently detailed feedback is provided so that corrective action can be taken. This may be a minor operating adjustment or it may involve a complete redesign of the system.

A good example of such a system is variance analysis:

1 Standard costs are developed and a budget produced detailing what should happen – this is the 'standard'.

2 Actual results are measured – this is the 'sensor'.

3 Actual results are compared against budget in the form of variance analysis – this is the 'comparator'.

4 Managers then decide which variances are significant and worth further investigation – this is the 'activator'.

5 Managers can then take appropriate action, whether this is changing the budget or addressing operational issues – this is 'feedback'.

In your assessment you will need to be practical and be focussed on controls within an accounting function, this is covered in more detail in chapter 3.

## 3.4 Systems and procedures best practice

As with most aspects of business administration, there are certain principles that have been built up over a long period. They include the following:

- There should be a smooth flow of work with no bottlenecks.

- Movement of staff should be kept to a minimum.

- Duplication of work should be avoided.

- The best and most effective use of existing specialist attributes should be made.

- Simplicity within systems should be sought. Complications usually lead to misinterpretations and/or mistakes.

- Machines should be used to help staff where appropriate.

Any system must be cost-effective. The benefits should be compared with the cost of implementation and subsequent supervision costs.

The establishment of systems and procedures will ensure that organisational objectives are attained. Data and information are constantly flowing within an organisation, some being generated internally and some stemming from external sources. All of this information must be processed and, to ensure that it is accomplished in the most effective, efficient and economical manner, a system needs to be established.

## 3.5 Systems and procedures manuals

Although they are not always immediately apparent, every organisation has systems, which are usually referred to as 'office procedures' that outline the operations necessary to perform a task associated with the receipt, recording, arrangement, storage, security and communication of information.

Sometimes these procedures are formalised by the preparation of 'laid-down' or written procedures in an office manual format stating the system, as it should be. These written instructions should indicate clearly what is required to be done, when, where and how. The preparation requires careful examination of the systems and procedures. This close attention can only be of benefit in that strengths and weaknesses are revealed.

There are, however, advantages and disadvantages associated with manuals.

A list of the advantages would include the following:

- Supervision is easier.

- It helps the induction and training of new staff.

- It assists the organisation in pinpointing areas of responsibility.

- Once they are written down, systems and procedures are easier to adapt and/or change in response to changing circumstances.

The disadvantages include:

- The expense in preparing manuals both in the obvious financial terms and the perhaps less obvious cost of administrative time.

- To be of continuing use an office manual must be updated periodically, again incurring additional expense.

- The instructions that are laid down in the office manual may be interpreted rather strictly and implemented too rigidly.
Within any organisation it is often beneficial for employees to bring a degree of flexibility to their duties to cope with particular circumstances.

### 3.6    The review of office procedures

Systems should be kept under continuous review and altered as necessary to reflect changes in the organisation, advances in technology, or indeed suggestions from the staff as to how systems can be improved. The decision to review the office procedures could stem from weaknesses that may have already been highlighted (for instance, too much paperwork).

A review may be divided into two parts:

(i)    an overview of the office and the role it plays within the organisation, which will consider:

- the purpose of the office

- what actually happens within the office

- who does what within the office

- the techniques and methods employed by staff in carrying out assigned responsibilities

- the quality of performance

(ii)    a detailed step-by-step examination of the procedures themselves.

The establishment of such information is vital as a first stage. After this a more detailed analysis of the day-to-day routine may be attempted.

In your assessment there is a requirement to consider the impact that changes to the environment might have on the accounting function.  This is considered more specifically in chapter 7.

**KAPLAN** PUBLISHING

## 3.7 Wider environmental factors – legislation and regulations

The law constitutes a set of environmental factors that are increasingly affecting organisations and their decision-making. They can also affect the accounting function. Most of the nations of the world are, or are becoming, regulated economies.

Government, or self, regulation of business has four principal aims:

- **To protect business entities** – e.g. laws putting limits on market dominance by acting against monopolies and restrictive practices and providing financial assistance to selected ailing industries and companies.

- **To protect consumers** – with many detailed consumer protection regulations covering packaging, labelling, food hygiene and advertising, and much more.

- **To protect employees** – with laws governing the recruitment of staff and health and safety legislation that regulates conditions of work.

- **To protect the interests of society at large against excessive business behaviour** – e.g. by acting to protect the environment.

Also at the most basic level, perhaps, laws are passed that enable Government to levy taxes, whereas company law affects the corporate structure of the business and prescribes the duties of company directors.

Managers cannot plan intelligently without a good working knowledge of the laws and regulations that affect their own companies and the businesses they operate in. In addition to those laws that apply generally to all companies, such as laws regulating Corporation Tax or Value Added Tax, there are laws specifically used to deal with individual industries, e.g. Petroleum Revenue Tax in the offshore oil and gas industry.

There is an almost endless list of laws or categories of legislation that affect business enterprises, in domestic, national or international dimensions.

The key point for your assessment is that the accounting system must make provision for the relevant regulation in place at any one time. For example if the VAT rate set by government was to change then the accounting system must change with that.

## 3.8 Regulations affecting accounting practice

The financial statements of limited companies must usually be prepared in accordance with the legal framework relevant to that company, for example:

- The Companies Act 2006 in the UK.

- In addition companies are also required to comply with a generally accepted financial reporting framework, which is the International Financial Reporting Standards (IFRS), which are issues by the International Accounting Standards Board (IASB).

## 3.9 The IASBs conceptual framework

The framework states that the objective of the financial statements is to provide information about the reporting entity that is useful to existing and potential investors, lenders and other creditors in making decision about providing resources to the entity.

The IASB's Framework also suggests that financial statements should have certain qualitative characteristics.

The Framework splits qualitative characteristics into two categories:

(i) Fundamental qualitative characteristics

- Relevance
- Faithful representation.

(ii) Enhancing qualitative characteristics

- Comparability
- Verifiability
- Timeliness
- Understandability.

## 3.10 Generally Accepted Accounting Practice (GAAP)

The concept of GAAP stems from US accounting. In the UK we publish financial statements, which show a 'true and fair' view. In the US the reference is to conforming to GAAP.

Although GAAP is not often referred to in the UK it comprises the whole set of accounting practices which have authoritative support amongst users of financial statements.

There will be crossovers between accounting standards and GAAP where standards reflect GAAP. However, there may be a GAAP that is not represented by a standard.

UK GAAP extends further than accounting standards alone to include the requirements of the Companies Act and The Stock Exchange.

# 4 Further 'Test your understanding' questions

##  Test your understanding 3

1    Outline the structure of your accounting function.

2    Explain quality control as a control system.

3    Outline the elements of a budgetary control system in which the financial performance of a department is compared with the budget.

4    What is the main function of an accounting system?

# 5 Summary

This chapter was a general introduction to systems and the accounting function in particular. It provides the theoretical background than you need to properly understand the relationships that exist for the accounting function.

## Test your understanding answers

 **Test your understanding 1**

**(a) Direct supervision of staff**

Jersey could opt to directly monitor the activities of its staff in order to ensure their work is of appropriate quality. This could be effective at stopping the production of poor quality speakers and the associated waste that would be involved in this. The fact that Jersey only has a small number of staff would also tend to make this approach work well.

However, there would be several problems associated with this control. Firstly, each group of workers has highly specialised skills. This may make it difficult for Jersey's supervisor to understand what each group does and monitor their activities effectively. In addition, the fact that each worker may undertake the same job as their colleagues but using a different technique, will increase the complexity of the monitoring role.

While the workforce is small, there is only one supervisor. They may have insufficient time available to supervise all staff. Hiring of additional supervisors would have cost implications for Jersey.

Finally, additional supervision may have a negative impact on the motivation of employees, who are used to having autonomy over the way they perform their jobs. A sudden change to being closely monitored could cause further job dissatisfaction.

**(b) Performance targets**

Setting performance targets could be of great use to Jersey. This would likely involve offering incentives for staff (such as pay rises and bonuses) depending on how well they perform their jobs. For Jersey, the number of defective units produced by each employee could be measured and a bonus could be offered if this was below a pre-agreed level.

This could be a very practical approach for Jersey, as it links employee rewards with the objectives of the company itself. It should be easy to implement and would prevent the production of units that were defective, reducing waste. The offer of an additional bonus or extra pay may also help to improve general motivation as workers are currently only adequately paid and have few other benefits or prospects.

Note that this may not improve the output of each worker, which is another issue for Jersey. Workers may spend longer on each unit in order to ensure the quality and thus receive their bonus, leading to a further fall in productivity.

**(c)  Reliance on self-control of workers**

Relying on individual staff to monitor their own activities may be problematic. It has the advantage of being cheap for Jersey, as it does not require any further staff to be hired. In addition, the staff are clearly skilled at their jobs, making it easier for them to understand the best way to approach individual tasks.

However, staff seem to be relatively de-motivated. This means that they are less likely to be concerned about the quality of their output. Unless they are offered an incentive by Jersey, there is no reason why they would focus on higher quality production.

In addition, there is no agreed 'best practice' for each of the four teams. Each worker is likely to see their method as superior to those of their colleagues, whether this is in fact correct or not. This means that they are unlikely to change their working practices to ones that would improve output and quality.

Note: this exercise is not indicative of the style of tasks in the synoptic assessment. However, it is useful to help you start thinking about how to control an organisation and what might go wrong. In the sample assessment tasks will focus much more on **accounting** tasks and activities.

**Test your understanding 2**

**The impact of the new customers on the finance function and key risks**

Firstly, there will be a significant increase in the volume of transactions that will need to be processed within the finance team. There are two aspects to this that will need to be addressed: ensuring that there is adequate employee resource to deal with the processing of orders and invoices as well as the ability of our systems to deal with the volume of data.

Secondly, there will be a potential detrimental impact on our cash flows. As we already know our small independent retailers often pay late and it is likely that these new customers follow the same trend.

Thirdly, there will be an increase in the recoverability risk that the business faces. By their nature small independent businesses are more likely to become insolvent or simply cease to trade than larger corporations.

Lastly, and on a positive note, one key impact will be that our brand will benefit from an increased presence in the market. Although this benefit might be limited if hotels and coffee shops simply sell our cakes by the slice or serve our desserts, as the end consumer will be unaware of the fact that it is one of our products.

**Measures to mitigate any additional risk**

1　**Recruit appropriate qualified people for the finance department:**

　It would be sensible to recruit an appropriate experienced and qualified credit controller to ensure that all new customers are assessed as to their credit worthiness and that the receivables are monitored and chased for payment as required in a timely manner.

2　**Ensure sound credit control procedures are in place:**

　All potential customers should be assessed as to their creditworthiness prior to being accepted. This might involve purchasing credit agency reports or performing an internal assessment by looking at financial statements. In addition there should be procedures in place for the regular monitoring of outstanding debts and for chasing up late payments through telephone calls and letters.

## Test your understanding 3

1    This should be based on your own business.

2    Quality control is the control system of setting quality standards, measuring performance against those standards and taking corrective action when necessary. The standard aimed for will depend on the nature of the product, the market for which the goods are produced and the standards achieved by competitors in the same market.

3    The elements of the control system are:

- standard: the budget (e.g. standard costs)

- sensor: the costing system, which records actual costs

- feedback: the actual results for the period, collected by the costing system

- comparator: the 'performance report' for the department, comparing actual with budget (e.g. variance analysis)

- effector: the manager of the department, in consultation with others, takes action to minimise future adverse variances and to exploit opportunities resulting from favourable variances.

4    The main function of an accounting function is to take inputs and convert them in to meaningful accounting information, which is useful to the various stakeholders of an organisation.

# The use of key financial reports

2

## Introduction

For your exam it is vital that you have an understanding of financial statements and management reports and their relevance to the organisation. Much of the information in this chapter will be familiar to you from your Financial Statements of Limited Companies (FSLC), Management Accounting: Budgeting (MABU) and Management Accounting: Decision and Control (MDCL) studies.

| PERFORMANCE CRITERIA |
| --- |
| 1.2 Discuss the purpose of the key financial reports and their use by a range of stakeholders |

## CONTENTS

1 Introduction

2 The purpose of financial statements

3 The purpose of management reports

4 User groups

# 1 Introduction

The accounting function in an organisation fulfils a number of important roles least of which is the supply of information for a variety of uses and users.

Here we shall consider the purpose of key financial reports and their use. Many of the issues covered here have already been discussed in more detail within the 'Financial Statements of Limited Companies' (FSLC) and 'Management Accounting: Budgeting' (MABU) units.

# 2 The purpose of financial statements

## 2.1 Introduction

The main purpose of financial statements is to provide information to a wide range of users.

- The statement of financial position provides information on the financial position of a business (its assets and liabilities at a point in time).

- The statement of profit or loss provides information on the performance of a business (the profit or loss which results from trading over a period of time).

- The statement of other comprehensive income shows income and expenses that are not recognised in profit or loss.

- The statement of changes in equity provides information about how the equity of the company has changed over the period.

- The statement of cash flow provides information on the financial adaptability of a business (the movement of cash into and out of the business over a period of time).

## 2.2 Stewardship

Financial statements also show the results of the stewardship of an organisation.

Stewardship is the accountability of management for the resources entrusted to it by the owners or the Government.

This applies to the financial statements of limited companies as well as to central and local government and government funded bodies such as the National Health Service.

## 2.3 Needs of users

All users of financial statements need information on financial position, performance and financial adaptability. However, many different groups of people may use financial statements and each group will need particular information. Users of financial statements may include investors, management, employees, customers, suppliers, lenders, the government and the public.

- Investors need to be able to assess the ability of a business to pay dividends and manage resources.

- Management need information with which to assess performance, take decisions, plan, and control the business.

- Employees and their unions need information to help them negotiate pay and benefits.

- Customers need to be assured that their supply will continue into the future.

- Suppliers need to be assured that they will continue to get paid and on time and the financial statements will help with this.

- Lenders, such as banks, are interested in the ability of the business to pay interest and repay loans.

- HM Revenue and Customs uses financial statements as the basis for tax assessments.

- The public (especially pressure groups) will look at the financial reports and statements to aid their understanding of profits an organisation may be making from activities to which the pressure group are opposed.

## 2.4 Legal requirements

The law requires limited companies to prepare financial statements annually. These financial statements must be filed with the Registrar of Companies and are then available to all interested parties. Most businesses, whether incorporated or not, are required to produce financial statements for submission to HM Revenue and Customs.

In the UK, the form and content of limited company accounts is laid down within the Companies Act.

The preparation of limited company accounts is also subject to regulations issued by the Accounting Standards Board if the company is still following UK standards or the International Accounting Standards Board if the company has adopted International Standards.

The financial statements of limited companies must usually be prepared within the legal framework relevant to that company.

In the case of UK companies, the Companies Act 2006 (CA06) contains guidance and rules on:

- formats for the financial statements
- fundamental accounting principles
- valuation rules.

The Companies Act has been amended to take account of the companies who have adopted International Financial Reporting Standards (IFRSs). It allows companies to use the format of accounts set out in IAS 1 *Presentation of Financial Statements* if they have adopted IFRS or continue to use the format in the CA06 if they have not.

## 2.5 Evaluating financial statements

As well as looking at key figures (e.g. profit) and movements from one period to another (e.g. revenue growth), the main way of interpreting financial statements is through ratio analysis. This has been covered in a number of units before and is recapped in chapter 5.

# 3 The purpose of management reports

## 3.1 The needs of management

Management accounting provides information for planning, controlling and decision making.

### Planning

Planning involves establishing the objectives of an organisation and formulating relevant strategies that can be used to achieve those objectives.

In order to make plans, it helps to know what has happened in the past so that decisions about what is achievable in the future can be made.

For example, if a manager is planning future sales volumes, he needs to know what the sales volumes have been in the past.

Planning can be either short-term (tactical planning) or long-term (strategic planning).

**Decision making**

Decision making involves considering information that has been provided and making an informed decision.

In most situations, decision making involves making a choice between two or more alternatives.

Managers need reliable information to compare the different courses of action available and understand what the consequences might be of choosing each of them.

**Control**

As discussed in chapter 1, control is often facilitated using 'feedback'.

Here, management prepare a plan, which is put into action by the managers with control over the input resources (labour, money, materials, equipment and so on).

Output from operations is measured and reported ('fed back') to management, and actual results are compared against the plan in control reports.

Managers take corrective action where appropriate, especially in the case of exceptionally bad or good performance.

Feedback can also be used to revise plans or prepare the plan for the next period.

## 3.2 Key reports

The nature of management accounting reports produced varies considerably from one organisation to another but could involve the following:

- Budget reports, detailing budgetary plans for future periods.

- Variance reports comparing actual and budget performance, to facilitate effective control.

- Reports of key performance indicators to ensure that management focus on what is important to the success of the organisation.

- One-off reports that look at individual decisions – for example a report considering a shut-down decision could examine the relevant costs associated with the different alternative courses of action.

Given this, the key issue with any of these reports is whether they are useful to management – are they fit for purpose? This discussed in more detail in the next section.

### 3.3    Evaluating a management report

If you are presented with a management report and asked to discuss it, then you may need to consider some or all of the following:

**The basis of preparation**

It is worth considering why a report has been prepared (planning, control or decision making) and who prepared it.

For example, suppose a manager has produced a future budget for their division to help justify why that division should be given greater investment.

It would be reasonable to suggest that the manager may have been over-optimistic with future forecasts because of the personal benefit they stand to gain from the result.

Note: we are not necessarily suggesting that the manager is acting unethically but simply that they will be biased.

On a related point, it is well known that participation in budgeting and target setting can result in budget padding as managers want to set themselves easy targets, thus increasing their chances of gaining a bonus.

Alternatively, under this heading, you could also consider the experience and qualifications of the person concerned in making future forecasts.

**The methods used**

This is particularly important for reports associated with decision making. As you know, a key concept when making decisions is the use of contribution.

For example, a report that looks at how best to deal with a scarce resource should rank options by looking at the contribution per unit of that scarce resource.

However, if a director in the scenario suggests that we should look at gross profit rather than contribution, then their opinion can be criticised on that basis.

**The figures used**

If a report uses historic figures, then you could question whether these have been verified in any way – for example, are they drawn from audited accounts?

Most reports will include future forecasts and plans. Given this you should look to question any assumptions made.

For example

- If revenue has grown by 3% for each of the last three years, then using future growth of 10% may be unrealistic or over-optimistic unless there are valid reasons for the increase, such as the introduction of new products.

**KAPLAN** PUBLISHING

- If sales volume is expected to grow by 7% but direct materials is only forecast to increase by 5%, then we have a problem as direct materials is a purely variable cost so would be expected to go up in line with production volume. Now this could be due to optimistic budgeting or planned efficiencies due to using better quality materials for example.

- Similarly if sales volume is expected to grow by 7% and administration costs are also budgeted to grow by 7%, then this would be surprising as one would expect a significant proportion of administration costs to be fixed in nature not variable.

- Even with fixed costs you have to be careful – suppose the cost of administration for next year is the same as for last year. This might seem reasonable, given they are fixed costs, except that the impact of future inflation had not been incorporated. Maybe an increase of just a few per cent would be more realistic?

- Are sales expected to increase without any corresponding increase in marketing or other investment? Try to look for cause and effect relationships.

In all of the above you would need to look carefully at the scenario to see what assumptions about the future had been made and whether they could be justified or not.

**The impact on people concerned**

This is particularly important when looking at control:

- Target setting

  If targets are being set, then will they be viewed as fair, stretching but achievable?

  If not, say because they relate to factors outside the manager's control, then the likely result will be that staff are demotivated rather than motivated.

  What level of participation in target setting was involved?

  How much pressure/incentive do managers have to hit targets? If excessive, then control problems could arise.

- Assigning responsibility

  If the report involves variances, then is there an attempt to assign responsibility? Has this been done fairly?

  Has the budget been flexed correctly?

  How aggressive is the tone of the report?

**Test your understanding 1**

Good Choice Hotels runs a chain of hotels throughout the UK.

John Patel (Finance Director) has been reviewing Good Choice Hotels' systems for budgeting and control and has decided to start trying to evaluate more precisely the performance of different aspects of the business – i.e. housekeeping (room cleaning and servicing), the bar, the restaurant and so on. He has designed some performance reports comparing actual results with budget with a view to running some pilots to explore how control could be improved.

On 15th May 20X6 Jane Seagar, the Head of Housekeeping in Hotel 2, received her first quarterly performance report from John Patel, together with an explanatory memorandum. These are given below.

The Head of Housekeeping had not been involved in setting the original budget – that was done by the hotel Manager – had never seen the budget, nor had she (or the hotel manager) been informed that there would be a performance report. She knew she was responsible for her department and had made every endeavour to run it as efficiently as possible, so found the report very upsetting.

> **Memorandum**
>
> To       Jane Seagar, Head of Housekeeping, Hotel 2
>
> From     John Patel, Finance Director
>
> Date     15 May 20X6
>
> Attached is the quarterly performance report for your department for the first 3 months of 20X6.
>
> The company has adopted a responsibility accounting system so you will be receiving one of these reports every quarter. Responsibility accounting means that you are accountable for ensuring that the expenses of running your department are kept in line with the budget.
>
> Each report compares the actual expenses of running your department for the quarter with our budget for the same period. The difference between the actual and forecast will be highlighted so that you can identify the important variations from budget and take corrective action to get back on budget.
>
> Any variation in excess of 5% from budget should be investigated and an explanatory memorandum sent to me giving reasons for the variations and the proposed corrective actions.

**Performance Report: Housekeeping – Hotel 2**
**Three months to 31 March 20X6**

| | Actual | Original Budget | Variation (over)/ under | % |
|---|---|---|---|---|
| Number of guests | 6,850 | 6,570 | (280) | 4.3 |
| Housekeeping expenses | £ | £ | £ | % |
| Cleaning materials | 2,730 | 2,628 | (102) | 3.9 |
| Room consumables – soap, shampoo, tea bags, sugar, milk | 20,750 | 19,710 | (1,040) | 5.3 |
| Cleaning staff wages | 76,000 | 75,000 | (1,000) | 1.3 |
| Head of Housekeeping's wages | 8,750 | 9,000 | 250 | 2.8 |
| Equipment depreciation | 750 | 750 | – | – |
| Laundry costs | 27,300 | 26,280 | (1,020) | 3.9 |
| Allocated hotel costs | 5,200 | 5,000 | (200) | 4.0 |
| Total cost | 141,480 | 138,368 | (3,112) | 2.2 |

**Comment:  We need to have an urgent discussion about your over-spending!**

**Task**

Evaluate the performance report by looking at

- the way it was prepared and who was involved,
- its contents and tone, and
- the effect it had (and could have going forwards) on Jane Seagar.

**Test your understanding 2**

Smalley plc makes and sells three models of specialist lorries – A, B and C - for use by armed forces. The company has a traditional costing system where overheads are absorbed using direct labour hours. Smalley plc normally has sufficient skilled workers to cope with changes in demand but a sickness bug has struck down a third of the workforce and it will be at least a month until the workforce is back at full strength.

Given this, the Directors need to decide how best to utilise the limited resource of skilled labour available over the next month. At the recent Board meeting there were differences in opinion on how to do this:

- Director W argued that the decision was simple – Lorry B has the highest gross profit per vehicle, so should be prioritised.

- Director X felt the company should manufacture in their standard mix to minimise upsetting major customers.

- Director Y put forward the view that contribution was more appropriate as a basis for decision-making.

- Director Z argued that the products should be ranked using contribution per labour hour and supplied the following schedule:

|  | Lorry A | Lorry B | Lorry C |
|---|---|---|---|
|  | £ | £ | £ |
| Selling price per unit | 183,000 | 225,000 | 200,000 |
| Material cost | 68,000 | 110,000 | 85,000 |
| Contribution per lorry | 115,000 | 115,000 | 115,000 |
| Contribution / labour cost | 134 | 153 | 127 |
| Ranking | 2 | 1 | 3 |

Assumptions
- All labour costs and all production overheads are fixed.

**Task**

1. Discuss what the basis of Smalley's decision-making should be, including reference to the views of Directors W, X and Y.

2. An explanation of Director Z's figures, including a discussion of the assumptions she has made.

# 4 User groups

## 4.1 The purpose of accounting

The purpose of accounting is to provide information to users of financial statements. Legally, company financial statements are drawn up for the benefit of the shareholders, so they can assess the performance of their Board of Directors. However, in practice many other groups will use these financial statements. These groups, and their needs, are described below.

## 4.2 Management

Management will be interested in an analysis of revenues and expenses that will provide information that is useful when plans are formulated and decisions made.

Once the budget for a business is complete, the accountant can produce figures for what actually happens as the budget period unfolds, so that they can be compared with the budget. Management will also need to know the cost consequences of a particular course of action to aid their decision making.

One key area of difference between external users and management is the need for management to monitor key performance indicators. These are referred to as KPIs. KPIs vary from business to business and are not in any way regulated.

For example a motor trader might feel that a KPI should be the volume of cars sold. This would then be measured as a KPI. The accounting function would need to accommodate the recording of a KPI as needed.

## 4.3 Shareholders and potential shareholders

This group includes the investing public at large and the stockbrokers and commentators who advise them. The shareholders should be informed of the manner in which management has used their funds that have been invested in the business. This is a matter of reporting on past events. However, both shareholders and potential shareholders are also interested in the future performance of the business and use past figures as a guide to the future if they have to vote on proposals or decide whether to sell their shares.

Financial analysts advising investors such as insurance companies, pension funds, unit trusts and investment trusts are among the most sophisticated users of accounting information. The company contemplating a takeover bid is yet another type of potential shareholder.

### 4.4    Employees and their trade union representatives

These use accounting information to assess the potential performance of the business. This information is relevant to the employee, who wishes to discover whether the company can offer him safe employment and promotion through growth over a period of years. The information is also useful to the trade unionist, who uses past profits and potential profits in his calculations and claims for higher wages or better conditions. The viability of different divisions of a company is of interest to this group.

### 4.5    Lenders

This group includes some who have financed the business over a long period by lending money which is to be repaid at the end of a number of years, as well as short-term payables such as a bank which allows a company to overdraw its bank account for a number of months.

Financial information is also used by suppliers of raw materials, which permit a company to buy goods from them and pay in, say, four to twelve weeks' time.

Lenders are interested in the security of their loan, so they will look at an accounting statement to ensure that the company will be able to repay on the due date and meet the interest requirements before that date. The amount of cash available and the value of assets, which form a security for the debt, are of importance to this group. Credit rating agencies are interested in accounts for similar reasons.

### 4.6    Government agencies

These use accounting information, either when collecting statistical information to reveal trends within the economy as a whole or, in the case of HMRC, to assess the profit on which the company's tax liability is to be computed.

### 4.7    The business contact group

Customers of a business may use accounting data to assess the viability of a company if a long-term contract is soon to be placed. Competitors will also use the accounts for purposes of comparison.

### 4.8    The public

From time to time other groups not included above may have an interest in the company e.g. members of a local community where the company operates, environmental pressure groups and so on.

# 5 Additional 'Test your understanding' questions

##  Test your understanding 3

1   What are the four statements that would be seen in a set of financial statements?

2   What is meant by the term 'stewardship'?

3   Why would a bank look at a set of financial statements?

# 6 Summary

This chapter considered the purpose and evaluation of financial statements and the end users concerned. It demonstrates the role of accounting within the organisation.

## Test your understanding answers

 ### Test your understanding 1

**The way the report was prepared**

**A lack of participation in target setting**

The first problem with the report was the fact that, while the hotel manager was involved in setting hotel budget, the targets involved no participation by the Housekeeping Head. She will feel that this has been imposed upon her.

It is generally agreed that participation in target setting by the Head of Housekeeping would have resulted in targets being seen as more reasonable, targets potentially being more realistic and greater ownership of the targets in the process.

There is a risk that participation may result in staff trying to get easier targets for themselves and budget "padding" but is generally the case that the advantages outlined above outweigh such concerns.

**Communication**

The second problem with the way the report was prepared is that nothing was communicated to the Head of Housekeeping in advance, resulting in the nasty surprise seen. At the very least the idea of a pilot should have been discussed with the Hotel Manager.

Greater communication would also have resulted in greater buy-in from the Hotel Manager, vital if variances are supposed to be subsequently investigated and action taken.

**The report contents and tone**

**Flexing budgets**

The first problem with the figures is that the budget has not been flexed before calculating variances.

To make a meaningful "like for like" comparison the budget figures should be adjusted to reflect the actual number of guests that stayed in the hotel over the period.

Given the actual number of guests was 4% higher than expected it is no surprise that many costs were also higher. Flexing budgets allows you to effectively separate out the volume difference and see what other differences still remain.

For example, looking at cleaning materials, a revised (flexed) target would be

$$2,628 \times 6,850/6,570 = 2,740$$

Compared to this figure the actual cost of 2,730 shows an underspend of £10 rather than an overspend of £102.

However, when flexing one needs to be careful to distinguish between fixed and variable costs – for example, equipment depreciation will be a fixed cost so does not need adjusting before making a comparison.

**Controllable factors**

The second main problem with the content of the report is that it includes many costs that are uncontrollable.

A key principle with responsibility accounting is that people should only be assessed with respect to factors that they can control and/or are responsible for. Being assessed on uncontrollable factors may result in demotivation as someone may fail to reach a target despite performing better than expected.

With the report used for housekeeping, the following costs are uncontrollable:

- Head of Housekeeping's wages – the head cannot set her own salary!

- Equipment depreciation – this will be determined by accounting policies.

- Laundry costs – while the housekeeping team sort what needs to be to the laundry the Head of Housekeeping cannot control either the amount of washing or the prices charged by the Laundry.

- Allocated hotel costs – this will be determined by overall hotel cost control (not just housekeeping) and the method of allocating costs. Neither can be controlled by the Head of Housekeeping.

**Emphasis on financial figures only**

If Good Choice Hotels really wants to evaluate the performance of housekeeping, then reports should also incorporate measures of quality, such as feedback from customer satisfaction surveys.

### Which variances to investigate

A fixed percentage of 5% has been set for investigation – this may not be an ideal system for deciding which variances should be investigated and which should not.

It seems an arbitrary figure and is being applied to all costs.

### The tone of the report

The memorandum has been presented in a somewhat authoritarian style based solely on accounting information and the tone of the final comment is particularly aggressive, implying that the Head of Housekeeping is being blamed for the variances.

### Impact on staff

The lack of participation may result in staff feeling resentment towards what they consider to be unfair targets.

This will be compounded if budgets are not flexed as targets will definitely be seen as unrealistic and unachievable.

If the tone and implied pressure to hit results continues, then staff may put more effort into finding excuses for poor cost control or even attempting to falsify data where possible, rather than focussing on doing a quality job.

The emphasis on financial aspects only may mean that the quality of cleaning falls as staff try to hit cost targets, undermining the customer experience.

### Preliminary recommendations

Before developing the pilot further, you should arrange meetings with relevant managers and staff to explain the concept, its benefits and how it will work going forwards.

If possible, heads should be included in the budget setting process to give greater buy-in and ownership.

The report should have controllable costs only and these should be flexed before variances are calculated. This will make it clearer what the Head of Housekeeping (and other heads) can be held responsible for.

The report should include non-financial data, especially customer feedback, as well to give a more balanced perspective.

**Test your understanding 2**

## 1. Basis of decision making

### Using gross profit (Director W)

The gross profit per lorry would include a share of all production costs and therefore can be said to reflect the profit per lorry after all production costs have been taken into account.

However, there are three main issues with using this measure as a basis upon which to decide the production schedule in this situation.

Firstly, gross profit includes costs that are mostly fixed in nature and therefore have to be incurred irrespective of which products are produced. Decisions should be based on future incremental cash flows.

Secondly, looking at gross profit per lorry in absolute terms does not take into account the fact that we are dealing with a constrained resource here (labour). Whilst, Lorry B might generate the highest levels of gross profit in absolute terms what is more important is how much benefit it generates in terms of a direct labour hour as this is the scarce resource.

Finally, production overheads will have been absorbed into the cost of each lorry based upon budgeted production overhead absorption rates. Given that we have a reduced level of production due to the sickness; it's likely that these rates will increase as overheads need to be shared over fewer lorries.

Therefore in this situation where we have a constrained resource it is not appropriate to base our decision on gross profit per lorry.

### Using contribution (Director X)

Because it's a contribution measure it, by definition, focuses on those production costs which change as the level of production changes. Ultimately contribution is so called because it's what "contributes" towards fixed costs and profit.

It is important when considering a production decision where there is a constraint, that the amount of contribution per unit of that constrained resource is calculated. This is because we need to ensure that we get the maximum benefit from using that resource, by prioritising those products which generate the greatest amount of contribution for each unit of that constrained resource.

In our situation our constrained resource is labour, so contribution per direct labour hour would be preferable.

### Producing in standard mix (Director Y)

The discussion concerning relevant costs and contribution above assumes that the primary objective is to maximise company profit by maximising contribution.

The main problem with this is that we may end up just making one type of lorry but larger customers may put in orders for all three types. Failing to meet their needs may result in a loss of goodwill and the risk that they may look to competitors going forwards.

There is thus an argument that all orders should be given equal priority.

### 2. Analysis produced by Director Z

### Methodology

Using contribution per labour hour ensures that we are taking into account both incremental cash flows (contribution) but also recognising the context of having a scarce resource.

This method is thus preferred to rank the two options and allocate labour.

Having said that, any contribution figure used should incorporate variable non-production overheads, such as distribution costs. However, the schedule focusses purely on production costs.

### Recommendations

Based on the analysis, available skilled labour should be used to make Lorry B first if available capacity is exceeded each week until either demand is reached or the month is over and the workforce is back to full strength. If it is the former scenario, then Lorry A should be prioritised second.

### Assumptions

The first assumption is that all production overheads are fixed. This can be challenged as it is highly likely that at least some overheads are variable – for example, electricity costs.

The second assumption is that all labour costs are fixed, which under normal circumstance is reasonable as most staff are likely to be salaried.

However, in times of peak demand, it may be that staff are paid extra as overtime, resulting in a variable element to labour costs.

With both of the comments regarding cost behaviour we are looking only at the short term. In the long run all costs can be considered variable as, for example, the number of staff can be increased or decreased to meet production needs.

**Test your understanding 3**

1    Statement of financial position, statement of profit or loss, statement of changes in equity and statement of cash flow.

2    Stewardship is the accountability of management for the resources entrusted to it by the owners or the Government.

3    A bank is normally, in this context, a lender. Consequently they will tend to be interested in the accounts to check the businesses ability to pay any loans outstanding and that that assets on which they depend for security are still recorded at good value.

# Internal controls and weaknesses in accounting systems

## Introduction

In this chapter we look at specific examples of controls within different accounting systems.

It is very likely that you will get up to two tasks on internal controls and the resulting weaknesses in your assessment.

This chapter needs to be studied carefully. You need to be able to suggest good controls and spot weaknesses caused by the absence of those controls.

| PERFORMANCE CRITERIA | CONTENTS |
|---|---|
| 2.1 Discuss how internal controls can support the organisation | 1 Internal control systems |
| 3.1 Examine an organisation's accounting system and its effectiveness | 2 The purchases cycle |
| | 3 The sales cycle |
| 3.2 Evaluate the underpinning procedures of an accounting system, assessing the impact | 4 Payroll |
| | 5 Further issues with cheque payments |
| | 6 Further issues with cash receipts |
| | 7 The effect of weaknesses |

# 1 Internal control systems

## 1.1 Internal control

### 🔍 Definition of internal control

'The process designed and effected by those charged with governance, management and other personnel to provide reasonable assurance about the achievement of the entity's objectives with regard to reliability of financial reporting, effectiveness and efficiency of operations and compliance with applicable laws and regulations.' (ISA 315)

### 💡 Examples

The following examples show some of the ways that internal controls could help a company achieve its objectives and mitigate risk:

- Quality control can prevent the production of poor quality goods
- Credit control can limit the level of bad debts
- Controls over inventory ordering can prevent stock-outs and ensure an optimal level of inventory to minimise holding costs
- A compliance department can implement policies to ensure the business complies with relevant laws and regulations
- Controls over payroll can ensure employees are paid the correct amount, avoiding disputes with staff and incorrect payment of payroll taxes which could result in penalties from HMRC.

###  Test your understanding 1

For the risks below, list some controls which may help minimize these risks.

- Non-payment by customers
- Producing damaged/poor quality products
- Paying too much for supplies

Internal control consists of the following components:

- the control environment
- the entity's risk assessment process
- the information system, including the related business processes, relevant to financial reporting, and communication
- control activities; and
- monitoring of controls.

## 1.2 The control environment

The control environment includes the governance and management function of an organisation.

It focuses largely on the attitude, awareness and actions of those responsible for designing, implementing and monitoring internal controls.

Elements of the control environment include the following:

- communication and enforcement of integrity and ethical values
- commitment to competence
- participation by those charged with governance
- management's philosophy and operating style.

## 1.3 The entity's risk assessment process

The risk assessment process forms the basis for how management determines the business risks to be managed, i.e. threats to the achievement of ongoing business objectives.

These processes will vary hugely depending upon the nature, size and complexity of the organisation.

Threats to business objectives can lead to misstatement in the financial statements, e.g. non-compliance with laws and regulations may lead to fines and penalties, which require disclosure or provision in the financial statements.

If the company has robust procedures for assessing the business risks it faces, the risk of misstatement overall, will be lower.

## 1.4 The information system

The information system is all of the business processes relevant to financial reporting and communication. It includes the procedures within both information technology and manual systems.

The information system includes all of the procedures and records which are designed to:

- initiate, record, process and report transactions
- maintain accountability for assets, liabilities and equity
- resolve incorrect processing of transactions
- transfer information to the general/nominal ledger
- ensure information required to be disclosed is appropriately reported.

### 1.5 Control activities

Control activities are policies and procedures that help ensure that management directives are carried out. Control activities are a component of internal control.

Whilst ISAs provide definition and advice on internal controls, for the ASAC unit it is possible to identify eight categories of internal controls that are relevant and that will be useful whilst carrying out a review of an accounting function. These controls are applicable to both computerised and non-computerised environments.

Here is a list of typical internal controls. You should learn this list.

Later the text applies these controls to specific systems. Computer based controls are equally important and are discussed in the following chapter.

(i)     **Organisation** – there must be a well-defined organisational structure showing how responsibility and authority are delegated. This was discussed in chapter 1.

(ii)    **Segregation of duties** – a fundamental form of control in any enterprise is the separation of responsibilities so that no one person can fully record and process a transaction.

This can be achieved by ensuring that the custodial function, the authorisation function, the recording function and the execution function are kept separate.

(The mnemonic CARE might be useful to you in remembering these four functions.)

For example, warehouse staff should not be responsible for the inventory count as this would not detect if goods were being stolen by staff throughout the year.

(iii)   **Physical controls** – these are concerned with the custody of assets and records and are concerned with ensuring that access to assets and records is only permitted to authorised personnel.

For example, keeping cash in a safe to prevent theft.

(iv) **Authorisation and approval** – all transactions require authorisation or approval by a responsible person. Limits on authorisations should be set down in writing.

For example, a manager signing off an employee's timesheet to confirm that the hours stated have been worked and can be paid. This should ensure the employee is not claiming for hours not worked.

(v) **Arithmetical and accounting** – these controls include those that check the arithmetical accuracy of records such as control accounts, cross totals, reconciliations and sequential controls over documents.

For example, sequence checks on sales invoices ensure the number sequence is complete and no invoices are missing.

(vi) **Personnel** – the proper functioning of the system depends upon the employment of well-motivated, competent personnel who possess the necessary integrity for their tasks.

For example, performing background checks on potential applicants to see if they have a criminal record.

(vii) **Supervision** – an important aspect of any control system is the existence of supervisory procedures by the management.

(viii) **Management** – these are controls exercised by the management outside the day-to-day routine of the system.

Examples are the use of monitoring procedures through the use of budgetary control and other management accounting techniques as well as the provision of internal audit procedures.

You may find **SPAM SOAP** a useful mnemonic to remember these eight categories of internal control.

## 1.6 Monitoring of controls

This is the process of assessing the effectiveness of controls over time and taking necessary remedial action. Clearly if a control is not implemented properly or is simply considered ineffective then misstatements may pass undetected into the financial statements and/or adversely affect management decision making.

Monitoring can be either ongoing or performed on a separate evaluation basis (or a combination of both). Either way, it needs to be effective for the system to work. Monitoring of internal controls is often the key role of internal auditors.

## 1.7 Limitations of internal controls

No system of internal controls will ever mitigate risks entirely due to the inherent limitation of controls.

- Human error
- Unusual transactions tend to be outside the scope of control systems
- Collusion
- Special considerations in small companies
  - Informal nature/lack of documentation
  - Limited numbers of staff make segregation of duties difficult.

## 1.8 Internal audit

Internal audit is not specifically in the syllabus, but some knowledge of it is useful as one of its key roles is the testing of internal controls and the methods that an internal auditor uses will help you spot weaknesses in systems.

There are two types of test that are used by auditors in the course of their work:

- **Compliance tests** are tests of controls and provide evidence as to whether or not the controls on which the auditor wishes to rely were functioning adequately during the period under review.

- **Substantive tests** are tests of transactions, account balances and the existence of assets and liabilities and their valuation (e.g. inventories, non-current assets and receivables) and other procedures such as analytical review, which seek to provide audit evidence as to the completeness, accuracy and validity of the information contained in the accounting records or in the financial statements.

## 1.9 Internal control questionnaires (ICQs)

As their name suggests, internal control questionnaires (ICQs) are checklists of questions that are designed to discover the existence of internal controls and to identify any possible areas of weakness.

The questions are framed so as to discover any situation where there is no subdivision of duties between essential functions, where controls do not exist, or where the aspects of managerial supervision – so essential to efficient operations – are deficient.

You should try to memorise as many of the typical ICQ questions as possible as they will help you spot weaknesses in systems. In most assessment tasks the weakness are fairly standard (no authorisation for example) so if you have as many standard weaknesses ready as you can you will be in good shape to do well.

**KAPLAN** PUBLISHING

# 2 The purchases cycle

## 2.1 Internal control objectives within the purchases cycle

All orders for goods and services should be properly authorised. Goods and services should be ordered in accordance with the purchaser's needs and on the most favourable terms that can be obtained.

All goods ordered should be received in a satisfactory condition with evidence of their receipt, which can be used as a basis for entries in inventory records and recording the liability arising from such transactions.

Control should be established over the process of returning goods and making claims on suppliers.

Purchase invoice documentation should be validated before a liability is recorded.

Purchases invoices should only be paid if the original purchase was authorised, the goods were received in good condition and the payment was authorised.

The validated transactions should be recorded accurately in the accounting records.

## 2.2 Overall supervisory controls

If an internal control system is to work satisfactorily, there must be certain overall disciplines which enable the framework of controls to be maintained.

In particular, there must be segregation of duties and appropriate supervision.

- Segregation of duties means that the persons who raise orders should be independent of the ledger keeping function, the stock recording and control subsystem and the cheque drawing/approval/signing functions.

- Supervision means that there must be overall systems of review by a responsible official.

## 2.3 Internal control questionnaire

The internal control questionnaire is a useful tool for identifying the main internal controls that exist in an organisation.

An internal control questionnaire will be used as the basis for questioning the members of staff who operate the system under review to identify what controls are in place.

Below we outline a typical internal control questionnaire for the purchases system. This is an excellent list of potential weaknesses (assuming a no answer) and strengths (assuming a yes answer) and so very useful in your assessment. The more you can remember from this list the better!

| **Purchases and payments to suppliers** | |
|---|---|
| Client: Normanton Ltd | |
| Year end: 30 September 20X6 | Prepared by: B E Mignano |
| Cycle: Purchases | Date: 7.9.X6 |
| | *Yes/No or N/A* |
| 1 **To ensure that all orders are raised to minimise errors** | |
| Are the orders raised in the order/purchasing department which is independent of all other departments? | |
| Are the orders requisitioned by a user department which is separate from the ordering department and stores? | |
| Are orders raised on authorised order forms which are pre-numbered serially and sequentially controlled? | |
| Is the supplier's price list checked to ensure that the correct quality and quantity of goods are being ordered at the correct price? | |
| Is a supplier's file maintained which will confirm details of discounts? | |
| Are all orders issued checked regularly to ensure that they have been fulfilled? | |
| Are unfulfilled orders checked to ensure that they are being satisfactorily progressed by the supplier? | |
| Is the official order signed by a responsible official? | |
| 2 **To ensure that goods received are correctly controlled** | |
| Are goods received in a stores department that is independent of the user and purchasing departments? | |
| Does the organisation use official goods received notes? | |

Is the goods received note correctly filled in when an order is received and signed off by a responsible official?

Are the goods received notes sequentially pre-numbered and is there control over them?

Is the delivery note which accompanies the goods from the supplier signed and returned to the supplier?

Is a copy of the delivery note sent by the supplier retained and filed?

Is the goods received note raised by the company matched and filed with the delivery note sent by the supplier?

3 **To ensure that invoices received are valid and agree with the goods delivered**

Are the invoices arithmetically checked?

Is the invoice compared to the purchase order and quantities, qualities and prices checked?

Is the invoice compared to the goods received note and supplier's delivery note to ensure that the correct quantities and quality were received?

Is the invoice stamped with a 'grid' so that the above checks are correctly evidenced on the face of the invoice?

Is the invoice correctly coded so that goods received are allocated to the correct nominal ledger code?

Are the invoices received allocated an internal sequential number and filed sequentially?

4 **To ensure that payments to suppliers are correctly made**

Are the persons who sign the cheques different from those who handle the authorisation of the invoices?

Are there two responsible officials who act as cheque signatories?

Is close control maintained over the custody of the cheques?

Are all cheques issued in sequential order?

Are spoilt or cancelled cheques retained?

Are all cheques stamped 'A/C payee'?

Are cheques presented for signature with relevant authorising documentation, e.g. an authorised invoice?

Is the number of the cheque used to pay the invoice written on the face of the invoice?

If BACS are used to pay suppliers, do two responsible officials sign the BACS authorisation?

Does company policy forbid the use of cash to pay suppliers' invoices?

Note that the internal control questionnaire outlined above is a fairly detailed questionnaire which is designed to assess a fairly 'advanced/ideal' system. In many smaller organisations, it will not be possible or even necessary to have a system which contains many of these features.

 **Test your understanding 2 – Purchases**

### Miller Ltd

Miller Ltd is a company engaged in pharmaceutical manufacturing. The purchasing department is managed by Mr Wurm, the buyer, and his assistant Walter Green. The value of purchase contracts placed annually is about £3 million. When goods are required the stock records clerk (Frederica) sends a purchase requisition to Mr Wurm, who gets Walter to type out an order form. Walter enters a serial number, sequentially-numbered after the last purchase order, and photocopies the order. The original is sent to the supplier and the copy is kept in a file.

When the goods arrive, they are taken into stock and the supplier's despatch note is sent to Walter from the goods inwards supervisor. Walter then marks off the items received on the order and sends the despatch note to the stock records section. They then use it to write up the stock ledger and file it in chronological sequence.

(a) What weaknesses does the system possess, briefly indicating the effect of that weakness?

(b) What outline recommendations would you make to improve the system? You may assume that the company has enough manpower to implement your recommendations.

**Test your understanding 3 – Payments to suppliers**

**Melchior Manufacturing Supplies Ltd**

At monthly intervals the purchase ledger clerk of Melchior Manufacturing Supplies Ltd, Mrs Thorborg, lists the ledger balances. She then compares them with a file of suppliers' statements. Those statements that agree with the list of balances are extracted and placed in a file. Those that do not agree with the listed balances are left in the original file.

Mrs Thorborg then prepares a list of payments for all the suppliers who have sent statements as follows.

(1)  Where the statement agrees with the balance, the statement is attached to the list.

(2)  Where there is a disagreement, Mrs Thorborg computes a 'round sum amount' (which is generally slightly less than the balance on the ledger) and enters this amount on the list of payments. She leaves these statements in the file.

(3)  The list of payments is then passed to Mr Lehmann, the assistant accountant, who writes out the cheques.

(4)  The cheques, list and statements are then sent to Mrs Turner, the commercial director, who signs them after checking against the statements (where these are attached) and the list.

(5)  The cheques are then passed to the managing director, Mr Widdop, the other signatory, who signs the cheques and sends them back to Mr Lehmann, who then posts them to the parties concerned.

**Required:**

The internal auditors have made various comments regarding the poor quality of the accounting controls. Identify those areas that you think would have been likely to attract adverse comment from the internal auditors.

Note: You are not asked here to make recommendations.

# 3 The sales cycle

## 3.1 Internal control objectives

Customers' orders should be properly controlled and recorded so that no losses of business opportunity are allowed to occur.

Controls should exist over goods delivered so that proof of delivery is obtained and all deliveries are accurately charged to the customer.

All claims made by customers should be validated and all goods returned to stock properly evidenced.

All invoices and credit notes should be validated before entry in the records.

Procedures should exist to ensure that invoices are paid for, overdue debts are followed up and bad debts promptly identified.

No sales should be made to non-creditworthy customers.

## 3.2 Specimen ICQ – sales and trade receivables

As before, the ICQ gives an excellent list of the types of controls that could be used.

| Client: | Normanton Ltd | | |
|---|---|---|---|
| Year end: | 30 September 20X6 | Prepared by: B E Mignano | |
| Cycle: | Purchases | Date: 7.9.X6 | |
| | | | Yes/No or N/A |
| 1 | **To ensure that all orders received are processed in such a way that keeps errors to a minimum** | | |
| | Are persons responsible for preparation of sales orders independent of credit control, custody of stock and recording sales transactions? | | |
| | Are standard forms used to record orders? | | |
| | Are sales orders pre-numbered? | | |
| | Do sales order clerks check the goods ordered are available in quantity and quality required? | | |
| | Are standard prices, delivery and payment terms in written form for the use of sales order clerks? | | |

| | | |
|---|---|---|
| | Are special orders (special qualities, quantities, prices) authorised by a responsible official? | 55 |
| 2 | **To ensure that sales orders are not accepted in respect of a bad credit risk** | |
| | Is the credit controller independent of the sales order clerks? | |
| | Are new credit customers vetted for creditworthiness by reference to independent persons or organisations? | |
| | Are orders from existing customers checked for payment record, sales ledger balance and credit limit? | |
| | Are credit limits set by responsible officials for all credit customers? | |
| | Is the credit approval evidenced on the sales order by the signature of a responsible official? | |
| | Is the work of a credit control clerk independently checked? | |
| 3 | **To ensure that goods are only despatched to customers after proper authorisation** | |
| | Is warehouse/despatch department independent of sales order preparation, credit control and invoicing? | |
| | Do warehouse personnel release goods from the warehouse on the basis of sales orders signed by authorised sales order and credit control personnel? | |
| | Is the despatch of goods evidenced by the preparation of a goods despatch note? | |
| | Are goods despatch notes pre-numbered? | |
| | Are two copies of the goods despatch notes sent to the customer for one to be returned as evidence of receipt? | |
| | Is a copy of the despatch note sent to a stock control department to update stock records? | |
| | Is stock counted periodically and compared with stock records? | |
| 4 | **To ensure that all goods despatched are invoiced at authorised prices and terms** | |
| | Is sales invoicing independent of sales order preparation, credit control, warehouse and despatch departments? | |
| | | |

| | |
|---|---|
| Are copies of sales orders received by sales invoicing? | |
| Is a sequence check carried out on sales orders? | |
| Is a sequence check carried out on goods despatch notes? | |
| Are goods despatch notes matched with sales orders and unmatched orders followed up? | |
| Do invoicing clerks have details of current prices, terms and conditions, including special agreements with particular customers? | |
| Are sales invoices independently checked before despatch? | |
| **5** **To ensure that all sales invoices are properly recorded in individual customers' accounts in the sales ledger** | |
| Is the sales ledger clerk independent of sales order preparation, credit control, warehouse, despatch and sales invoicing? | |
| Is a sales ledger control account maintained independent of the sales ledger clerk? | |
| Are differences between extracted list of sales ledger balances and control account balances investigated by a responsible official? | |
| Are monthly statements of amounts outstanding prepared and despatched to customers? | |
| Is an aged debtor listing prepared and reviewed by a responsible official? | |
| Are sales ledger balances made up of identifiable sales invoices and other items? | |
| Are bad debt write-offs and discounts authorised by a responsible official other than the sales ledger clerk? | |

**Test your understanding 4 – Sales Cycle**

**Gustavus plc**

Gustavus plc sell a variety of electrical equipment on a wholesale basis to some 1,500 credit customers. Cash sales are not a feature of the business.

Sales orders are received by telephone and are recorded on a pre-numbered order form in two parts. Part 1 is sent to the customer as acknowledgement of the order. Part 2 is used by the manager of the sales office as an action copy. He authorises the order after checking the account balance with the accounts department to ensure that the credit limit is not exceeded. The order is then passed to the warehouse where the goods are picked and sent to despatch.

The order form is then passed to the invoice typing section in the sales office and three-part invoice sets are typed. Each set is numbered by reference to a number register and the top copy is given to the customer with the goods at the collection point. The second copy is an accounts copy and the third is filed in the customer file in the sales office. There are no other procedures in relation to sales order processing.

**Required:**

Comment on the weaknesses inherent in the sales system.

 **4 Payroll**

### 4.1 Internal control objectives

The payroll cycle embraces the following:

- maintenance of payroll
- authorisation of hours worked
- payroll preparation
- distribution of pay
- payroll approval
- cheque signing, and
- identifying liabilities to third parties for payroll costs and paying these when due.

The objectives of the key internal controls in the payroll cycle are as follows:

(a)    Wages and salaries are computed for the client's employees only and in accordance with authorised rates of pay and conditions.

(b)    Wages and salaries computed should be in agreement with records of work performed, i.e. overtime claims, bonus calculations, etc.

(c)    Payroll is correctly computed and paid to the appropriate employees.

(d)    All records of transactions are accurately maintained within the accounting system.

(e)    There are controls to ensure that all payroll deductions, PAYE income tax payable, National Insurance Contributions, etc are computed and paid over on the due dates.

## 4.2    Internal control questionnaire – payroll

| Client: | Normanton Ltd | | |
|---------|---------------|---|---|
| Year end: | 30 September 20X6 | Prepared by: B E Mignano | |
| Cycle: | Purchases | Date: 7.9.X6 | |
| | | | Yes/No or N/A |
| **1** | **Fundamental controls of a payroll system** | | |
| | Is a permanent record kept for each employee containing details of engagement, dismissal, changes in rates of pay, etc? | | |
| | Are these details and any changes in details evidenced in writing by a responsible official? | | |
| | Are timesheets kept for each employee giving details for each payment period of normal hours and overtime hours worked? | | |
| | For piecework employees, are details kept of amounts produced as a basis for payment? | | |
| | For each payment period, are the calculations which make up gross pay checked for each employee against the timesheets and records of rates, etc? | | |
| | Is the calculation for the total amount of the payroll checked for each payment period? | | |
| | Are all payments for overtime approved by a responsible official? | | |
| | | | |

| | | |
|---|---|---|
| 2 | **To ensure the correct preparation and payment of the payroll** | |
| | Does a responsible official formally approve the total payroll by signing it? | |
| | Where employees are paid by cheque or BACS, does a responsible official check the total amount being paid to each employee? | |
| | Where wages are paid by cash, do two responsible officials authorise and sign the cheque to raise the cash? | |
| | Is the cash securely transported from the bank and securely held on the premises? | |
| | Does a responsible official oversee the correct cash being placed into each wages packet? | |
| | Are unclaimed wages securely held in the company's premises until collected? | |
| 3 | **Controls over accounting for payroll** | |
| | Are payroll liabilities reconciled with the source total payroll (i.e. PAYE and NIC deductions included)? | |
| | Is PAYE and NIC paid on the due date? | |
| | Do adequate procedures exist to ensure that payroll is analysed and entered in the appropriate nominal ledger accounts? | |

 **Test your understanding 5 – Payroll**

**Bingham**

You have been asked by the senior in charge of the audit of Bingham Manufacturing Limited to describe certain aspects of the work you will carry out in auditing the company's wages system. Employees of Bingham Manufacturing are paid on the basis of hours worked and quantities produced. The hours worked are recorded on clock cards and the quantities produced are confirmed by the foreman. Wages are paid in cash each Friday for the previous week's work. Appointment of employees is authorised by the managing director, and the personnel department maintains employees' records and their rates of pay. The cashier is separate from the wages department.

Previous years' audits have highlighted weaknesses in internal controls in the company's wages system. This has allowed an employee in the wages department to perpetrate a fraud by creating fictitious employees on the payroll and misappropriating the wages. Some of your audit tests have been designed to detect whether this fraud is still taking place.

A 'starters and leavers' test is carried out to ensure that employees are not paid before they commence employment or after they have left.

**Required:**

State the principal controls you would expect to exist in a wages system and explain their purpose.

---

 **Test your understanding 6 – Payroll**

**Burnden Limited**

Burnden Limited manufactures a range of components and spare parts for the textile industry. The company employs 150 hourly-paid workers and 20 administrative staff, including the three directors of the company. There are two wages clerks who deal with the weekly payroll of the hourly-paid employees. They are directly responsible to the assistant accountant.

The company uses a computerised time clock at the factory gate to record the hours worked by the production employees. Each employee has a card with a magnetic strip with his own identification code on it. This card is inserted in the computerised time clock on the arrival and departure of each worker, whereupon it records on the card the hours worked. The cards are collected weekly by the wages clerks, who simply insert them individually into the microcomputer, which then reads them and prepares the payroll. The production manager keeps the unused clock cards in a locked cabinet in his office.

Wages are paid one week in arrears. The wages clerks compile the payroll by means of the microcomputer system, and pass the payroll to the assistant accountant who scrutinises it before drawing the wages cheque, which is passed to one of the directors for signature. Any pay increases are negotiated locally by representatives of the employees. If any alterations are required to the standing data on the microcomputer, then the wages clerks amend the records. For example, when a wage increase has been negotiated, the rates of pay are changed by the wages clerks.

The cheque is drawn to cover net wages and the cashier makes arrangements for collecting the cash from the bank.

The wages clerks then make up the wages envelopes.

---

Whenever there is assistance required on preparing wages, the assistant accountant helps the wages clerks. The payment of wages is carried out by the production manager who returns any unclaimed wages to the wages clerks who keep them in a locked filing cabinet. Each employee is expected to collect his unclaimed wages personally.

New production employees are notified to the wages department verbally by the production manager and when employees leave, a note to that effect is sent to the wages department by the production manager. All statutory deductions are paid to the appropriate authorities by the chief accountant.

Administrative staff are paid monthly by credit transfer to their bank account. The payroll is prepared by the assistant accountant and the bank credit transfers are authorised by a director. Any increases in the salaries of the administrative staff are notified to the assistant accountant verbally by the chief accountant. The employment of administrative staff is authorised by the financial director.

You have recently been appointed the auditor of Burnden Limited for the year ended 31 December 20X8 and have just started your interim audit. You are about to commence your audit evaluation and testing of the wages system.

**Required:**

Describe the weaknesses in the present wages and salaries system, and suggest, with reasons, improvements which could be made to the system (assuming that the only controls are those set out above).

# 5 Further issues with cheque payments

## 5.1 Introduction

Cheque payments are an important part of the system for incurring expenditure and so we need to consider the internal controls in this specific context.

It is necessary to remember the fundamental principle of internal control; namely, the need for a division of duties between authorisation, custodial, recording and execution functions.

### 5.2 Desirable internal controls

(a) **Division of duties**

   (i)   The persons who sign cheques should be different from the authorisation, recording and custodial functions.

   (ii)  There must be two responsible officials who act as cheque signatories. If pre-printed cheques are in use, or a cheque signing machine is installed, the control over the issue and custody of cheques must be closely supervised by a responsible official who is different from the recording or custodial function.

(b) **Custody**

   (i)   All cheques should be issued in sequential order and their sequence should be controlled.

   (ii)  Unused stocks of cheque books must be kept under lock and key.

   (iii) Spoilt or cancelled cheques must be retained.

   (iv)  All cheques should be crossed 'A/c payee only' to minimise the chance of fraud if the cheque is lost.

(c) **Authorisation**

   (i)   No cheque should be prepared without supporting documentation, e.g. an approved invoice, a signed payroll or an authorised cheque requisition.

   (ii)  The cheque signatories' authority should be laid down in writing and be in accordance with the bank mandate.

   (iii) The system of cheque payments must be supervised by a responsible official who will oversee the preparation of regular bank reconciliations and carry out spot checks thereon.

# 6 Further issues with cash receipts

### 6.1 Introduction

The cash receipts system is an important part of the income cycle. It is necessary to consider the internal control aspects of this part of the system. As with cash payments, one should consider the importance of a proper subdivision of duties between authorisation, custodial and recording functions.

### 6.2 Internal control

**(a) Custodial procedures**

    (i)    All post should be opened by at least two responsible officials.

    (ii)   All cheques and postal orders should be crossed restrictively to the company's bankers.

    (iii)  A cash diary should be maintained of daily amounts of cash received.

    (iv)  All monies received should be banked intact on that business day.

**(b) Separation of duties**

    (i)    The persons who are responsible for opening the post, preparing the paying-in details and controlling the sales ledger should be separate functionaries.

    (ii)   There should be an independent check on cash receipts by a suitable official who can spot-check the details in the cash diary with the paying in records.

**(c) Recording controls**

    (i)    The entries in the cash receipts book should be proved by regular bank reconciliations.

    (ii)   The bank reconciliations should be reviewed and spot-checked on a regular basis by some responsible official remote from the recording functions.

# 7 The effect of weaknesses

### 7.1 Introduction

From the syllabus and the sample synoptic assessment, it is clear that you need to be able to go further than simply spot weaknesses in accounting systems in most tasks.

You are also required to be able to describe what the effect of those weaknesses might be on the organisation.

### 7.2 A wide perspective

The effect that a weakness might have should be considered widely. You could consider the effect on:

- Assets
- Liabilities
- Income

- Expenses
- Theft or fraud
- Morale
- Efficiency of system
- Reputation of business
- Time taken to produce information.

You should ask yourself what bad things could happen!

The sample synoptic made it very clear if this was needed and provided a separate box for this extra requirement. So if the task asks for weaknesses only then simply do that. If you are asked to explain the effect, then do that too.

Some of the examples above ask for "effect" and some don't. Similarly some asked for recommendations but others didn't, so you must read the question carefully. Note, you would not get penalised for giving an effect when it isn't asked for and it does improve your answer but it does use up time.

# 8 Additional 'Test your understanding' questions

 **Test your understanding 7**

1    Can you identify four of the eight categories of internal control?

2    Internal checks are a feature of internal control. What are they designed to ensure?

3    Describe the essence of an internal check.

4    What is an operational or 'value for money' audit?

5    Briefly explain the two types of test that are used by auditors in the course of their work.

6    What are ICQs?

7    An internal control evaluation (ICE) summary may be used in conjunction with ICQs or in substitution for them. What is the principal difference between an ICQ and an ICE?

# 9 Summary

This has been a very important chapter and in some ways goes to the heart of the analysis of the accounting systems.

The division of responsibilities is a key element to internal control and you should always be aware of any shortcomings in this respect when analysing a system.

The internal control questionnaire is a very good way of gaining information about a system and its shortcomings. When doing your project, it is a technique which you should seriously consider employing.

## Test your understanding answers

 **Test your understanding 1**

Non-payment by customers

- Credit checks on all new customers
- Credit limits set for all customers
- Regular review of balances against credit limits to ensure not breached
- Reducing/altering payment terms for poor payers

Production of damaged/poor quality products

- Choose suppliers with good market reputation (approved supplier list)
- Regularly review level of returns/credit notes issued to determine whether problem exists
- Instigate appropriate training techniques for production staff
- Implement adequate quality control procedures

Paying too much for supplies

- Check taking advantage of any prompt payment / bulk discounts
- Compare all invoices received to goods received note (GRN) prior to payment
- Marking paid invoices as such to avoid duplicate payments

 **Test your understanding 2 – Purchases**

(a) **Weaknesses in the system**

(i) The purchase orders are not multipart, pre-numbered documents (the numbers are added manually). As a result of this weakness, unauthorised orders can be placed. The lack of original documentation makes the system susceptible to loss or irregular alteration.

(ii) The orders are neither priced, nor are they checked by Mr Wurm before they are despatched.

This could lead to incorrect pricing being committed too or incorrect goods being ordered.

(iii)   Mr Wurm does not sign the orders as the company's authorised signatory. The effect of this is as for (ii) above.

(iv)   There is no goods received note system to evidence the arrival of goods. Goods could be invoiced for but not received and we could not prove otherwise.

(v)   The acceptance of goods in the goods inwards section is done without reference to the purchase order; Walter only matches them up later. Goods that have not been ordered could be accepted and potentially subsequently paid for.

(vi)   There is no review of outstanding purchase orders in order to chase up unfulfilled orders. Production delays could occur.

**(b)   Recommendations**

(i)   The purchase orders should be a three-part document and sequentially-controlled. Unissued order pads should be kept under lock and key. Sequential control should then be maintained over books of purchase orders in issue. Spoilt and unused copies should be retained and the completeness of the sequential numbering monitored frequently.

(ii)   The purchase orders should be priced by reference to suppliers' catalogues before despatch. This enables the amount eventually invoiced by the supplier to be checked.

(iii)   Purchase requisitions should be checked before being processed. Similarly, purchase orders should be signed by Mr Wurm as evidence of authority before being despatched.

This ensures that unauthorised purchases cannot be made.

(iv)   A copy of the purchase order should be sent to the goods inwards department in order to provide authority for the acceptance of the goods.

(v)   When goods arrive they should be checked against the copy purchase order and evidenced on a pre-numbered, three-part goods received note (GRN). One part (top) of the GRN should be used to update the order file i.e. to indicate which orders have been fulfilled and which are still outstanding. The second part can be used to write up the stock ledger. The third part can be kept as a master copy in serial number order.

(vi)   Mr Wurm should review the order file weekly and check on the position of outstanding orders.

**Test your understanding 3 – Payments to suppliers**

Matters likely to cause adverse comment from the auditors:

(a) Mrs Thorborg appears to operate in a most lackadaisical fashion in that she:

    (i) does not appear to claim cash discounts for early payment

    (ii) makes no attempt to reconcile bought ledger accounts

    (iii) makes round sum payments and is therefore likely to aggravate the problem of account balances that disagree

    (iv) does not attach invoices for payment; thus there is no attempt to identify specifically the transactions that are being settled and the same invoice could therefore be paid twice.

(b) There is a lack of evidence for the first cheque signatory, as Mrs Turner does not see the statements for balances that disagree.

(c) Mr Widdop does not receive supporting evidence for payment. Consequently he may not notice errors or be aware of any lapses in control.

(d) The signed cheques are sent to Mr Lehmann who could suppress or alter them for his own benefit.

(e) The payment of invoices or statements does not alert the company to errors made by the supplier. Thus it is possible to pay for items not ordered and charged to the company in error.

 **Test your understanding 4 – Sales Cycle**

**Weaknesses in the system**

- There is no separation of duties between the functions of recording and authorisation of sales orders.

- The validation procedures appear to be inadequate as there is no evidence of formal procedures such as validation of prices and stock availability.

- There are no procedures to ensure that the customer signs for the goods collected which would serve as proof of delivery.

- Invoices are not pre-numbered; this is a serious control weakness as transactions can be suppressed without trace.

- Invoices are not checked for arithmetical accuracy before being despatched.

- There are no procedures for dealing with unsatisfied orders.
- There are no procedures to update the order file with details of orders despatched to customers.

 **Test your understanding 5 – Payroll**

**Controls**

The principal controls in a wages system and their purpose would include the following:

There should be a proper division of duties in the wages system. Employees who calculate wages should not be responsible for making up the wage packets.

There is proper control over custody of cash for wages and unclaimed wages.

Wages are only paid to employees for work done i.e. not in advance. Employees are paid at a rate authorised by management.

There is appropriate authorisation over employee appointment and dismissal.

Deductions are correctly calculated and paid promptly to the relevant authorities i.e. HM Revenue and Customs and pension companies.

Payments are made to employees actually registered with the company.

The transactions are correctly recorded in the books of account, including the allocation of the wages expense between sales, manufacturing, administration, etc.

**Aim**

The aim of these controls is to ensure that employees are paid at authorised rates for work done, that the transactions are recorded accurately in the accounting records, that the employees and other authorities are paid the correct sums and that the risk of fraud and error is minimised.

**Test your understanding 6 – Payroll**

**Weaknesses and improvements (These may need to be separated in an assessment)**

The weaknesses in the company's present wages and salaries system and suggestions for improvements are as follows:

- There are two wages clerks dealing with the production payroll. To improve control within the wages department, the duties of these clerks should be rotated during the year. Neither of the clerks should be responsible for all functions in the department.

- Personnel records should be kept for each employee giving details of engagement, retirement, dismissal or resignation, rates of pay, holidays etc, with a specimen signature for the employee. It does not appear that these records are maintained at present and they would be essential in the event of failure or corruption of the computer system.

- The production manager verbally notifies the wages department of new employees. As he also controls the unused clock cards and pays out the wages he could introduce a fictitious employee. It is important that there is written authorisation from the chief accountant for the appointment and removal of all employees. The unused clock cards should also be kept in a secure place by someone other than the production manager. They should be issued weekly by a responsible official.

- The wages clerks appear to amend pay rates without any authorisation. Changes in rates of pay should be authorised in writing by an official outside the wages department.

- The clocking-in and out procedures do not seem to be supervised. There should be supervision of the cards and timing devices.

- The production manager pays out wages alone. It would be preferable if the two wages clerks paid out the wages. A surprise attendance at the payout should be made periodically by an independent official. It would also be preferable that an employee should not be allowed to take the wages of another employee without written authorisation. Unclaimed wages should be recorded immediately in a register and held by someone outside the wages department until claimed or until a predefined period after which the money should be rebanked.

- The payroll is not authorised. It should be signed by the person preparing it. The director should check that it has been authorised before signing the wages cheque. He should also sign the payroll. Further, the payroll should be carefully scrutinised by the assistant accountant who should carry out random checks on rates of pay, amendments to employees etc.

- Access to the computer payroll system does not appear to be restricted. Access should be controlled by passwords which should be changed regularly.

- A manual back-up system should be available in the event of computer failure.

- There is a security risk in drawing large amounts of cash from the bank and keeping this on the premises. If possible, the company should transfer the employees onto a bank giro transfer system.

- There are weaknesses in the monthly payroll. The assistant accountant should sign the payroll as preparer and the director should authorise the bank credit transfer only after checking an authorised payroll.

- Salary increases should be notified in writing by the chief accountant after authorisation by a director. Personnel records should be kept as for production staff and appointments and dismissals should be authorised only by directors.

- If any overtime is worked it should be authorised by the production manager.

### Test your understanding 7

1   You could choose any four of the following types of internal control: organisation, segregation of duties, supervision, management, physical controls, authorisation and approval and personnel. The proper functioning of the system depends upon the employment of well-motivated, competent personnel who possess the necessary integrity for their tasks.

2   Internal checks are designed to ensure that all transactions and other accounting information that should be recorded have been recorded, any errors or irregularities in processing accounting information are highlighted and assets and liabilities recorded in the accounts do actually exist and are recorded at their correct amount.

3       The essence of an internal check is to ensure that no one person carries too much responsibility and that each person's work is reviewed or checked by another. This is achieved by a division of responsibilities. The absence of internal checks leads to errors remaining undiscovered and can also lead to fraudulent acts, which are committed because the fraudster feels free of any form of supervision.

4       An operational or 'value for money' audit monitors the organisation's performance at every level to ensure optimal functioning according to pre-determined criteria. It concentrates on the outputs of the system and the efficiency and effectiveness of the organisation.

5       There are two types of test that are used by auditors in the course of their work:

Tests of controls provide evidence as to whether or not the controls on which the auditor wishes to rely were functioning adequately during the period under review.

Substantive procedures (or substantive tests) are those tests of transactions, account balances and the existence of assets and liabilities and their valuation e.g. stocks, fixed assets and debtors and other procedures such as analytical review, which seek to provide audit evidence as to the completeness, accuracy and validity of the information contained in the accounting records or in the financial statements.

6       As their name suggests, internal control questionnaires (ICQs) are checklists of questions that are designed to discover the existence of internal controls and to identify any possible areas of weakness. An important feature of the ICQ is the way in which questions are phrased; an affirmative answer indicates a strength and a negative answer a weakness.

7       The principal difference between an ICQ and an ICE is that the latter concentrates on the most serious weaknesses that could occur within a system through the use of 'key' questions.

# Internal controls in a computerised environment

## Introduction

Most businesses have accounting systems within a computerised environment. In principle there is little difference in the accounting function but some different internal controls are necessary.

The scenarios in the assessment may include computer aspects but essentially the tasks will be the same as in the previous chapter. You will still have to spot weaknesses and make recommendations.

| PERFORMANCE CRITERIA |
| --- |
| 2.1 Discuss how internal controls can support the organisation |
| 3.3 Evaluate the risk of fraud arising from weaknesses in the internal control system |

| CONTENTS |
| --- |
| 1 Information systems controls |
| 2 Integrity controls |
| 3 Contingency controls |
| 4 Assessing and managing risk |

# 1 Information systems controls

## 1.1 Risks to information systems

> ### Q Definition
>
> The British Computer Society defines security as 'the establishment and application of safeguards to protect data, software and computer hardware from accidental or malicious modification, destruction or disclosure'. Security is the protection of the system from harm. It relates to all elements of the system, including hardware, software, data and the system users themselves.

There are three basic concerns relevant to the computerised information system. Security should maintain:

(i)    the availability of the computerised service itself

(ii)   the integrity of the data that it processes and stores, and

(iii)  the confidentiality of the data before, during and after processing.

Controls are procedures or system features that help to ensure that the system operates in accordance with the requirements of the organisation and the user. The issue of the information system's security is based on the following three elements:

- **physical** – the operation of computer equipment can be severely impaired where it is subject to events such as fire, flooding and improper environmental conditions, e.g. heat

- **people** as a threat, and

- the **data/information** that might be lost or damaged.

The security measures adopted should perform the following functions:

- the avoidance or prevention of loss

- the deterrence of as many threats as possible

- easy recovery after any loss

- identification of the cause of any loss after the event, and

- the correction of vulnerable areas to reduce the risk of repeated loss.

## 1.2 General controls

General controls relate to the environment within which computer-based systems are developed, maintained and operated and are generally applicable to all the applications running on the system. You should memorise as much of this list as possible:

- **Personnel recruitment** policies to ensure honesty and competence.

- **Segregation** of duties between different types of job, to minimise tampering with programs or data.

- Proper **training** programmes for new staff and for new systems developments.

- **Physical** security of hardware and software against accidental or malicious damage or natural disasters.

- **Authorisation** procedures for program amendments and testing.

- **Back-up procedures** (maintaining copies of files off-site, back-up facilities).

- **Access** controls. (e.g. firewalls and anti-virus checkers).

- Measures to ensure the system is not accessed during data **transmission** (hacking).

- Controls to ensure that the computing resources are used **efficiently**.

## 1.3 Data security

A critical element of effective data protection is the need for security. There is a range of issues that should be considered:

- the nature of the personal data and the harm that would result from access, alteration, disclosure, loss or destruction

- the place where the personal data is stored

- reliability of staff having access to the data.

Data security measures involve different aspects:

- **Physical security**, such as the security of data storage facilities, from flood as well as unauthorised access

- **Software security**, such as maintaining a log of all failed access requests, and

- **Operational security**, with regard to such things as work data being taken home by employees, and periodic data protection audits of the computer systems.

Under the terms of the **Data Protection Act 1998**, the need for privacy is recognised by the requirements that all personal data on individuals should be held only for clearly designated purposes. Accuracy and integrity must be maintained and the data must be open to inspection. Only legitimate parties can access data and information must be secured against alteration, accidental loss or deliberate damage. Furthermore, the Act states that data must be obtained fairly, to precise specifications and must not be kept for longer than required.

## 1.4 Physical security

Computer systems consist of a mixture of electronic and mechanical devices that can be severely impaired when they are subject to events such as fire, flooding, and improper environmental conditions. As well as covering these threats, physical security also covers the prevention of theft and accidental or malicious damage caused by external parties or internal staff.

The organisation must assess the physical risks applicable to them, and put in place appropriate controls. These controls may be designed to detect the risk or may be designed to prevent it, and might include the following:

- **Fire systems and procedures** – systems of fire alarms, heat and smoke detectors can alert staff to the risk or presence of fire in time for preventive action to be taken. The fire control system might also trigger automatic fire extinguishing equipment, though the use of water sprinkler systems in offices with computer hardware is inappropriate due to the damage they can cause to electrical equipment.

- **Location of hardware** away from sources of risk – not siting computer facilities in areas susceptible to flooding or natural disasters is common sense, but there are other controls that may be less obvious e.g. locating equipment where it cannot be seen through windows from a public area may reduce the risk of theft.

- **Regular building maintenance** – attention to roofs, windows and doors will reduce the risk of water penetration and make forcible entry more difficult. Training – staff should be given copies of relevant policies and procedures, and trained in the implementation of them. Specific training should cover evacuation drills, fire control and fighting, safe behaviour, first aid, how to deal with a bomb threat and general risk identification and management.

- **Physical access controls** – there are a number of steps that can be taken to prevent the access of unauthorised persons to computer facilities.

  Examples include security guards to check identification and authorisation, CCTV, using badge readers or coded locks on access doors from public areas and electronic tagging of hardware.

Environmental threats can come from extremes of temperature, excessive humidity and interruptions or inconsistencies in the power supply. The mechanisms that can be used to control the computer environment include heating and air-conditioning systems, smoothed power supplies and uninterruptable power supplies (UPS).

## 1.5 Individual staff controls

No matter what the size of organisation, or the type of hardware involved, where activities are undertaken that are important to the commercial fabric of the organisation, individual staff functions must be specifically defined and documented where they involve data processing of any form.

This is vital, as it may be the only control in smaller organisations that will prevent, minimise or lead to the detection of fraudulent manipulation of data during processing, destruction of data, the accidental incorrect processing of data and unauthorised access to personal or confidential data that may be in contravention of the Data Protection Act 1998, or may be otherwise unlawful.

It is necessary to restrict access to the system, to protect the confidentiality of the software and data. Access must be limited to those with the proper authority, and a number of controls are available. These include the physical access controls that we have already outlined as well as the following:

- **Logical access system** – unauthorised people can get around physical access controls and gain access to data and program files unless different controls are used to deter them. Measures such as identification of the user, authentication of user identity and checks on user authority are alternative ways of achieving control.

- **Personal identification** – the most common form of personal identification is the PIN (personal identification number), which acts as a form of password. Users should be required to log in to the system using a unique user name and a password that is kept secret and changed frequently. Other, more sophisticated personal identification techniques that are coming into use include fingerprint recognition, eye retina 'prints' and voice 'prints'. Usage logs – the system should be designed to automatically record the log-in and log-off times of each user, and the applications accessed. Periodic checks should be made for unusual patterns, such as a day-shift worker accessing the system at night.

- **Storage of CDs, removable data storage devices in secure locations** – given that one of the risks that the organisation is trying to counteract is the physical destruction of the installation, it is sensible to put in place controls to ensure that back-up data is stored in a fire-proof environment on-site, and occasionally some form of master back-up is removed from the installation site completely.

---

 **Test your understanding 1**

You are a trainee management accountant in a small manufacturing company. Your head of department is going to a meeting and has asked you to provide some information for him.

Write a briefing report for the head of department which:

(a) examines the factors that you consider most affect the security of an organisation's computer systems

(b) identifies ways in which the risks associated with computer security might be successfully managed.

---

# 2 Integrity controls

## 2.1 Sources of error

It is important to identify how errors might occur during the operation of a system other than as a result of failing to establish proper administrative controls. Errors will fall into the following classes:

1 **Data capture**/classification errors – these occur before data is ready for input to a system and arise because of:

- incorrect classification of data (e.g. allocating a production cost as an administrative cost)

- measuring mistakes (e.g. recording the arrival of ten tons of raw material when only nine tons was delivered)

- incorrect spelling (of a customer's name)

- transposition (recording a receipt as £50,906 instead of the actual figure of £50,960).

2 **Transcription errors** – these arise during the preparation of data for processing.

For example, data which has been written down previously or which is passed on orally may be incorrectly recorded on data input forms.

3  **Data communication faults** – if the system operates over a wide area network (WAN) then the original input at the terminal/PC may become corrupted during transmission either during online processing or where the information is stored in a batch file and transmitted over the WAN later for processing. Similar issues need to be considered for local area networks (LANs) but far fewer problems arise due to the greater level of resilience inherent in LANs.

4  **Data processing errors** – these can arise due to programming error, system design and/or data corruption on the system itself.

Because the above errors are likely to occur throughout the life of a system, with varying degrees of seriousness, we must take specific measures to identify when they occur and to ensure that corrections are made to the data, either before or after processing has occurred.

## 2.2  System activities

The purpose of the controls is to ensure as far as possible that:

- the data being processed is complete
- it is authorised
- the results are accurate
- a complete audit trail of what was done is available.

The areas in which we would expect controls to be assigned to provide protection to the system are concerned with input, file processing and output.

| Input activities | File processing activities | Output activities |
|---|---|---|
| • data collection and preparation<br>• data authorisation<br>• data conversion (if appropriate)<br>• data transmission<br>• data correction<br>• corrected data re-input | • data validation and edit<br>• data manipulation, sorting/merging<br>• master file updating | • output control and reconciliation with predetermined data<br>• information distribution |

Controls in these areas are vital and must deal with errors or problems as they arise instead of delaying their resolution to a later processing stage. Inaccurate data represents a waste of both computer time and human effort and may lead to further unforeseen errors occurring and misleading final results.

## 2.3 Data integrity

Data integrity means completeness and accuracy of data. For decisions to be made consistently throughout the organisation, it is necessary for the system to contain controls over the input, processing and output of data to maintain its integrity.

While computer systems are made up of physical items, the input of data and the output of information is designed for the benefit of human beings and is subject to their interpretation. Security risks arise where input and output occurs. Risks may arise due to innocent events such as running the wrong program, or inadvertently deleting data that is still of value to the organisation.

More importantly, as more and more systems consist of networks of computers either in the form of Local Area Networks and/or Wide Area Networks, the risks of unauthorised users hacking into those systems increases significantly.

This type of activity is referred to as 'hacking' and encompasses anything from the unauthorised accessing of personnel information to the manipulation of important accounting or other financial information.

Many of the security controls described in the previous section will have some effect on data integrity. Data controls – should ensure that data is:

- collected in full and with accuracy

- generated at the appropriate times

- kept up-to-date and accurate on file, and

- processed properly and accurately to provide meaningful and useful output.

Information can only be reliable if the underlying data is also reliable. Controls should be exercised to ensure that data could only be derived in the first instance from properly identified and responsible data providers. In order to remain reliable, such data must subsequently be processed and maintained in an adequately controlled environment.

Input data can get lost or it might contain errors. Human error is usually the biggest security weakness in the system. Controls ought to be applied to reduce the risk.

The extensiveness of the input controls will depend on the method used to process the input data and the cost of making an error.

If the consequences of input errors would be costly, the system should include more extensive controls than it would if the cost of making an error was insignificant.

## 2.4    Input controls

### Input controls

Input controls will be designed with a view to completeness, authorisation, accuracy and compliance with audit needs. The controls will use the following techniques:

- **Verification** – determines whether the data has been properly conveyed to the system from the source (unlike validation which is concerned with whether the data is correct or not).This procedure is normally carried out by a system user to check the completeness and accuracy of data. The main types of error found in data verification are copying errors and transposition errors, e.g. where a value £369,500 might have been entered as £365,900. Similarly, transposition errors in the text might be found where a customer's name might have been entered wrongly (Smtih instead of Smith).Various checks are used including:

- **Type checks** – every entry must comply with the prescribed format, e.g. dates may be defined as consisting of 2 digits, 3 alphabetic characters and 2 further digits such as 04DEC04. Any other form of input will result in an error.

- **Non-existence checks** – data fields requiring entry may have a separate validation table behind them such that the data being input must exist on that table, e.g. a supplier account number must exist already before the system will accept that number on an invoice.

- Checks for **consistency** – where data is originally entered and does not require on-going maintenance, the fact that it is still consistent with the original data input should be checked within an appropriate timescale, e.g. batch totals should not be altered once input, payee codes for suppliers paid by BACS should be confirmed by print-out against source data on a half-yearly basis.

- Avoiding a **duplication** error – the system may check, for example, that only one invoice has been received from a supplier with the supplier's invoice number currently being input.

- **Range checks** – a minimum and maximum value could be established against which input can be checked.

- Input **comparison** between document and screen.

- Checking **batch and hash totals**. A batch total is the total of (say) invoice values, which are to be processed in a batch. The total actually processed should equal the total on the manually added batch header document. . A hash total is the same as a batch total except it lacks inherent meaning. It is (say) the total of the account numbers added up. The idea of these two controls is that the operator can use them to verify that all invoices were processed at the right amount and in the right accounts.

- **One-for-one** checks between data lists.

**Validation**

Validation is the application, normally by the computer software, of a series of rules or tests designed to check the reasonableness of the data. Computers are unable to check the completeness and accuracy of data, as they are unable to see or read the source data. Instead, they must be programmed with rules and tests to apply to data to check its reasonableness.

Techniques used in validation include:

- **Comparison of totals**, e.g. checking that the total of debits equals the total of credits on a journal voucher.

- **Comparison of data sets**, e.g. a one-for-one check between two computerised files of data to identify and reject any differences.

- **Check digits** – are commonly used in supplier, customer and account numbers. The computer would perform the calculation on the code input, and compare the digit calculated with the check digit input. The idea here is to try and prevent the wrong number being entered since if it were, then the check digit would not tally and so the transaction would be rejected by the computer.

- **Sequence numbers** – often documents such as invoices, orders and credit notes have sequential numbers to avoid omission of a document. The software can be programmed to reject any document that is out of order, or to periodically report any missing documents.

- **Range checks** – the computer might be programmed with an acceptable range for each piece of data, e.g. if products are priced between £3.49 and £12.99, the sales system might be told to reject unit prices lower than £3.00 and higher than £20.00.

- **Format checks** – the software might be programmed to expect certain data to be alphabetic, numeric or a combination of the two. A numeric field would then reject the letter O being input instead of the number 0, or the letter I (lower case L) instead of the number 1.

  File controls – should be applied to make sure that:
  - correct data files are used for processing
  - whole files or data on a file are not lost or corrupted
  - unauthorised access to data on files is prevented
  - if data is lost or corrupted, it can be re-created.

### Data communication/transmission controls

If a system operates over a WAN, then the original input at the terminal/PC may become corrupted during transmission, either during on-line processing or where the information is stored in a batch file and transmitted over the WAN later for processing. Similar issues need to be considered for LANs but far fewer problems arise due to the greater level of resilience inherent in LANs.

Controls are necessary where data is transmitted in any form. The less sophisticated the techniques used for transmitting data, the higher the level of separate controls that need to be designed to identify errors and ensure that incorrect data is not processed.

## 2.5    Processing controls

These should ensure the accuracy and completeness of processing. Data processing errors can arise due to programming error, system design and/or data corruption on the system itself. Because these errors are likely to occur throughout the life of a system, with varying degrees of seriousness, specific measures should be taken to identify when they occur and to ensure that corrections are made to the data, either before or after processing has occurred.

Programs should be subject to development controls and to rigorous testing. Periodic running of test data is also recommended. Other processing controls include the following:

- **standardisation** – structured procedures for processing activities
- **batch control** documents – information about the batch that is entered prior to processing
- **double processing** – repeat of processing with comparison of individual reports.

## 2.6    Output controls

These are controls to ensure that the produced output is checked against the input controls to ensure completeness and accuracy of processing.

The system output, particularly in hard copy form, must be controlled so that the recipient receives complete and accurate information. There are a number of features that can be built into each report to ensure this:

- Batch control totals – the totals of accepted and rejected data. Exception reports – reporting abnormal transactions that may require further investigation (e.g. a report of all employees paid more than £3,000 in a particular payroll run).

- Start of report/page number/end of report markers – it should be impossible for a user to receive a report with pages missing without realising immediately. This is often used in error reports, where careless staff might 'lose' some pages from a report of the errors they have made. Nil return reports – if there is nothing to report, a report should be produced that says so. This is particularly important for error, exception and security control reports. A person committing a fraud might steal the report that showed evidence of their action, then claim there was no report produced because there were no items to report.

- Distribution lists – the header of each report should show the distribution list for the report, the number of copies, the copy number and the planned recipient of the report.

## 2.7    Application controls

These can be incorporated in the software of the system to ensure that applications preserve the integrity of data. These controls include the following:

- **Passwords** – are a set of characters that may be allocated to a person, a terminal or a room, which have to be keyed into the system before access is permitted. They may be built in to the system to allow individual users access to certain parts of the system but not to others. This will prevent accidental or deliberate changes to data.

- **Authorisation levels** – certain actions may require a user to have authorisation attached to their user-name. This type of control is commonly used for the production of cheques. Authorisation is also often necessary when rolling forward the system defaults at the end of a month or year, due to the complicated nature of correcting such a move when it is done in error.

- **Training and supervision** – staff should receive adequate training to prevent them from making the most common mistakes. They should also be made aware of any tasks that they should not attempt.

- **Audit trails** – software should be written in such a way that a clear logic exists in the sequence of tasks it performs, and data at different stages of processing is kept rather than being over-written. In this way the sequence of events can be evidenced for the benefit of any observer trying to check that the system works correctly.

---

### Test your understanding 2

Controls are invariably incorporated into the input, processing and output stages of a computer-based system.

(a) State the guidelines which should normally be followed in determining what controls should be built into a system.

(b) Identify and briefly describe one type of control which might be used to detect each of the following input data errors:

(i) Errors of transcription resulting in an incorrect customer account code.

(ii) Quantity of raw material normally written in pounds weight but entered in error as tons.

(iii) Entry on a despatch note for a product to be despatched from a warehouse which does not stock that particular product.

(iv) A five-digit product code used instead of a six-digit salesman code.

(v) Invalid expenditure code entered on an invoice.

---

## 2.8 Systems integrity

Systems integrity relates to the controlling and monitoring of the system in order to ensure that it does exactly what it was designed to do. Factors include:

- project management
- operations management
- systems design
- personnel
- procedure control
- hardware configuration.

These factors are all relevant to the system achieving what it was designed to do.

Some of the controls that we have already discussed in earlier chapters are applicable to the integrity of the system.

There is an overlap with control measures that apply to security of the system and to system integrity because, obviously, the loss of security to a system will result in the loss of integrity of the system also.

### (a) Administrative systems

Administrative controls relate to personnel and support functions. For some positions, segregation of duties is a security requirement involving division of responsibility into separate roles. The selection process for personnel (both recruitment for new staff and movement within an organisation) should reflect the nature of the work. If sensitive information is handled, positive vetting might be applied. Staff should all have detailed job descriptions, with those responsible for control clearly identifiable. Other controls include job rotation, enforced vacations, system logs and supervision.

Administrative procedures should be clearly documented and adhered to. These include health and safety procedures, especially fire drills, the operation of a 'clean desk' policy, logging document movements and the filing or shredding of documents.

The physical security of the site is vital. Visitors need to be authorised and accompanied whilst in the building. Access to more sensitive facilities can be controlled by devices such as magnetic swipe cards. Placement of hardware should ensure that the screens and documents are not visible to the 'passer by'. Access to specific terminals can be restricted by the use of devices such as passwords.

Procedures to be followed in the event of interruptions to processing should be documented and observed. Computer-based information should be backed up frequently, with the copies stored in separate locations, in fire-proof safes. Recovery plans should identify procedures for all eventualities from the retrieval of a corrupt file through to complete system failure due to, for example, fire. These plans should clearly identify the people responsible to effect the procedures.

### (b) On-line and real time systems

In this kind of processing, transactions are input as and when they arise. There is no attempt to accumulate and batch similar transactions. This gives rise to particular control problems. Traditional batch controls are not normally applicable, while the number of people inputting transactions from widely scattered terminals makes security difficult to ensure.

The following controls may be used in on-line and real time systems.

- Using passwords with a logical access system.

- Transaction log – the totals of data on the transaction log (which may be a daily or weekly log) can be matched to movements on master file control accounts.

- Supervisory controls, i.e. regular physical supervision by management. This is particularly important for situations where there is a lack of segregation of computer operator duties.

- Physical restriction of access to terminals – terminals may be kept in separate locked buildings or offices. The terminals themselves may require a key to be inserted before the terminal can be used.

- Documentation of transactions. All transaction or input documents should be recorded and signed or initialled by appropriate personnel within the user department. Pre-numbering of documents is also important so that sequence checks can be performed and reports of duplicated or missing data can be produced.

- Matching transactions to master file data. An on-line system enables full matching of transaction data to master file data.

### (c) Systems integrity in a network environment

The complexity of local and wide area networks allows for many more breaches of security than a single computer and each breach can, of course, involve many computers. The main risks on a networked system are:

- Hardware/software disruption or malfunction.

- Computer viruses – usually unwittingly distributed by opening an infected e-mail message, but also catchable from infected CDs and USB devices. Once the virus comes into contact with a system it replicates itself onto the system and lies dormant until either the use of the system, some defined event or transaction or a certain date activates it. The replication of the virus makes it very difficult to find its original source.

- Unauthorised access to the system – hacking is usually associated with people who are not employees of the organisation, but who gain access to an organisation's data for mischievous or malicious intent. However, in its widest term – a person who gains access to a computer without permission – it can also be applied to company employees themselves. Hacking has been made possible by organisations using always-on broadband telecommunications networks that are accessible to the hacker via powerful workstations and modems.

- Electronic eavesdropping – which has become more of a risk as more organisations implement wireless network configurations. Possible controls include many that we have already discussed and some that are specific for the risks outlined above. They include:

- **Physical access controls** – the use of strict controls over the locking of the rooms in which the computers are located and the distribution of keys to authorised personnel only. This is vital where the computers are used either to access sensitive data files or to alter or develop programs. Secondly, machine access – the restriction of access to and use of computers by keys, cards and badges.

- **User identification** – this includes the positive confirmation of the identity of the user and the proof of his or her identification (authentication). The former includes the input of the name, employee number and account number. The latter includes the input of something that is known (e.g. passwords, question-and-answer sequences), or something that is possessed (badges, cards), or something personal to the user (e.g. finger print, hand or voice features, signature).

- **Data and program access authorisation** – after identification of the user, the type of privileges are checked to ensure that the user has the necessary authority. Privileges cover the type of files and programs that can be accessed, and the activities allowed during access. The user is denied access if he or she is not specifically authorised.

- **Program integrity controls** – ensure that unauthorised access and alterations cannot be made to programs.

- **Database integrity controls** – controls and audit techniques that protect database management systems software and data against unauthorised access, modification, disclosure and destruction.

- **Anti-virus software** – (regularly updated with new releases) detects known viruses and destroys them. Each common virus will be known and identifiable by the anti-virus software. However, it must be recognised that such software only protects against known viruses. All emails, removable disks and CDs should be checked before they can be used internally. Most organisations implement stringent internal procedures to make sure that unauthorised disks and CDs are not used within the organisation. Failure to comply with these requirements usually leads to disciplinary action, including dismissal.

- **Surveillance** – the detection of security violations by direct observation, by review of computer logs or by use of the operator's console to display current program and data usage.

- **Communication lines safeguards** – while impossible to fully protect communication lines, controls such as encryption, phone tap and bug checks should go a long way to prevent penetration of the system via the communication lines.

- **Encryption** – is a control to translate a message into coded form using a code key that is only known to the sender and recipient of the message. This is a useful control for preventing eavesdropping, particularly in a wireless network.

- **Firewalls** – are security devices that effectively isolate the sensitive parts of an organisation's system from those areas available to external users.

- **Administrative considerations** – procedures that ensure that controls and safeguards are effective in preventing, deterring and detecting unauthorised or fraudulent systems data and program access and modification.

---

### Test your understanding 3

On a number of occasions, you will be aware that a new virus has been reported that might be spread by e-mail and do considerable damage. Opening the e-mail will run the virus, and might also forward it to all the addresses in your address book. Next time this happens, carefully make a note of all the steps your organisation has taken to deal with this contingency. What would you do if you suspected an e-mail you had been sent contained a virus?

# 3 Contingency controls

## 3.1 Disasters affecting the computer system

In computing terms, a disaster might mean the loss or unavailability of some of the computer systems. In a modern business there are few areas unaffected by computing and consequently few that will not suffer if its performance is impaired. Also, risks are increasing; an organisation now has to cope with the risks of hacking, virus infection and industrial action aimed at the computing staff.

Losses that can be expected due to the non-availability of computer systems increase with time; it is therefore important to make plans to keep downtime to a minimum.

Management commitment is an essential component of any contingency plan because it will almost certainly involve considerable expense. Various stand-by plans must be considered; the choice will depend on the amount of time that the installation can reasonably expect to survive without computing.

The key feature of any disaster recovery plan is the regular back up of data and software. If, at the time of disaster, there are no back-up copies, then no amount of stand-by provision will replace them.

The contingency plan must specify what actions are to be taken during a disaster and during the time that computer systems are unavailable up to the time that full operations are restored. The plan must be as detailed as possible; should state who is responsible at each stage, when it should be invoked, and where copies may be found. The more care that is taken with a contingency plan, the better the organisation will be able to survive a computing disaster; it also concentrates the mind on computer security and the risks faced, with an increased likelihood that counter measures will be installed which will reduce the risks.

## 3.2 Contingency controls

Contingency controls are those which correct the consequences of a risk occurring, rather than preventing or reducing the risk. It is the process of planning for catastrophes and in the computing environment this usually means the breakdown of the computer system. For organisations that rely upon their computer systems to carry on their business the loss of those systems, even for a short period, can be disastrous, therefore good contingency plans should be put in place.

The plan should include:

- standby procedures – so that essential operations can be performed while normal services are disrupted

- recovery procedures – to return to normal working once the breakdown is fixed

- management policies to ensure that the plan is implemented.

A number of standby plans merit consideration and are discussed below. The final selection would be dependent upon the estimated time that the concern would function adequately without computing facilities.

- Distributed support, where computing is spread over several sites so that, if one site is lost, the others can cope with the transferred work. This approach implies compatibility and spare capacity to cope with the loss of the largest installation.

- Reciprocal agreement with another company. Although a popular option, few companies can guarantee spare capacity, or continuing capability and compatibility, which attaches a high risk to this option.

- A more expensive, but lower risk, version of the above is the commercial computer bureau. This solution entails entering into a formal agreement, which entitles the customer to a selection of services.

- Empty rooms or equipped rooms. The former allows the organisation access to install a back-up system, which increases the recovery time but reduces the cost. The latter can be costly, so sharing this facility is a consideration.

- Relocatable computer centres. This solution involves a delay while the facility is erected and assembled and also larger computers cannot usually be accommodated.

The effectiveness of the contingency plan is dependent on comprehensive back-up procedures for both data and software. The contingency plan must identify initial responses and clearly delineate responsibility at each stage of the exercise – from damage limitation through to full recovery.

## 3.3 Backing up

Information on your computer is vulnerable: hard disks can fail, computer systems can fail, viruses can wipe a disk, careless operators can delete files, and very careless operators can delete whole areas of the hard disks by mistake. Computers can also be damaged or stolen. For these reasons backing up your data is essential. This involves making copies of essential files, together with necessary update transactions and keeping them on another computer, or on some form of storage media so that copies can be recreated. Your organisation will have procedures and you will have been taught how to do this.

To ensure that you can back up easily you will probably have your own 'workspace' – an area of a disk that contains your work. This helps segregate your unique work from files or information that are held by a number of people.

It is important to get into the habit of backing up in different ways for different reasons to increase the reliability of your backed-up data. You should consider backing-up:

- when you have done a large amount of work over a short period – in which case you should back up all the contents of your 'workspace'

- when you have completed a major body of work – you should clean up the directory containing the files (to get rid of files that are not needed) and just back up that directory

- on a regular basis, back up your whole 'workspace' and the essential system files.

Where the data is maintained by batch processing, the Grandfather/ Father/ Son method of backing-up will be used. The principle of this method is that at any point in time the last two back-ups made should be available plus all of the batches that have been processed since the older of the back-ups was made. These would be in the form of master and data discs that would be separately labelled and stored. Once the Grandfather disc becomes older than that, it can be re-used as the latest disc for back-up purposes and becomes the Son.

These days, where it is more likely that the data is maintained on-line, data will be backed-up each day, so that if the normal storage medium fails, the information is available for the system to be restored to the last point of data entry prior to the back-up being taken. Copies of all data files should be taken on a frequent and regular basis and kept off-site or in a fireproof safe. The data can then be restored in case of data loss or corruption.

**Software backup** – copies of system software and applications should also be taken and stored off-site. Thus the computer system can be re-created on new hardware in case the building is damaged or destroyed. Software can also be restored in case it becomes corrupted or accidentally deleted.

Procedures to be followed in the event of interruptions to processing should be documented and observed. Computer-based information should be backed up frequently, with the copies stored in separate locations, in fireproof safes. Recovery plans should identify procedures for all eventualities from the retrieval of a corrupt file through to complete system failure due to, for example, fire. These plans should clearly identify the people responsible to effect the procedures.

**Test your understanding 4**

List and give a brief explanation of the control techniques and safeguards to protect a system where multiple users have access to centralised data through terminal devices at remote locations linked to a central computer system via telephone lines or other communication links.

## 3.4 Advantages and disadvantages of contingency planning

The main argument in favour of contingency planning is that it places the management team in a better position to cope with the change by eliminating or at least reducing the time delay (and hence lost profits) in making a response to an emergency. The emergency may be a lost opportunity or a definite threat. Specific reserve plans help managers to respond more rationally to the event. A crisis can lead to decisions being made within a very short time span and without full information. Early evaluation of the demands of low probability events and the alternative remedies allows more detailed consideration and consequently should reduce the likelihood of panic measures.

Although contingency planning does force managers to consider unlikely events that can result in beneficial spin-offs, it can also result in negative attitudes. Events with low probabilities may be threats and focusing attention on these threats could be demoralising and demotivating.

# 4 Assessing and managing risk

## 4.1 Managing risk

In general terms, risk would be taken as meaning anything that could cause the organisation to make a financial loss. It can be defined as the 'chance of bad consequences'. The types of risk include disasters outside the control of the organisation, poor trading, mismanagement, errors because of human or machine problems and misappropriation of resources, physical assets or intangible assets.

You must understand the concept of risk and how it may be assessed in the planning of controls within an organisation.

The following step-by-step process is a useful framework for the risk assessment process:

- Identify risks.

- Quantify risks.

- Identify counter measures (some of the possibilities are listed below).

- Cost counter measures.

- Choose which counter measures are required.

- Draw up contingency plans.

- Implement the plan to manage the risk.

- Monitor, review and update the plan.

- Constantly watch for new risks – encourage all staff to report situations where they feel there might be a risk.

The counter measures that an organisation can adopt include the following possibilities:

- Transfer the risks (by means of an insurance policy) – limited liability is another way of transferring risk.

- Decide to live with the risks, if the counter measures cannot be justified.

- Modify a system so as to eliminate the risks.

- Reduce the probability of risk by introducing controls e.g. two signatures on payments.

- Reduce the exposure to risk by removing the organisation from risky situations.

- Adopt measures that reduce the cost associated with a risk (e.g. by ensuring an adequate back-up system).

- Enable recovery by implementing recovery procedures appropriate to the situation e.g. relocation plans and computer disaster recovery plans.

# 5 Additional 'Test your understanding' questions

##  Test your understanding 5

1 Why do organisations adopt security measures?

2 Describe the three elements of the information system's security.

3 Outline the terms of the Data Protection Act.

4 What are usage logs?

5 Identify four of the techniques used in data validation.

6 What do you understand by the term 'data integrity'?

7 What sort of documents need sequence controls?

8 To maintain systems integrity, what types of control may be used in on-line and real time systems?

9 What type of control is encryption?

# 6 Summary

Computer systems require special attention in any organisation for two reasons. Firstly, the fact that the audit trail through a computer system is not visible as in a manual system may lead to problems of control. Secondly, any errors in a computer system of a systematic nature can have a very serious impact on the accuracy of the records, whereas in a manual system the damage is likely to be far more localised to one specific area.

You should therefore ensure that the computer systems of an organisation are very well controlled with tight security over all the key functions.

# Test your understanding answers

 **Test your understanding 1**

**BRIEFING REPORT**

To:       Head of Department

From:   Trainee management accountant

Date:    2nd November

**Security of an organisation's computer system**

The factors, which most affect the security of an organisation's computer system, can be divided into three groups – physical, systems and human.

**Physical aspects** – these relate to the security risks to which the computer hardware is exposed. These risks mainly come from outside the system and include theft, fire, dust, humidity, flooding and wind and earth movement damage to the building housing the computer.

**Systems aspects** – these relate to risks, which are inherent in the system itself and include loss of data, loss of software and possibly damage to equipment, all caused by system malfunctioning brought about by either hardware or software failure or errors.

**Human aspects** – these include risks from inside and outside the organisation and risks arising from both intentional and unintentional actions. For example a large multi-user networked computer system is at risk from outside 'hacking' as well as from employees within the organisation. Unintentional damage to equipment, data and software etc may be caused by accidents e.g. spilling drinks into equipment, accidental changes to data e.g. correcting the wrong file or deleting a file, running the wrong software, forgetting to run a particular process etc. Intentional aspects include setting up fake accounts, causing unauthorised payments either as credit or cheques to be made, allowing favourable discount terms to particular clients and damage such as the deletion or corruption of data files and software.

## Managing the risks associated with computer security

Managing the risks associated with computer security involves reducing the risks and the effects to the lowest possible levels. Three stages are necessary.

**Risk assessment** – a full examination of all the risks in the three groups above is made. Particular types of computer systems and particular locations and environments each have their own problems. The risks are, of course, different for a centralised system as against a distributed computing system.

Another factor is the importance of the work being done on the computer. For example if a personnel department computer went down, it would not be as serious as if the computer monitoring a production line failed and there would not be such a need to get the personnel computer up and running again quickly.

**Risk minimisation** – this comprises the actions, which may be taken when the risks to a computer system have been assessed. These actions include both taking physical and system precautions and providing fall-back and remedial measures. The list of actions includes:

- securing the building(s) housing equipment with bars, strong doors, locks, monitoring systems, access control, etc.

- provision of an environment suitable for reliable computer operation, having clean air at the correct temperature and humidity and an electrical power supply that is both continuous and smooth

- strict control of the quality of new software and on any modifications required to existing software

- vetting of all computer staff appointments and the taking out of 'fidelity guarantees' with suitable insurance companies

- access control for the system from terminals, etc. This will normally involve a system of passwords changed on a regular basis

- a high level of training and education of computer staff

- automated operating procedures with built in checks (probably utilising job control language 'programs') so that operators do not have to trust to memory and are given minimum scope for error

- fully documented systems and procedure manuals including precise statements of actions to be taken for system recovery after breakdowns

- provision of standby facilities and a reciprocal processing agreement with another organisation.

(If the computer failed and it was expected that it would not be repairable for quite some time, then back-up disks would be transferred and processing carried out on the other organisation's computer, overnight or at the weekend – and vice versa.)

**Risk transference** – it is impossible to eliminate all risks, but it is possible to transfer the element of uncovered risk to another party through the medium of insurance i.e. in the event of a computer catastrophe, the losses caused would be covered by insurance.

 **Test your understanding 2**

(a) **Systems controls should be designed according to the following guidelines:**

- All transactions should be processed.

- All errors in transactions should be reported. Errors should be corrected and re-input. Fraud should be prevented.

- The likelihood of error should be estimated. This will depend partly on the location in which the source document is prepared and the type of person originating it.

- The importance of errors should be assessed. In accounting systems, 100% accuracy may be required. In other systems (e.g. market surveys), a degree of error may be acceptable.

- The cost of control should be considered in relation to the cost of an error. The cost of 100% accuracy is, in practice, usually too high. The controls should not interfere unduly with the progress of work. The controls should be as simple as possible, and acceptable to users. Auditors should be consulted and the system designed to meet their requirements.

(b) **Incorrect customer account code**

This should be detected by a check digit. The account code would include an extra digit derived by calculation from other digits. On input to the computer, the program would perform the calculations and, if the digit derived was not the check digit, an error would be reported. The system selected should minimise the possibility of undetected error.

**Raw material quantity**

This should be detected by a reasonableness check. Upper and lower limits would be set, outside which a quantity should not lie. Since the entry of kilograms instead of tonnes would result in a value 1000 times as big as the correct one, it would be detected.

**Product not stocked**

This would be detected by an on-file check. On input, the despatch note details would be referred to the stock master files, which would indicate that the product was not held in the warehouse shown.

**Five-digit product code**

This would be detected by a format check. The validation program would have parameters for the size of fields, and would report the product code as being a digit short.

**Invalid expenditure code**

This would be detected by a range check. The validation program would have parameters showing the upper and lower values of expenditure codes. Comparison of the code with the parameters would reveal that it was not in the permissible range.

---

 **Test your understanding 3**

Did you note that your organisation has anti-virus software? Does the information systems department give you clear instructions on the procedure to adopt? If a machine was infected, what happened?

You would not open the e-mail under any circumstances but should contact the IS department immediately. They should be able to identify and remove the virus. In some situations you might have to delete it yourself. This means deleting it from your inbox and then deleting it from your 'deleted items' folder.

**Test your understanding 4**

The control techniques and safeguards used to protect a system where multiple users have access to centralised data through terminal devices at remote locations linked to a central computer system via telephone lines or other communication links are as follows.

- **Terminal physical security** – this covers two aspects. Firstly, terminal room access – the use of strict controls over the locking of the rooms in which the terminals are located and the distribution of keys to authorised personnel only. This is vital where the terminals are used either to access sensitive data files or to alter or develop programs. Secondly, terminal machine access – the restriction of access to and use of terminals by keys, cards and badges.

- **User identification** – this includes the positive confirmation of the identity of the user and the proof of his identification (authentication). The former includes the input of his name, employee number and account number. The latter includes the input of something that is known (e.g. passwords, question-and-answer sequences), or something that is possessed (badges, cards), or something personal to the user (e.g. finger print, hand or voice features, signature).

- **Data and program access authorisation** – after identification of the user (above), the privileges he has as to what he can access (files and programs) and what he can do during access have to be checked to ensure that he has the necessary authority. The user must be denied access if not specifically authorised.

- **Surveillance** – the detection of security violations by direct observation, by review of computer logs or by use of the operator's console to display current program and data usage.

- **Communication lines safeguards** – while impossible to fully protect communication lines controls such as encryption, phone tap and bug checks should go a long way to prevent penetration of the system via the communication lines.

- **Encryption** – the transformation of a message or of data for the purpose of rendering it unintelligible to everyone but the correct users who are able to translate the message back to its original form. Program integrity controls – controls, which ensure that unauthorised access and alterations cannot be made to programs.

- **Database integrity controls** – controls and audit techniques, which protect database management systems software and data against unauthorised access, modification, disclosure and destruction.

- **Administrative considerations** – procedures, which ensure that controls and safeguards are effective in preventing, deterring and detecting unauthorised or fraudulent systems data and program access and modification.

### Test your understanding 5

1    They adopt security measures to avoid or prevent loss; to deter as many threats as possible; for easy recovery after any loss; to identify the cause of any loss after the event; and to correct vulnerable areas to reduce the risk of repeated loss.

2    The information systems security is based on three elements. The people, the data/information elements and the physical elements, which acknowledge that the operation of computer equipment can be severely impaired where it is subject to events such as fire, flooding and improper environmental conditions, e.g. heat.

3    Under the terms of the Data Protection Act 1998, the need for privacy is recognised by the requirements that all personal data on individuals should be held only for clearly designated purposes. Accuracy and integrity must be maintained and the data must be open to inspection. Only legitimate parties can access data and information must be secured against alteration, accidental loss or deliberate damage. Furthermore, the Act states that data must be obtained fairly, to precise specifications and must not be kept for longer than required.

4    Usage logs are part of the system, which is designed to automatically record the log-in and log-off times of each user, the applications accessed and any applications or files where access has been denied. Periodic checks are made for unusual patterns, such as a day-shift worker accessing the system at night.

5    The techniques used in data validation include comparison of totals, comparison of data sets, check digits, sequence, range checks and format checks.

6   Data integrity means completeness and accuracy of data. For decisions to be made consistently throughout the organisation, it is necessary for the system to contain controls over the input, processing and output of data to maintain its integrity.

7   Documents such as invoices, orders, petty cash vouchers and credit notes need sequential numbers to avoid omission of a document.

8   The following controls may be used in on-line and real time systems.

- Using passwords with a logical access system.

- Transaction log – the totals of data on the transaction log (which may be a daily or weekly log) can be matched to movements on master file control accounts.

- Supervisory controls, i.e. regular physical supervision by management. This is particularly important for situations where there is a lack of segregation of computer operator duties.

- Physical restriction of access to terminals – terminals may be kept in separate locked buildings or offices. The terminals themselves may require a key to be inserted before the terminal can be used.

- Documentation of transactions. All transaction or input documents should be recorded and signed or initialled by appropriate personnel within the user department. Pre-numbering of documents is also important so that sequence checks can be performed, and reports of duplicated or missing data can be produced.

9   Encryption is a control to translate a message into coded form using a code key that is only known to the sender and recipient of the message. This is a useful control for preventing eavesdropping, particularly in a wireless network.

# Ratio analysis

**5**

## Introduction

In both of the units 'Financial Statements of Limited Companies' and 'Management Accounting: Decisions and Control' you considered the use of ratios to assess performance.

Within the synoptic assessment you may get tasks asking you to do exactly the same thing – assess performance. However, in addition to this you will also get tasks that ask you to analyse accounting ratios in order to relate problems in them back to the system of internal control.

The assumption behind this is the idea that poor controls can lead to poor decisions or mistakes, which then manifest themselves in the financial statements of a business.

In this chapter we revise key ratios and then consider the link to internal controls.

| PERFORMANCE CRITERIA |
| --- |
| 2.1 Evaluate how information from the financial statements may indicate weaknesses in internal controls |

| CONTENTS |
| --- |
| 1 Profitability ratios |
| 2 Liquidity ratios |
| 3 Investor ratios |
| 4 Interpreting financial ratios |
| 5 Question styles |
| 6 The link between ratios and internal controls |

# 1 Profitability ratios

## 1.1 Introduction

Ratios calculated from financial statements help to interpret the information they present. We can break down the ratios into categories to make our discussion more structured. To begin with we look at ratios relating to profitability.

## 1.2 Return on capital employed (ROCE)

Return on capital employed is frequently regarded as the best measure of profitability, indicating how successful a business is in utilising the funding it has received.

$$\text{Return on capital employed} = \frac{\text{Profit from operations}}{\text{Total equity} + \text{Non-current liabilities}} \times 100$$

A low return on capital employed is caused by either a low profit margin or a low asset turnover or both.

## 1.3 Return on shareholders' funds

$$\text{Return on shareholders' funds} = \frac{\text{Profit after tax}}{\text{Total equity}} \times 100\%$$

This looks at the return earned for ordinary shareholders. We use the profit after preference dividends and interest (i.e. the amounts that have to be paid before ordinary shareholders can be rewarded).

## 1.4 Gross profit percentage

$$\text{Gross profit percentage} = \frac{\text{Gross profit}}{\text{Revenue}} \times 100\%$$

The gross profit percentage focuses on the trading account. A low margin could indicate selling prices are too low or cost of sales is too high.

## 1.5 Expense/revenue percentage

$$\text{Expense/revenue percentage} = \frac{\text{Specified expense}}{\text{Revenue}} \times 100$$

The expenses/revenue percentage focuses on individual expenses in relation to revenue.

## 1.6 Operating profit percentage

$$\text{Operating profit percentage} = \frac{\text{Profit from operations}}{\text{Revenue}} \times 100$$

A low margin indicates low selling prices or high costs or both.
Comparative analysis will reveal the level of prices and costs in relation to competitors.

## 1.7 Asset turnover

$$\text{Asset turnover (non-current assets)} = \frac{\text{Revenue}}{\text{Non} - \text{current assets}}$$

OR

$$\text{Asset turnover (net assets)} = \frac{\text{Revenue}}{\text{Total assets} - \text{Current liabilities}}$$

This is a measure of how fully a company is utilising its assets.

A low turnover shows that a company is not generating a sufficient volume of business for the size of the asset base.

This may be remedied by increasing sales or by disposing of some of the assets or both.

# 2 Liquidity ratios

## 2.1 Current ratio

This is a common method of analysing working capital (net current assets) and is generally accepted as a good measure of short-term solvency. It indicates the extent to which the claims of short-term payables are covered by assets that are expected to be converted to cash in a period roughly corresponding to the maturity of the claims.

$$\text{Current ratio} = \frac{\text{Current assets}}{\text{Current liabilities}}$$

The current ratio should ideally fall between 1:1 and 2:1.

## 2.2 Acid test ratio (quick ratio)

This is calculated in the same way as the current ratio except that inventories are excluded from current assets.

$$\text{Acid test ratio} = \frac{\text{Current assets} - \text{Inventories}}{\text{Current liabilities}}$$

This ratio is a much better test of the immediate solvency of a business because of the length of time necessary to convert inventories into cash (via revenue and receivables).

Contrary to what might be expected, this ratio may fall in a time of prosperity since increased activity may lead to larger inventories but less cash; conversely, when trade slows down inventories may be disposed of without renewal and the ratio will rise.

Although increased liquid resources more usually indicate favourable trading, it could be that funds are not being used to their best advantage (e.g. large cash balance).

### 2.3 Inventory holding period in days

Inventory turnover can also be calculated in terms of days. This is calculated as follows:

$$\text{Inventory turnover period} = \frac{\text{Inventories}}{\text{Cost of sales}} \times 365 \text{ days}$$

### 2.4 Trade receivables collection period

This is computed by dividing the trade receivables by the average daily sales to determine the number of days sales held in receivables. It is usually calculated as:

$$\text{Average collection period} = \frac{\text{Trade receivables}}{\text{Revenue}} \times 365 \text{ days}$$

A long average collection period probably indicates poor credit control, but it may be due to other factors such as overseas sales where the collection period will be much longer, or a deliberate decision to extend the credit period to attract new customers.

### 2.5 Trade payables payment period

This is computed by dividing the trade payables by the average daily purchases to determine the number of days purchases held in payables.

$$\text{Average payment period} = \frac{\text{Trade payable}}{\text{Cost of sales}} \times 365 \text{ days}$$

Note: If only cost of sales (rather than purchases) is available in the information given this can be used as an approximation to purchases.

If the payables period is very low, then the business might not be making the best use of its cash by paying suppliers early.

If the period is very long then this is a free source of credit but the business must be careful not to harm relations with suppliers.

### 2.6 Working capital cycle

Inventory days + Receivable days – Payable days

This is the length of time between paying out cash for inventory and receiving the cash for goods or services supplied.

The longer the period of time that cash is tied up in working capital the more cost that is incurred by companies either directly, by virtue of bank interest, or indirectly, as a result of the inability to invest cash surpluses into higher interest yielding accounts.

# 3 Investor ratios

### 3.1 Gearing

Gearing measures the extent to which a business is dependent on non-equity funds, as opposed to equity funding. A high gearing ratio means that the business has a high proportion of borrowed funds in its total capital.

Gearing gives an indication of long-term liquidity and the financial risk inherent within the business. Highly geared companies have to meet large interest commitments before paying dividends and may have problems raising further finance if expansion is necessary.

$$\text{Gearing} = \frac{\text{Non - current liabilities}}{\text{Total equity} + \text{Non - current liabilities}} \times 100$$

### 3.2 Interest cover

$$\text{Interest cover} = \frac{\text{Profit from operations}}{\text{Finance costs}}$$

Interest on debt has to be paid before shareholders can receive dividends. Therefore a good measure of risk is to compare available profit with the amount of interest to be paid.

### 3.3 Dividend cover

$$\text{Dividend cover} = \frac{\text{Profit after tax}}{\text{Dividend}}$$

Dividend cover looks at how many times the dividend could have been paid out of current profits. Therefore a good measure of risk as it indicates how much profit could fall by before the dividend is compromised.

# 4 Interpreting financial ratios

There are some more general points on ratio analysis which should be particularly noted.

## 4.1 Caution in interpretation

Dogmatic conclusions should be avoided. For example, a reduction in the inventory holding period may be a good thing, but if it is likely to cause loss of customer goodwill or production dislocations due to inventory shortages, it may not be such an advantage.

Ratios rarely answer questions but they can highlight areas where questions might usefully be asked.

## 4.2 Statement of financial position figures

Many of the ratios considered in this chapter involve the use of statement of financial position figures. These ratios should be interpreted with caution since the statement of financial position shows the position at a specific moment only and this may not be typical of the general position.

This point is particularly important where the ratio is derived from a statement of financial position figure in conjunction with a figure from the statement of profit or loss and other comprehensive income.

This is because the first figure relates to a moment in time whereas the second is a total for a period.

A sensible way to try to avoid possible distortions here is to use the average figure for the statement of financial position figure. So, for example, the receivables collection period would relate credit sales to the average of the trade receivables figures at the beginning and at the end of the year.

However in many industries the existence of recurrent seasonal factors may mean that averaging beginning and end of year figures will not solve the problem.

It may be for example, that the date up to which a business draws up its final accounts has been selected because it is a time when inventory levels are always low, so that inventory is relatively easy to value.

In such cases, averaging the inventory figures for two consecutive year end dates would simply be averaging two figures which were totally untypical of inventory levels throughout the rest of the year. Averaging monthly figures would usually be the solution to this problem. However, outsiders would not typically have access to such information.

## 4.3 Other financial ratios

There are an almost infinite number of ratios which can be calculated from a set of final accounts. The ones shown above are those most commonly used in practice and include those which have been specifically identified by the FNST study guide. It should be noted, however, that there are many other ratios which could be useful in particular contexts.

## 4.4 Partial sightedness of ratios

It is usually unwise to limit analysis and interpretation only to information revealed by ratios.

For example, revenue for a business could double from one year to the next. This would be a dramatic and important development, yet none of the ratios whose use is advocated in most textbooks would reveal this, at least not directly.

However, this significant increase in turnover would be fairly obvious from even a superficial glance at the final accounts.

# 5 Question styles

In the synoptic assessment, as well as calculating ratios, you may be given a range of statements and asked to identify which

- reflect what the ratios are showing, or

- explain why ratios are different, from one period to another or between companies, or

- summarise cause and effect correctly.

When explaining why ratios have changed, try to refer to the underlying drivers of business performance where possible.

For example:

- A higher gpm could be due to a rise in prices and/or a drop in production costs per unit, but why might they have happened?

- Higher prices could be due to the introduction of new products or greater brand awareness or improvements in quality or greater market power over customers.

- Lower costs could be due to new machinery or improvements in efficiency or economies of scale or a more motivated workforce or fewer quality problems.

Let us look at a range of question styles. Firstly, a traditional question along the lines of ones you have met before:

 **Test your understanding 1 – Financial Statements of Limited Companies style**

You work for Grudem Ltd, a book publisher. The directors are looking to invest in Zusak Ltd, a chain of shops.

The Finance Director has asked you for assistance and has given you Zusak's statement of profit or loss and the summarised statement of financial position for the past two years prepared for internal purposes. These are set out below.

**Zusak Ltd**
**Summary statement of profit or loss**
**for the year ended 31 March**

|  | 20X4 | 20X3 |
| --- | --- | --- |
|  | £000 | £000 |
| Revenue | 8,420 | 7,595 |
| Cost of sales | (3,536) | (3,418) |
|  |  |  |
| Gross profit | 4,884 | 4,177 |
| Distribution costs | (1,471) | (1,016) |
| Administrative expenses | (1,224) | (731) |
|  |  |  |
| Profit from operations | 2,189 | 2,430 |
| Finance costs | (400) | (480) |
|  |  |  |
| Profit before tax | 1,789 | 1,950 |
| Tax | (465) | (569) |
|  |  |  |
| Profit for the period | 1,324 | 1,381 |

**Zusak Ltd**

**Summary statement of financial position as at 31 March**

|  | 20X4 £000 | 20X3 £000 |
|---|---|---|
| **ASSETS** | | |
| **Non-current assets** | | |
| Property, plant and equipment | 15,132 | 13,880 |
| Current assets | 4,624 | 3,912 |
| **Total assets** | **19,756** | **17,792** |
| **EQUITY AND LIABILITIES** | | |
| **Equity** | | |
| Ordinary shares of £1 each | 6,000 | 5,000 |
| Share premium | 2,000 | 1,000 |
| Retained earnings | 4,541 | 3,937 |
| **Total equity** | 12,541 | 9,937 |
| **Non-current liabilities** | | |
| Long term loan | 5,000 | 6,000 |
| Current liabilities | 2,215 | 1,855 |
| **Total liabilities** | 7,215 | 7,855 |
| **Total equity and liabilities** | **19,756** | **17,792** |

Prepare working papers that include:

(a) a calculation of the following ratios of Zusak Ltd for each of the two years:

(i) return on capital employed

(ii) operating profit percentage

(iii) gross profit percentage

(iv) asset turnover (based on net assets)

(b) an explanation of the meaning of each ratio and a comment on the performance of Zusak Ltd as shown by each of the ratios

(c) a conclusion on how the overall performance has changed over the two years.

Next some 'statements' style questions:

 **Test your understanding 2**

The Return on Capital Employed (ROCE) for DF has increased from 12.3% to 17.8% in the year to 31 March 20X5.

**Which one of the following independent options would be a valid reason for this increase?**

| | |
|---|---|
| Significant investment in property, plant and equipment shortly before the year end. | |
| Revaluation of land and buildings following a change of policy from cost model to revaluation model. | |
| Property, plant and equipment acquired in the previous period now operating at full capacity. | |
| An issue of equity shares with the proceeds being used to repay long-term borrowings. | |

 **Test your understanding 3**

The following information is available for 2 potential acquisition targets that are situated in the same country and operate in the same industry.

| | A | B |
|---|---|---|
| Revenue | $375m | $380m |
| Gross profit margin | 28% | 19% |
| Profit for the year/revenue margin | 11% | 11% |

**Which one of the following statements is NOT a valid conclusion that could be drawn from comparing the above information?**

| | |
|---|---|
| A's gross profit margin is better than B's as it is able to benefit from economies of scale. | |
| The difference between the gross profit margin of A and B may be due to how they classify their expenses between cost of sales and operating costs. | |
| A may have improved their gross profit margin by significant investment in new and efficient machinery, but could be suffering from high finance costs as a result of financing the investment with long-term borrowings. | |
| B may be selling a significantly higher volume of products than A, but at a lower price. | |

**KAPLAN** PUBLISHING

**Test your understanding 4**

ABC is a small private entity looking for investment. It has been trading for more than 10 years manufacturing and selling its own branded perfumes, lotions and candles to the public in its 15 retail stores and to other larger retailing entities. Revenue and profits have been steady over the last 10 years however about 15 months ago ABC set up an online shop and also secured a lucrative deal with a boutique hotel chain to supply products carrying the hotel name and logo.

Extracts from the statement of profit or loss of ABC are provided below:

|  | 20X2 | 20X1 |
|---|---|---|
|  | $000 | $000 |
| Revenue | 6,000 | 3,700 |
| Gross profit | 1,917 | 1,095 |
| Profit before tax | 540 | 307 |

The revenue and profits of the three business segments for the year ended 31 December 20X2 were:

|  | Retail operations | Online store | Hotel contract |
|---|---|---|---|
|  | $000 | $000 | $000 |
| Revenue | 4,004 | 1,096 | 900 |
| Gross profit | 1,200 | 330 | 387 |
| Profit before tax | 320 | 138 | 82 |

The online store and hotel contract earned a negligible amount of revenue and profit in the year ended 31 December 20X1.

**Which THREE of the following statements could be realistically concluded from the extracts provided above?**

| | |
|---|---|
| The revenue growth is principally due to the online store and hotel contract. | |
| The gross profit margin would have fallen in 20X2 if the new operations had not been introduced. | |
| The online store should have a better gross profit margin than retail operations as it does not have the shop overheads. | |
| The hotel contract attracts a higher gross profit margin than the other operations. | |
| The hotel contract appears to require significant overheads in comparison to revenue when compared with other segments. | |
| The increase in profit before tax margin is principally due to the hotel contract. | |

**Test your understanding 5**

LW, a listed entity, operates in the manufacturing sector. LW operates in a mature market and has not experienced growth in volume for the past five years. It is currently considering ways that it can increase revenue by diversifying its product range however it has yet to implement any new strategy.

The following ratios have been calculated based on LW's most recent financial statements for the year ended 31 December 20X3.

|  | 20X3 | 20X2 |
|---|---|---|
| Gross profit margin | 39.4% | 36.6% |
| Operating profit margin | 12.6% | 14.4% |
| Quick ratio | 0.5 | 1.1 |
| Inventories holding period | 141 days | 112 days |
| Payables payment period | 154 days | 98 days |

LW was involved in a major dispute with one of its key customers in 20X3 regarding the non-settlement of amounts owed by the customer. The dispute was eventually settled close to the reporting date and the majority of the cash has since been received, however LW incurred significant legal fees in the process and had to stop supplying the customer for a period of time.

**Which THREE of the following statements could be realistically concluded from the extracts provided above?**

| Stopping supplies to the significant customer will have contributed to the increase in inventory holding period. | |
|---|---|
| The impact of the cost of the dispute can be seen in the operating profit margin, which has fallen despite an increase in gross profit margin for the year. | |
| The increase in gross profit margin is likely to have been achieved by increasing selling prices. | |
| The increase in payables payment period will have resulted in a reduction in cash and cash equivalents. | |
| The reduction in quick ratio is principally due to the significant increase in inventory holding period. | |
| The reduction in quick ratio is principally due to the significant increase in payables payment period. | |

# 6   The link between ratios and internal controls

An important aspect of the synoptic assessment syllabus is the link between a ratio change (often a deterioration) and the business' internal control system.

Ideally you can follow the line of possible cause and effect from both directions:

## From control issue to ratios

Suppose there is an error in the annual inventory stock-take that results in closing inventory being **undervalued** – which ratios could be affected?

- If closing inventory is undervalued, then cost of sales will be overstated and gross profit understated.

- An obvious result is that ratios involving profit will be affected:
  - GPM will be lower
  - ROCE will most likely be lower (note: the impact on ROCE is not clear cut as profit will be lower, but so will capital employed)
  - Interest and dividend cover will be lower.

- There will also be an impact on working capital ratios
  - The current ratio will be lower (note that the quick ratio does not contain inventory so will be unaffected)
  - Inventory days will be lower as we have lower inventory and higher cost of sales.

Alternatively, suppose a cut-off error at the end of an accounting period means that a sales invoice has been recognised for the period when it should be deferred to the next period.

- The error means that both sales (and hence, profit) and receivables (debtors) are overstated.

- Profitability ratios will improve
  - GPM will be higher
  - ROCE will be higher.

- Liquidity ratios will be larger
  - Both current and quick ratios will get larger
  - Receivables days (and the length of the operating cycle) will be longer.

- Investor ratios will improve
  - Both interest cover and dividend cover will be higher.

 **Test your understanding 6**

A dishonest credit controller has been found to be writing off debts owed to his employer by friends of his.

**Identify the impact of the fraud on the following ratios**

|  | Higher | Lower | No change |
|---|---|---|---|
| Gross profit margin | | | |
| Payables days | | | |
| Quick ratio | | | |
| Interest cover | | | |

**From ratio to potential causes**

If, for example, the receivable days ratio has worsened from one year to the next then this might be tracked back to poor control over the collection of cash from receivables. You would be expected to realise that and (potentially) suggest improvements to rectify the situation.

 **Test your understanding 7**

The quick ratio has declined from last year to this. During the year end audit a number of errors were detected.

**Identify which of the following errors would have contributed to the quick ratio being lower.**

| | |
|---|---|
| Year-end inventory over-valued during the stock take | |
| A sales invoice was posted twice to the sales day book | |
| A purchase of a non-current asset was mistakenly posted to purchases | |
| A purchase invoice received after the year end had been posted to this year by mistake | |

# 7 Additional 'Test your understanding' questions

 **Test your understanding 8**

**Data**

Magnus Carter has recently inherited a majority shareholding in a company, Baron Ltd. The company supplies camping equipment to retail outlets. Magnus wishes to get involved in the management of the business, but until now he has only worked in not-for-profit organisations.

He would like to understand how the company has performed over the past two years and how efficient it is in using its resources. He has asked you to help him to interpret the financial statements of the company which are set out below.

**Baron Ltd – Summary statement of profit or loss for the year ended 31 March**

|  | 20X1 | 20X0 |
|---|---|---|
|  | £000 | £000 |
| Revenue | 1,852 | 1,691 |
| Cost of sales | (648) | (575) |
| Gross profit | 1,204 | 1,116 |
| Expenses | (685) | (524) |
| Profit from operations | 519 | 592 |
| Tax | (125) | (147) |
| Profit for the period | 394 | 445 |

**Baron Ltd – Summary statement of financial positions as at 31 March**

|  | 20X1 | 20X0 |
|---|---|---|
| **Assets** | £000 | £000 |
| Non-current assets | 1,431 | 1,393 |
| Current assets | | |
| Inventories | 217 | 159 |
| Trade receivables | 319 | 236 |
| Cash | 36 | 147 |
| Total assets | 2,003 | 1,935 |
| **Equity and liabilities** | | |
| Equity | | |
| Share capital | 500 | 500 |
| Retained earnings | 1,330 | 1,261 |
| | 1,830 | 1,761 |
| Current liabilities | | |
| Trade payables | 48 | 44 |
| Taxation | 125 | 130 |
| | 173 | 174 |
| Total equity and liabilities | 2,003 | 1,935 |

**Task**

Prepare a report for Magnus Carter that includes:

(a) A calculation of the following ratios for the two years:

(i) gross profit percentage

(ii) net profit percentage

(iii) receivable turnover in days

(iv) payable turnover in days (based on cost of sales)

(v) inventory turnover in days (based on cost of sales).

(b)   For each ratio calculated:

   (i)   a brief explanation in general terms of the meaning of the ratio

   (ii)   comments on how the performance or efficiency in the use of resources has changed over the two years.

(c)   Outline three areas where the ratios might indicate potential for control weakness.

 **Test your understanding 9**

### Data

Jonathan Fisher is intending to invest a substantial sum of money in a company. A colleague has suggested to him that he might want to invest in a private company called Carp Ltd which supplies pond equipment to retail outlets. You have been asked to assist him in interpreting the financial statements of the company which are set out below.

**Carp Ltd – Summary statement of profit or loss for the year ended 30 September 20X9**

|  | 20X9 £000 | 20X8 £000 |
|---|---|---|
| Revenue | 3,183 | 2,756 |
| Cost of sales | (1,337) | (1,020) |
| Gross profit | 1,846 | 1,736 |
| Expenses | (1,178) | (1,047) |
| Profit from operations | 668 | 689 |
| Finance costs | (225) | (92) |
| Profit before tax | 443 | 597 |
| Taxation | (87) | (126) |
| Profit for the period | 356 | 471 |

**Carp Ltd – Summary statement of financial positions at 30 September**

|  | 20X9 | 20X8 |
|---|---|---|
|  | £000 | £000 |
| **Assets** | | |
| Non-current assets | 4,214 | 2,030 |
| Current assets | | |
| Inventories | 795 | 689 |
| Trade receivables | 531 | 459 |
| Cash | 15 | 136 |
| Total assets | 5,555 | 3,314 |
| **Equity and liabilities** | | |
| Equity | | |
| Share capital | 700 | 500 |
| Retained earnings | 1,517 | 1,203 |
| Total equity | 2,217 | 1,703 |
| Non-current liabilities | | |
| Long term loan | 2,500 | 1,000 |
| Current liabilities | | |
| Trade payables | 751 | 485 |
| Taxation | 87 | 126 |
| Total liabilities | 3,338 | 1,611 |
| Total equity and liabilities | 5,555 | 3,314 |

**Task**

(a)   Calculate the following ratios for the two years:

    (i)    gearing

    (ii)   net profit percentage

    (iii)  current ratio

    (iv)  return on shareholders' funds (after tax).

(b)   Using the ratios calculated, comment on the company's profitability, liquidity and financial position and consider how these have changed over the two years.

(c)   Identify and explain two areas where the ratios might indicate poor internal controls.

# 8   Summary

By comparing the ratios of different companies, or of one company year-on-year, users of the financial statements will develop a more thorough understanding of a particular company and will therefore be able to make better decisions.

In this chapter we have covered the following categories of ratios:

- profitability
- liquidity
- investor ratios.

We have also considered the important link between deterioration in ratios and weak internal control.

## Test your understanding answers

 **Test your understanding 1**

**Working papers**

(a) **Calculation of the ratios**

| | 20X4 | 20X3 |
|---|---|---|
| Return on capital employed | $\dfrac{2{,}189}{17{,}541} \times 100 = 12.5\%$ | $\dfrac{2{,}430}{15{,}937} \times 100 = 15.2\%$ |
| Operating profit percentage | $\dfrac{2{,}189}{8{,}420} \times 100 = 26\%$ | $\dfrac{2{,}430}{7{,}595} \times 100 = 32\%$ |
| Gross profit percentage | $\dfrac{4{,}884}{8{,}420} \times 100 = 58\%$ | $\dfrac{4{,}177}{7{,}595} \times 100 = 55\%$ |
| Asset turnover | $\dfrac{8{,}420}{17{,}541} = 0.48$ | $\dfrac{7{,}595}{15{,}937} = 0.48$ |

(b) **Explanation and comment**

*Return on capital employed*

- This ratio shows in percentage terms how much profit is being generated by the capital employed in the company.

- The company is showing a lower return on capital employed in 20X4 compared to 20X3 and hence is generating less profit per £ of capital employed in the business.

*Operating profit percentage*

- This ratio shows in percentage terms how much net profit is being generated from revenues.

- The ratio has decreased over the two years.

- This could be explained either by a decrease in the gross profit margin or by an increase in expenses, or both.

- In fact, the ratio of distribution costs and admin expenses as a percentage of revenue has increased from 23% in 20X3 to 32% in 20X4.

20X4:                                    20X3:

(1,471 + 1,224)/8,420 × 100              (1,016 + 731)/7,595 × 100

= 32%                                    = 23%

*Gross profit percentage*

- This ratio shows in percentage terms how much gross profit is being generated from the company's revenues and thus indicates the gross profit margin on sales.

- The ratio has improved over the two years with an increase in the percentage from 55% to 58%.

- The company is increasing its revenue without significantly cutting its margins.

- This may be due to increasing its sales price or reducing the cost of sales or both.

*Asset turnover*

- This ratio shows how efficient the company is in generating revenue from the available capital employed/net assets.

- The ratio has stayed the same between the two years and so a similar level of revenue has been generated from the available capital employed/net assets in 20X4 than in 20X3.

- The new investment that has been made in property, plant and equipment and current assets in 20X4 has generated a proportional increase in sales.

**(c)  Overall**

The ratios show that the return on capital employed has deteriorated in 20X4 and that the company is thus generating less profit from the capital employed/net assets.

Although there are increased margins there is less control over expenses and this has contributed to the deteriorating position. Control of expenses needs to be addressed by management.

The efficiency in the use of assets has remained the same in 20X4 and the increased investment in assets that has taken place in 20X4 has yielded benefits in terms of increased sales.

**Test your understanding 2**

| | |
|---|---|
| Significant investment in property, plant and equipment shortly before the year end. | |
| Revaluation of land and buildings following a change of policy from cost model to revaluation model. | |
| Property, plant and equipment acquired in the previous period now operating at full capacity. | ✓ |
| An issue of equity shares with the proceeds being used to repay long-term borrowings. | |

**Notes**

Statement 1 is incorrect.

A significant investment in PPE shortly before the year end would result in a large increase in capital employed with little effect in profit.

Statement 2 is incorrect.

A revaluation of land and buildings will increase capital employed (revaluation reserve is part of equity) but will have no positive effect on profit.

Statement 3 is correct.

The impact on capital employed would be in the previous period and therefore in the current year's ratio the improvement in profitability would be reflected.

Statement 4 is incorrect.

An issue of shares to repay long-term borrowings would have no effect on capital employed (as both equity and debt are included in the calculation). There would be a saving in finance costs, however the profit used in the ROCE calculation does not include finance costs and therefore the ratio would not be affected.

## Test your understanding 3

| | |
|---|---|
| A's gross profit margin is better than B's as it is able to benefit from economies of scale. | ✓ |
| The difference between the gross profit margin of A and B may be due to how they classify their expenses between cost of sales and operating costs. | |
| A may have improved their gross profit margin by significant investment in new and efficient machinery, but could be suffering from high finance costs as a result of financing the investment with long-term borrowings. | |
| B may be selling a significantly higher volume of products than A, but at a lower price. | |

**Notes**

A's revenue is similar, and slightly lower, than B's so economies of scale is not a valid explanation of the difference in gross profit margins.

## Test your understanding 4

| | |
|---|---|
| The revenue growth is principally due to the online store and hotel contract. | ✓ |
| The gross profit margin would have fallen in 20X2 if the new operations had not been introduced. | |
| The online store should have a better gross profit margin than retail operations as it does not have the shop overheads. | |
| The hotel contract attracts a higher gross profit margin than the other operations. | ✓ |
| The hotel contract appears to require significant overheads in comparison to revenue when compared with other segments. | ✓ |
| The increase in profit before tax margin is principally due to the hotel contract. | |

**Notes**

Statement 2 is incorrect.

The gross profit margin for retail operations in 20X2 is 30.0% (1,200/4,004) compared with 29.6% (1,095/3,700) last year.

Statement 3 is incorrect. The shop overheads would affect operating profit and profit before tax margins, but not the gross profit margin.

Statement 6 is incorrect. The online store has a higher profit before tax margin (138/1,096 = 12.6%) than the hotel contract (82/900 = 9.1%).

---

### ✎ Test your understanding 5

| | |
|---|---|
| Stopping supplies to the significant customer will have contributed to the increase in inventory holding period. | ✓ |
| The impact of the cost of the dispute can be seen in the operating profit margin, which has fallen despite an increase in gross profit margin for the year. | ✓ |
| The increase in gross profit margin is likely to have been achieved by increasing selling prices. | |
| The increase in payables payment period will have resulted in a reduction in cash and cash equivalents. | |
| The reduction in quick ratio is principally due to the significant increase in inventory holding period. | |
| The reduction in quick ratio is principally due to the significant increase in payables payment period. | ✓ |

**Notes**

LW are unlikely to have increased selling prices when there has been no growth in sales volume for the past five years, therefore statement 3 is not a realistic conclusion.

An increase in payables payment period would improve rather than worsen the cash position therefore statement 4 is not a realistic conclusion.

The quick ratio does not include inventory and therefore statement 5 is not a realistic conclusion.

**KAPLAN** PUBLISHING

**Test your understanding 6**

|  | Higher | Lower | No change |
|---|---|---|---|
| Gross profit margin |  |  | ✓ |
| Payables days |  |  | ✓ |
| Quick ratio |  | ✓ |  |
| Interest cover |  | ✓ |  |

Writing off debts unnecessarily means that both debtors and profit are too low. However, the bad debt expense account normally gets accounted for as part of admin or operating expenses below the gross profit line. Payables days will be unaffected.

 **Test your understanding 7**

| | |
|---|---|
| Year-end inventory over-valued during the stock take | |
| A sales invoice was posted twice to the sales day book | |
| A purchase of a non-current asset was mistakenly posted to purchases | |
| A purchase invoice received after the year end had been posted to this year by mistake | ✓ |

The first and third errors would not have affected the quick ratio and the second would have made it higher.

**Test your understanding 8**

**REPORT**

**To:**      Magnus Carter

**From:**    A Student

**Subject:** Interpretation of financial statements

**Date:**    23 June 20X1

This report has been prepared to support the interpretation of the financial statements of Baron Ltd and to compare and contrast the company performance over the two year period.

**(a)   Calculation of the ratios**

|  | 20X1 | | 20X0 | |
|---|---|---|---|---|
| Gross profit percentage | $\dfrac{1,204}{1,852}$ | = 65% | $\dfrac{1,116}{1,691}$ | = 66% |
| Net profit percentage | $\dfrac{519}{1,852}$ | = 28% | $\dfrac{592}{1,691}$ | = 35% |
| Receivables collection period in days | $\dfrac{319}{1,852} \times 365$ | = 63 days | $\dfrac{236}{1,691} \times 365$ | = 51 days |
| Payables payment period in days | $\dfrac{48}{648} \times 365$ | = 27 days | $\dfrac{44}{575} \times 365$ | = 28 days |
| Inventory turnover in days | $\dfrac{217}{648} \times 365$ | = 122 days | $\dfrac{159}{575} \times 365$ | = 101 days |

**(b)   Explanation and comment**

- *Gross profit percentage*

   This measure of profitability shows the percentage of gross profit in relation to revenue, it is often termed the gross margin.

   The ratio has remained fairly constant over the two year period with only a marginal decrease from 66% to 65%. It is expressed as:

   $$\frac{\text{Gross profit}}{\text{Revenues}} \times 100\%$$

   The company has achieved a greater volume of business without having to reduce its margins.

- *Net profit percentage*

  This measure of profitability shows the percentage of net profit in relation to revenue. It is influenced by the gross margin and the level of other costs in relation to revenue. There has been a significant fall in the net return over the period. The gross margin has only fallen marginally, however the expenses in relation to revenue have increased from 31% to 37% over the period and this has had an adverse effect on the performance.

  This indicates that the company is generating less net profit per '£' of revenue than previously achieved.

- *Receivables collection period*

  This is a measure of management control as it relates to the effectiveness of the credit control policy.

  The ratio shows the average number of days it takes to collect debts. It is expressed as:

  $$\frac{\text{Receivables}}{\text{Revenues}} \times 365 \text{ days}$$

  The collection period has increased over the two year period and it is taking 12 days longer to collect debts than previously experienced. This may be due to either customer cash flow problems or poor and less effective credit control.

- *Payables payment period*

  This ratio shows the average days it takes for the company to pay its suppliers. This period has remained similar over the two years. It indicates that the company can meet its demands from trade payables on a timely and regular basis.

## (c) Control issues

*Gross profit*

Gross profit has declined slightly from 66% to 65%. This could have many causes of course but it is possible that there is a control issue surrounding sales pricing. A reducing GP% could be due to reducing prices perhaps due to increased competitive pressure or increased discounts being given by sales people.

It is possible, therefore, that discounts levels are not being properly authorised or controlled by the sales manager.

*Receivable days*

Receivable days are considerably up on the previous year. This could easily be linked to poor control.

Specifically, it is possible that existing credit terms are not being properly enforced and procedures that are normally used to collect debts (warning letters for example) are not being followed.

It is also possible that new customers vetting is not taking place allowing more dubious customers to take excessive amounts of credit.

*Inventory days*

Inventory days are also up considerably. Purchase authorisation procedures may not be being followed allowing unnecessary or excessive quantities of inventory to be bought.

---

 **Test your understanding 9**

**Notes to Jonathan Fisher**

(a) **Calculation of ratios**

The following ratios for the company have been computed:

| | | 20X9 | | 20X8 | |
|---|---|---|---|---|---|
| (i) | Gearing<br>Debt/cap. employed | $\dfrac{2,500}{4,717}$ | × 100 = 53% | $\dfrac{1,000}{2,703}$ | × 100 = 37% |
| | or | | | | |
| | Debt/equity | $\dfrac{2,500}{2,717}$ | × 100 = 92% | $\dfrac{1,000}{1,703}$ | × 100 = 59% |
| (ii) | Net profit percentage | $\dfrac{668}{3,183}$ | × 100 = 21% | $\dfrac{689}{2,756}$ | × 100 = 25% |
| (iii) | Current ratio | $\dfrac{1,341}{838}$ | = 1.6:1 | $\dfrac{1,284}{611}$ | = 2.1:1 |
| (iv) | Return on shareholders' funds | $\dfrac{356}{2,217}$ | × 100 = 16% | $\dfrac{471}{1,703}$ | × 100 = 28% |

(b) • Gearing ratio: This measure represents the company's reliance on debt in relation to total equity. The gearing has increased over the two years and the company is now a 'high geared' organisation. There is a greater reliance on borrowed funds in the second year. This increases shareholder risk as when profits reduce, interest payments must still be met.

• Net profit percentage: The net return to revenue has fallen over the period. This is a result of a fall in the gross margin from 63% to 58%, the level of expenses to revenue remaining fairly constant.

• Current ratio: There has been a reduction in this measure of liquidity over the period, there has been a deterioration in the cash position and the acid test ratio has fallen significantly from 0.97 to 0.65. The business now has less current assets per '£' of current liabilities than previously.

• Return on shareholders' funds: The return has fallen over the two year period which has been influenced by the overall reduction in profitability as shown in the net profit percentage to revenue.

The company is not generating as much profit for each '£' worth of equity investment as it did in the previous year.

(c) The net profit percentage is well down on the previous year. Although this can have many causes, one possibility is poor control over expenses. Invoices may not be properly checked against orders or not authorised.

Gearing has increased significantly and this may well have been deliberate. However, management controls are common in this area. Raising debt finance should been properly discussed at board level and authorised by them. This may well have been the case but it is also possible the FD acted independently.

# Preventing and detecting fraud

## Introduction

Fraud is depressingly common and can take many forms. It is management responsibility to prevent fraud from happening and if it does happen to detect it quickly in order to mitigate the situation.

The risk of fraud needs to be assessed (which varies) and then appropriate steps taken.

| PERFORMANCE CRITERIA |
| --- |
| 2.3 Examine ways of preventing and detecting fraud and systemic weaknesses |
| 3.3 Evaluate the risk of fraud arising from weaknesses in the internal control system |

## CONTENTS

1   Introduction

2   Types of fraud

3   Implications of fraud

4   Detecting fraud

5   Preventing fraud

6   Fraud policy and contingency plans

# 1 Introduction

## 1.1 What is fraud?

 **Definition**

Fraud is an intentional act involving the use of deception to obtain an unjust or illegal advantage – essentially 'theft by deception'.

Fraud (intentional) should be contrasted with error (unintentional).

 **Example – Fraud or error**

If a purchase ledger clerk deliberately enters a false invoice from a friend into the purchase ledger, hoping that it will be paid so that the clerk and the friend can split the proceeds, this is a fraud. However if the clerk accidentally enters an invoice twice into the ledger, this is an error.

Note that fraud may be carried out by management, employees or third parties. For example:

- Managers may deliberately select inappropriate accounting policies.

- Employees may steal the proceeds of cash sales and omit to enter the sale into the accounting records.

- Third parties may send bogus invoices to the company, hoping that they will be paid in error.

Fraud is a criminal offence, punishable by a fine or imprisonment.

 **Test your understanding 1**

A safety inspector has found several safety violations in the manufacturing plant where you work. Correcting these will cost £30,000.

The inspector has offered to ignore the violations in return for a secret payment of £5,000, which your boss has asked you to organise. The workers will never be told about the safety violations and the inspector will file a report stating that the plant passes all the safety regulations.

What would you do?

## 1.2    Different types of fraud

Examples of fraud include:

- Crimes against consumers or clients, e.g. Misrepresenting the quality of goods; pyramid trading schemes; selling counterfeit goods.

- Employee crimes against employers, e.g. Payroll fraud; falsifying expense claims; theft of cash.

- Crimes against investors, consumers and employees, e.g. Financial statement fraud.

- Crimes against financial institutions, e.g. Using lost and stolen credit cards; fraudulent insurance claims.

- Crimes against government, e.g. Social security benefit claims fraud; tax evasion.

- Crimes by professional criminals, e.g. Money laundering.

- E-crime by people using computers, e.g. Spamming; Copyright crimes; hacking.

Types of fraud are discussed in greater detail below.

## 1.3    The Fraud Act (2006)

Fraud is a criminal act and can be broken down into three distinct offences.

- **Fraud by false representation**

  Is defined by Section 2 of the Act as a case where a person makes "any representation as to fact or law ... express or implied" which they know to be untrue or misleading.

- **Fraud by failing to disclose information**

  Is defined by Section 3 of the Act as a case where a person fails to disclose any information to a third party when they are under a legal duty to disclose such information.

- **Fraud by abuse of position**

  Is defined by Section 4 of the Act as a case where a person occupies a position where they are expected to safeguard the financial interests of another person, and abuses that position.

In all three classes of fraud, it requires that for an offence to have occurred, the person must have acted dishonestly, and that they had to have acted with the intent of making a gain for themselves or anyone else, or inflicting a loss (or a risk of loss) on another.

## 1.4 Prerequisites for fraud

Fraud generally occurs when someone has identified an opportunity, a weakness in the company's systems, and believes that the potential rewards will outweigh the risk of being caught.

There are thus three prerequisites for fraud to occur: dishonesty, opportunity and motive. All three are usually required – for example an honest employee is unlikely to commit fraud even if given opportunity and motive.

## 1.5 Fraud prevention

The aim of preventative controls is to reduce opportunity and remove temptation from potential offenders. Prevention techniques include the introduction of policies, procedures and controls, and activities such as training and fraud awareness to stop fraud from occurring.

The existence of a fraud strategy is itself a deterrent. This can be achieved through:

- **An anti-fraud culture**

  Where minor unethical practices are overlooked, for example, expenses or time recording, this may lead to a culture in which larger frauds occur. High ethical standards bring long term benefits as customers, suppliers, employees and the community realise they are dealing with a trustworthy organisation.

- **Risk awareness**

  Fraud should never be discounted, and there should be awareness among all staff that there is always the possibility that fraud is taking place. It is important to raise awareness through training programmes. Particular attention should be given to training and awareness among those people involved in receiving cash, purchasing and paying suppliers.

  Publicity can also be given to fraud that has been exposed. This serves as a reminder to those who may be tempted to commit fraud and a warning to those responsible for the management of controls.

- **Whistleblowing**

  Fraud may be suspected by those who are not personally involved. People must be encouraged to raise the alarm about fraud.

- **Sound internal control systems**

  Sound systems of internal control should monitor fraud by identifying risks and then putting into place procedures to monitor and report on those risks. This is the main emphasis within the synoptic assessment.

**KAPLAN** PUBLISHING

# 2 Types of fraud

## 2.1 Introduction

There are two main types of irregularity which are of concern when considering fraud:

- Theft – dishonestly appropriating the property of another with the intention of permanently depriving them of it. This may include the removal or misuse of funds, assets or cash.

  Some theft, particularly of tangible assets such as computer or telephone equipment, can be opportunistic and may not always involve deception. A theft does not therefore necessarily fit into the general perception of 'fraud'.

- False accounting – dishonestly destroying, defacing, concealing or falsifying any account, record or document required for any accounting purpose, with a view to personal gain or gain for another, or with the intent to cause loss to another or furnishing information which is or may be misleading, false or deceptive.

## 2.2 Theft

Any business assets can be stolen, whether by employees or management, acting alone or in collusion with third parties.

This may involve the theft of stock, commonly known as shrinkage. Computer equipment is particularly vulnerable here.

**Small scale theft**

There are incidences of theft that will go unnoticed because of the scale of the crime.

- Small amounts of cash taken from the till of a retailer or the petty cash box in an office might not be noticed because the sums involved are not significant enough to have any impact on the organisation.

- Many employees think nothing of taking pens and paper from the stationery cupboard to stock up their home supply.

**Larger scale theft**

There are thefts that are for significant amounts.

- The last cheques in the company's cheque book can be taken out and the thief can do a passable imitation of a couple of authorised signatures, clear the funds, withdraw and disappear.

  No one realises until the bank statement comes, so it may be weeks, or months before they realise they are missing a quarter of a million pounds.

- The theft of intellectual property, perhaps in the form of customer or price lists, also falls into this category.

- Staff who are sure of not being challenged may submit false expense claims, covering anything from private entertainment to large-scale projects.

- Theft from a company may also take the form of payroll fraud where payments to former or fictitious employees are diverted to the fraudster's own bank account.

**Collusion**

Collusion is a common element in frauds whereby individuals pool their resources to achieve their aims – specialist skills might not be available to the individual acting independently.

- Employees can collude with customers, with other employees or with friends. In the case of fraud involving collusion with a third party, money may be taken from unsuspecting customers on the promise of spectacular returns or as an advance fee.

- Or the customer may not be an innocent dupe but may in fact be acting in collusion with the staff member. Such cases may involve the payment of kickbacks or commission from a supplier as a reward for being awarded that contract. These are particularly difficult to detect since the kickback is paid directly to the employee and does not go through the company's books.

- Sometimes it happens that an employee has an undisclosed interest in a transaction that results in harm to the business because the price of the contract is not the best that the company could get.

## Computer fraud

There is a great deal of talk about computer fraud but in fact it could be argued that there is no such thing. What is usually meant is that fraud is carried out using a computer rather than traditional methods of paper and pen. The computer is simply the mechanism for perpetrating the fraud.

Computers may be used to disguise the true nature of a transaction by manipulating the date records and programs, to hack into an organisation's computer system to steal or manipulate information or for the unauthorised electronic transfer of funds.

On the Internet, fraudsters may pose as a legitimate business to obtain payment for goods that are either not delivered or are of significantly lower quality.

While there are legal obstacles to a successful prosecution, such as jurisdiction and privacy rights, computers also generate a great deal of admissible evidence.

Some companies are seeking to appoint 'computer fraud experts', but are having great difficulty in defining the special skills and experience such a person would require.

Computer fraud may be summarised as the use of information technology resources to commit or conceal a criminal offence or civil wrong.

Computer fraud typically includes:

- financial fraud

- sabotage of data and/or networks

- theft of proprietary information

- system penetration from the outside, including denial of service attacks

- unauthorised access by insiders, including employee misuse of Internet access privileges as well as malicious software (such as viruses, worms, trojans, time bombs, zombies), which is the leading cause of unauthorised users gaining access to systems and networks via the internet.

## 2.3 False accounting

The main aim of false accounting is to present the results and affairs of the organisation in a better light than the reality.

Frequently, there are commercial pressures to report an unrealistic level of earnings, which can take precedence over controls designed to prevent fraud.

Management may occasionally wish to '**window dress**' their statement of financial position (i.e. present either a better or worse picture than that which can be fairly presented) by a variety of devices. For example

- Payments are entered before the year-end but are not sent to creditors until after the year-end or the cashbook is kept open for some days after the year-end so that money received after the year-end is included in the cashbook balance.

- This will give an incorrect impression of the company's credit worthiness to a reader of the accounts.

The owners or managers of the company could '**cook the books**' by:

- a misuse of pension funds

- overvaluing assets

- not writing off bad debts and avoiding the effects on profits and assets

- understating depreciation

- understating expenses

- illegally supporting their own company by purchasing shares to force up their value.

Whatever the purpose of the fraud, the feature common to all cases is the need to falsify records, alter figures, and perhaps keep two sets of books. In every instance, it is only a matter of time before the 'hole' cannot be hidden any longer and the fraud is exposed.

Some of the most dramatic corporate collapses and high-profile fraud trials have been characterised by false accounting used to cover up extensive fraud or theft within the business.

Recent times have seen the end of huge multinationals such as Enron and WorldCom, both of which fraudulently inflated their profits by deliberately misstating revenues to disguise mounting losses.

Although the aim is always to present the business in a flattering light, the reasons for doing so can be as varied as the ways in which it is achieved. In some cases the purpose is to deceive the bank into providing more finance. The bank reconciliation may also be manipulated to cover up a theft. The target of the deception may be a customer, who is more likely to be attracted by a successful company, or it may be a regulator whose intervention can be prevented or delayed.

Another common practice is the abuse of a slush fund under the discretion of executive management.

False accounting is obviously carried out by insiders – either employees or management who are in a position to override the normal controls and to present figures that are simply not true. By contrast, fraud under the general heading of theft may be carried out by third parties as well as insiders.

 **Test your understanding 2**

Can you think of three ways that stock can be used to show a false increase in the value of the assets in the company?

## 2.4    Types of fraud – further examples

The following table outlines some of the various types of fraud.

| Type of fraud | Examples |
|---|---|
| False accounting | • Obtaining external financing by falsely improving the results. |
| | • Raising the share price by false means to aid acquisitions or to help a new issue of shares. |
| | • Obtaining more business by appearing more successful or less indebted. |
| | • Obtaining performance bonuses for managers by inflating profits. |
| | • Covering up internal theft by altering, adding, falsifying or deleting bank/stock/purchase or other records. A fictitious customer can be created. Orders can be sent, goods despatched on credit and the 'customer' can neglect to pay their bill. The debt is written off. |
| | • Hiding losses in the hopes that fortunes may reverse. Preventing or delaying intervention by a regulator. |

| Theft | <ul><li>Direct theft of cash, stock or assets – theft of stock, commonly known as stock shrinkage, can be significant. Computer equipment is particularly vulnerable.</li><li>Staff can make private telephone calls (to friends in Australia).</li><li>Employees can fiddle their time sheets and claim for overtime hours they did not work or claim a higher rate for the job.</li><li>Employees can claim to have purchased supplies in excess of the actual amount or there is no control on prices charged and the employee could be keeping a percentage of the takings.</li><li>Theft of intellectual property – customer lists, contract prices, etc.</li><li>False expense claims – this can be anything from claiming for private entertainment expenses to large-scale projects which relies on the claimant being sure that the expense will not be challenged. Expenses can also be deducted from takings without prior authorisation and could thus be inflated.</li><li>Payroll fraud – diverting ex-employee or fictitious employee payments to one's own bank account.</li><li>Rolling debtors' receipts – misappropriating debtors' receipts and substituting subsequent receipts. This is where takings are remitted at irregular intervals, and the rate that they are remitted could be kept permanently behind the rate at which they are actually received (known as teeming and lading). It could mean that substantial sums are available to the employee.</li></ul> |
|---|---|

| Third-party | • Customers ordering goods on credit with no intention of paying – includes some credit card frauds. |
| | • Kickbacks or commission from a supplier as a reward for awarding the contract to that supplier. These are particularly difficult to detect, since the kickback is paid direct from the supplier to the employee and does not go through the company's books. |
| | • Collusion with customers to charge lower prices or raise spurious credit notes. |
| | • Collusion with suppliers to accept under-deliveries of stock. |
| | • Related party transactions. A company employee or officer has an undisclosed financial interest in a transaction that causes harm to the business, often because the price of the contract is not the best the company could get. |
| Computer fraud | • Hacking/unauthorised access to bank accounts to transfer funds. |
| | • Setting up as a legitimate Internet business and obtaining payment for goods that are either never delivered or are of lower quality than advertised. |
| | • Theft of intellectual property, e.g. engineering drawings, by unauthorised access to a computer. |
| | • Publishing malicious claims about the company on anonymous bulletin boards, thus affecting the company's reputation. |
| | • Disguising the true nature of a transaction by manipulation of date records and programs held on a computer. |
| | • Hacking into an organisation's computer system to steal or manipulate information. |

# 3 Implications of fraud

## 3.1 Typical elements of fraud

Fraud investigations often reveal one or more of the following:

- Credit notes given to customers for undisclosed or inadequate reasons.

- High level of inventory losses accepted without investigation.

- Suppliers insist on dealing with only one employee in the department.

- Discrepancies in petty cash are not investigated or are written off to 'sundry' expenses.

- Payroll summaries are not checked by department heads or by the HR department.

- Excessive habitual overtime worked without relation to workload.

- High levels of sickness absence not investigated.

- Unduly friendly relations between some employees and their suppliers or service providers.

- Faulty goods are not returned to the supplier for credit or credit notes are not chased up.

- Excessive and constant level of returns to suppliers.

- Company assets are not checked against a fixed asset or stock register.

- Inadequate reconciliation of balance sheet accounts.

- Insufficient justification for balance sheet reserves.

- Unusually high levels of despatches or purchases just prior to the period end.

- Employees' expense claims are not checked and authorised by departmental managers.

- Management appears to condone petty fraud because 'everybody knows about it but never does anything about it'.

- Invoices from some suppliers seem high in relation to the goods or services rendered.

- Amounts are written off the sales ledger without authorisation or investigation.

- Management and supervision are remote from those they control.

- Some branches are in reality uncontrolled because of geography or because no manager has become involved in the branch.

 **Test your understanding 3**

To be in a position to combat fraud, you need to think like a fraudster. Make a list of the ways expenses can be fiddled.

## 3.2 The impact of fraud

The way the organisation is affected by the fraud depends on the type of fraud perpetrated.

| Type of fraud | Implications |
| --- | --- |
| Any fraud that is discovered and addressed. | <ul><li>Negative publicity can damage the organisation irrevocably by affecting the public's perceptions and consumer confidence.</li><li>Consideration must be given to what effect any publicity would have on suppliers and customers. Will suppliers withdraw credit? Will customers look elsewhere for their supplies? Whilst publicity will certainly deter other frauds within the company, its effects on outsiders must be managed. If the case goes to court the facts cannot be prevented from getting out.</li><li>Fraudsters may be arrested and, depending on the scale and seriousness of the fraud, may face a custodial sentence.</li></ul> |

| Theft of funds or assets from the organisation. | • Profits are lower than they should be. Because there is less cash or fewer assets the net asset position is weakened. Returns to shareholders are likely to be reduced as a result. |
| | • If the working capital is reduced it can be difficult for the organisation to operate effectively. In the most serious cases of fraud, otherwise successful businesses can collapse e.g. Barings. |
| Misrepresentation of the financial position of the organisation – results artificially enhanced. | • Too much of the organisation's profits may be distributed to shareholders. |
| | • Retained profits will be lower than expected, which could result in a shortfall in working capital – making day-to-day activities more difficult to perform effectively. |
| | • Investors making decisions based on inaccurate information may not achieve the expected returns. |
| | • Suppliers may extend credit while being misled about the financial position of the organisation. |
| Misrepresentation of the financial position of the organisation – results under-stated. | • Access to loans may be restricted where assets are under reported. |
| | • If the organisation is a listed company and quoted on the Stock Exchange, the share price might fall and market strength might be eroded. |
| | • Returns to investors may be reduced unnecessarily. |

**KAPLAN** PUBLISHING

# 4 Detecting fraud

## 4.1 Questions to pose

The starting point for most fraud detection is to ask yourself how someone could go about making money by defrauding your employer.

Someone who knows a lot of detail about the way the business works will probably be able to think of several ways in which a suspected fraud could have been committed. For each possible method of fraud a series of questions should then be asked.

- Who might be involved in this fraud?

- Why would this person risk their job, reputation and future livelihood by committing the fraud?

- How would the person attempt to cover up the fraud?

- Where would the loss appear in the company's accounts?

- Would the fraudster need accomplices either inside or outside the company to carry out the fraud?

- What would be the tell-tale signs to look for?

- Who is the best person in the company to look for suspicious signs of fraud?

- Is the company's policy to prevent future frauds or punish existing frauds?

- Is the investigation to be kept secret and if so how does this affect the answers to the above questions?

By answering the above questions for each method of perpetrating the suspected fraud, the company will be well on the way to evolving a fraud detection plan with clear objectives. In particular the following questions will have been answered:

- What are the most effective means of detecting whether fraud has taken place?

- Who should lead the investigation into the suspected fraud?

- What should the company do if fraud is confirmed? At what stage, if any, are the police or others within or without the organisation to be informed?

**Test your understanding 4**

Why might an employee be motivated to act against their company's interest?

### 4.2 Conditions for fraud

Fraud is found to be more frequent in organisations with some or all of the following characteristics:

- Domineering management with no effective overseeing board or committee.

- Climate of fear or an unhealthy corporate culture.

- High staff turnover rates in key controlling functions.

- Long-service staff in stores/purchasing departments.

- Chronic understaffing in key control areas.

- Frequent changes of legal advisers, auditors or professional advisers.

- Excessive reporting leading to insufficient time for analysis of data.

- Remuneration based very significantly on financial performance.

- Inadequate segregation of duties – e.g. where an individual orders goods, approves the invoices and then authorises the payments.

- Low staff morale/lack of career progression/weak management.

- Excessive hours worked by key staff with insufficient delegation of duties.

- Lack of effective procedures in HR, credit control, inventory control, purchasing or accounts departments. Consistent failure to correct major weaknesses in internal control.

- Management frequently override internal controls.

- Rumours that fraud is not dealt with effectively or at all.

- Inadequate internal reporting or management accounting.

- Loss of records or inadequate documentation about transactions.

- Unusual transactions having a large profit effect.

- Frequent transactions with related parties/no checking that suppliers are appropriate.

- Overly secret dealings with certain clients or suppliers.

- Mismatch between profitability and cash flow.

- Excessive pressure to meet budgets, targets or forecast earnings.

- Personnel not required to take their holiday entitlement.

- When an employee is on holiday leave, the work is left until the employee returns.

- Inadequate responses to queries from management, suppliers, auditors or bankers.

- An employee's habits change or their lifestyle is more affluent than would be expected from their employment.

- Lack of common-sense controls such as changing passwords frequently, requiring two signatures on cheques or restricting access to sensitive areas.

Effective fraud detection requires management to be sufficiently knowledgeable about the mechanics of the business and constantly aware of the need to be vigilant against fraud.

## 4.3 Uncovering fraud

Discovering fraud can be exceptionally difficult and perhaps the majority of frauds both with and without computers are found by accident. Well-operated controls should prevent fraud taking place but, as one of the ways fraud is committed is to circumvent controls, these may be inadequate to discover it is occurring.

There are some key ways of uncovering fraud:

- Perform regular control checks, e.g. stocktaking, cash counts. Often computers are used to cover up non-computer frauds. All frauds have a weak point in having to remove what has been taken (cash or other assets).

- Be aware that fraud might be occurring: have an attitude!

- Look out for signs that there may be a problem: late payments, work backlogs, incomplete audit trails, people with an extravagant life-style, people who are 'experts', confused decision making, multiple interlocking companies or deals, strange payments to countries with strict privacy laws, large transfers before public holidays.

- Don't look first for the complex: many frauds exploit simple missing elements of control.

- Look out for managers who say fraud can't happen in their department and say they have trustworthy staff.

## 4.4 Risk management

Risk management comprises risk assessment (identifying and analysing risk) and risk control (taking steps to reduce risk, provide contingency plans and monitor improvements). Risk management can be seen as a series of steps:

* **Risk identification** – producing lists of risk items.

* **Risk analysis** – assessing the loss probability and magnitude for each item. Clearly, stronger internal controls reduce the risk here.

* **Risk prioritisation** – producing a ranked ordering of risk items.

* **Risk-management planning** – deciding how to address each risk item, perhaps by avoiding, transferring, absorbing or reducing the risk (see below).

* **Risk resolution** – producing a situation in which risk items are eliminated or resolved.

* **Risk monitoring** – tracking progress toward resolving risk items and taking corrective action.

**Risk analysis** – no matter what process is used, the method is always the same:

* Identify the asset.

* Ascertain the risk.

* Determine the vulnerability.

* Implement the corrective action.

For example a table could be drawn up with the headings shown below.

| Area of risk | Probability | Impact | Controls | Net likely impact | Action |
|---|---|---|---|---|---|
| False accounting: Inflation of assets | | | | | |
| Theft: Expense statement frauds | | | | | |

The risks to and impact on the systems/applications supporting the organisation's operations may be identified as below:

**Threats**

* Attempts to access private information

* Malicious attacks

- Fraud
- Pranks
- User error
- Natural disasters
- Sabotage
- Systems/applications supporting the organisation's operations interrupted
- Customer loss of confidence
- Sensitive information disclosed
- Assets lost
- Integrity of data compromised
- Critical services and benefits operations halted
- Failure to meet contractual obligations.

**Potential damage**

Risks can be handled in a number of different ways.

- Ignore the risks and do nothing – appropriate where the effect of the risk is small and the chances of it occurring remote. Remember – sometimes accepting the risk is the appropriate corrective action.
- Purchase insurance against the risk.
- Transfer the risk – e.g. arranging for third parties to complete the riskier parts of the project.
- Protect against the risk – arrange for additional staff to be available at critical parts of the project to minimise the possibility of the project overrunning.

## 4.5 Grading the risk level

You might be expected to be able to grade the risk from low, through medium to high and this requires a little judgement.

It is difficult to provide precise guidance here but:

- The more desirable the asset the more likely it could be stolen. Cash, high value items or household goods are more prone to theft and hence would be rated as higher risk.
- The level of past incidence. If frauds have occurred in the past then they are more likely to reoccur.
- Cash based businesses are high-risk areas as it relatively easy to steal and any controls are highly dependent on the integrity of individuals.

- Complex accounting environments are more prone to fraud as fewer people understand what is happening.

- Weak control environments can encourage more fraud as there is a reduced chance of discovery.

---

 **Example – risk of fraud**

1   A taxi business (1). Customers can flag down a taxi and almost always pay cash for the journey. The taxis do not have a GPS system attached so no record is kept of the mileage covered. Petrol is bought by the driver from the cash taken from customers.

This is clearly very high risk. It is cash based and no verification is possible of mileage or the petrol consumed from which an estimate of fares could have been made.

2   A taxi business (2). Customers can only book using an application on their smart phones. Payment is made by bank transfer automatically. All petrol is bought at one location owned by the business where a record of miles covered and fuel used is kept.

This is low risk. The extra controls and the method of payment have improved the risk profile considerably. If petrol were being bought elsewhere then the MPG figures would reveal that.

You can see here that the type of business may not be relevant. The methods followed and the level of control is also a factor.

---

# 5   Preventing fraud

## 5.1   Prerequisites for fraud

As with any crime prevention strategy, the key to minimising the risk of fraud lies in understanding why it occurs, identifying business areas that are at risk and implementing procedures to address vulnerable areas.

As mentioned above, there are three prerequisites for fraud to occur: dishonesty, opportunity and motive.

One approach for reducing fraud is to target these three prerequisites.

## Motive

The motive for fraud is often simply dissatisfaction, based on being passed over for promotion, inadequate pay or a feeling of carrying more than a fair workload. Just giving employees the opportunity to air their grievances and discuss aspirations could be sufficient to reduce this problem. Employees may also be aware of other problems within the organisation and would welcome some forum where they could come forward.

Motivation to commit fraud will thus normally be prevented by:

- good employment conditions (e.g. pay)
- instant dismissal where appropriate
- sympathetic grievance procedures.

## Dishonesty

Dishonesty will be prevented by careful scrutiny of staff. The fight against fraud should start even before a new employee joins the company. References must be checked thoroughly. Take particular care where temporary employees, particularly those supplied through an agency, are to be employed permanently. Screening and reference checking are frequently overlooked in these circumstances. Fraud will be reduced in a culture of:

- severe disciplinary procedures for offenders
- moral leadership by management.

## Opportunity

Opportunity will be prevented by:

- separation of duties
- input and output controls on computer processing
- control over and testing of new computer programs
- physical security of assets and computer hardware
- controls over forms and documentation, e.g. cheques.

Most of the above controls are standard internal controls on preventing fraud. In addition to controls to prevent fraud it is important to have a system for detecting fraud covering such areas as:

- an audit trail
- logging of access to files, terminals, books and records
- good documentation of accounting procedures and programs.

Employees and third parties should be encouraged to report their suspicions of fraud or other irregular activity without fear of reprisal.

In fact, where the report is made in good faith, the whistleblower is now protected by law.

## 5.2    Prevention and deterrence

Prevention of fraud is a two-stage process:

1    ensure that opportunities for fraud are minimised (fraud prevention), and

2    ensure that potential fraudsters believe they will be caught (fraud deterrence).

**Prevention**

Fraud prevention – means examining all the key company systems and viewing them with the mind-set of a potential fraudster. The review will bring to light a number of weaknesses in the current systems that could be exploited by a fraudster. Having identified the weaknesses in the current systems, the company must then change those systems by introducing new or different controls.

Simple controls are often the most effective and frequently require little management time or effort. For example:

- Credit notes over a threshold amount must be explained to and authorised by a senior independent manager before issue.

- Inventory write-downs must be investigated before authorisation by an independent manager.

- Key balance sheet accounts must be reconciled monthly and the reconciliation reviewed regularly by senior managers.

- Fixed assets must be tagged and checked periodically – this can often be combined with the regular testing of electrical and lifting equipment.

- Ensure that no goods or assets leave a site without a despatch note or other documentation.

- Sickness absence must be monitored and controlled.

- Wherever practical, duties must be segregated so that no one person is responsible for both approving expenditure and authorising payment. Physical and electronic access to sensitive areas and procedures must be restricted.

- Employees must take their vacation entitlement and the work of employees on vacation must be covered by others.

- All employees' expense claims must be authorised by their immediate managers before payment.

- New employees must be screened and their references must be checked.

The introduction and enforcement of controls like these will reduce the opportunities for fraudsters. The controls themselves warn potential fraudsters that management is actively monitoring the business and that in turn deters fraud.

**Deterrence**

Fraud deterrence – only when potential fraudsters believe fraud will be detected and when whistle-blowers believe they will be protected will there be an effective deterrence of fraud. The most effective ways of detecting fraud have been found to be:

- Internal controls.

- Internal audit.

- Management review.

- Whistle-blowers.

- Change of management.

- Anonymous tip-offs.

- Outside information.

- Security of passwords.

- External audit.

- Access/exit controls – operating effective access controls within the premises is obviously essential. Never underestimate the role of security tags, CCTV cameras or other surveillance equipment. Pay particular attention to access controls over computer systems, which should include the rigorous use of passwords, firewalls and other measures to prevent or detect hacking into the system. Significant amounts of information are now held in databases and other formats to aid communication within companies. If not properly managed, this concentration of information constitutes an increased risk.

Fraud is difficult to prevent and detect, but all organisations should institute basic controls. These include:

- segregation of duties (often lost with computerised systems) employment of honest staff

- a control log or audit trail of all transactions carried out.

 **Test your understanding 5**

Lots of passwords are very basic. There are top ten password charts published in magazines. Can you guess what the most popular ones are?

**Test your understanding 6**

Steve works for Sciss Ltd, a manufacturer of cardboard boxes, as Head of the Production Department. He is awarded a bonus each year if profits exceed budget. Steve is able to view the accounts each month to see whether the department is exceeding the budget.

In the final month of the year, to maintain production, Steve had to order glue which cost £1,000. Within Sciss Ltd glue is not capitalised and recorded in inventory but is simply written off as an expense. Unfortunately this extra bill will be sufficient to reduce the year-end profit so that the department will not receive their bonus.

The employees have started using the glue, but Steve has hidden the invoice in his desk until the year-end accounts have been finalised.

For each of the following controls, identify which may have deterred Steve from acting in this way:

| | Yes/No |
|---|---|
| The matching of all orders to goods received notes. | |
| A year-end inventory count. | |
| The use of sequentially numbered orders. | |
| The use of sequentially numbered goods received notes. | |
| The matching of goods received notes to invoices. | |
| The use of sequentially numbered invoices. | |
| A sequence check on all orders and goods received notes. | |

# 6 Fraud policy and contingency plans

## 6.1 Fraud ethics policy

A fraud ethics policy is intended to show the company's desire to be open and honest in all its dealings, internally and externally. It should be clear that the company values integrity and effort, not merely financial performance, in all dealings with staff, customers and suppliers. It is important to emphasise that the policy applies consistently to all staff, whatever their level. Failure to comply with the policy will be considered a disciplinary offence.

What is considered acceptable and unacceptable behaviour may vary between countries and cultures, therefore specific guidance should be given on this, with reference to the core values of the organisation. The company should give its definition of fraud and provide a detailed list of examples of actions that it considers to be fraud.

The company should explain that unless authorised, personal interests in outside organisations should be avoided. Employees may not act as a director, officer, employee or partner of any other organisation outside the group. Relationships with parties of another organisation should be disclosed to management, who should then ensure that the individual is not involved in any activity in the area of the conflict of interest.

If employees find themselves in a position where there is a conflict of interest, this must be disclosed immediately.

The company must make it clear that employees may not accept gifts to a value in excess of what is laid down in the ethics policy. Employees should be advised to use discretion and common sense if accepting modest gifts. All gifts received must be reported and recorded by the company. A similar policy should exist for giving gifts to customers and for entertainment.

The policy should state that employees have a duty of confidentiality to the company and its clients. Information received in the course of employment must not be disclosed to persons outside the group. Information received must not be used for an employee's own benefit or the benefit of others. The policy should make it clear that employees are obliged to report suspicions of fraud or irregular activity.

Finally, the fraud ethics policy must state that all suspicions and reports of fraud will be treated seriously and investigated.

The fraud contingency plan will be implemented and appropriate action taken, which could include police involvement.

## 6.2    It's fraud – what now?

When faced with the suggestion that fraud has been perpetrated against them, companies react in different ways. For some, it is critical that no hint of the matter ever comes to light; they only want to recover the lost funds. Others believe that to maximise the impact of their corporate code of ethics, action should be taken and should be seen to be taken against the perpetrator and that this is more important than recovering the money.

Few companies have established and agreed procedures for handling suspected fraud. Yet, if the suspicion and supporting evidence are handled in the wrong way, considerable damage can be done to the organisation's finances and reputation.

## 6.3    Fraud contingency plan

Many organisations have disaster recovery procedures in place in the event of fire, bomb explosion or major computer failure. Few have established and agreed procedures for handling suspected fraud. Yet, if the suspicion and supporting evidence are handled in the wrong way, considerable damage can be done to the organisation's finances and reputation.

A fraud contingency plan provides the route map that enables the company to undertake an investigation that meets its objectives and protects its interests. This plan identifies fraud risks in each area from management, employees, third parties or through collusion; implements appropriate controls; determines who will lead the investigation as well as the objectives and powers of the investigation team; and decides on how to work with the police and handle publicity.

In the initial stages, an investigation is likely to be undertaken by company personnel and/or external investigators, perhaps forensic accountants.

At a later stage it is of particular benefit to use private organisations and forensic specialists to establish and assess the facts, which can then be handed over to the police in the event of a criminal prosecution.

No matter how suspicion was aroused, it is essential to ascertain as soon as possible who is implicated. Where the suspect is an employee, the designation and position of the suspect may determine the financial damage that could be caused, the reputation damage that could result if the matter became known publicly, the parties to be informed and the action to be taken.

Fundamental to any investigation is the documentary information, which may be what first aroused suspicion, and will subsequently provide the evidence that an irregularity has occurred. It is essential to ensure that this information cannot be destroyed, altered or removed from the company's control.

Internal and external publicity must be managed in order to avoid scare mongering, while those who need to know are kept informed. A carefully managed media strategy can help to deflect criticism and concerns about the organisation's stability.

## Test your understanding 7

NL is a qualified accountant. He works for the treasury department at B Bank. He manages a small department of six staff who specialise in foreign exchange transactions. Their work is very complex and only the cleverest people are recruited to the department.

Many managers of other departments do not understand the workings of the foreign exchange employees and leave NL to supervise all of their activities. NL started as a junior in the foreign exchange department ten years ago and has rapidly worked his way to the top.

NL reports to the board of B Bank at each board meeting. Reported profits by NL increase slightly each year, enough to warrant the bonus available according to the department's employment contracts – up to 200% of their salaries.

One Board member has become suspicious that reported profits have been manipulated.

Which THREE of the following controls would allay the board members suspicions?

| | |
|---|---|
| The department's reported profits should be independently scrutinized. | |
| The reported profit should be recalculated. | |
| NL should be supervised by at least one other Board member with foreign exchange experience. | |
| Reviewing other bank's foreign exchange profits to see if they too are generally rising each year. | |
| Verifying that NL is a qualified accountant and able to produce financial statements. | |

# 7 Additional 'Test your understanding' questions

## Test your understanding 8

1  Explain the term 'window dressing'.

2  The information systems security is based on three elements. What are they?

3  Identify five types of false accounting.

4  Give an example of collusion.

5  List as many types of computer fraud that you can.

6  How would you go about uncovering fraud?

7  Outline the four ways that risks can be handled.

8  What are the three prerequisites for fraud to occur?

9  What areas would be covered in a fraud policy statement?

# 8 Summary

This chapter has identified the risks and common indicators of fraud. You should understand how to evaluate a system and identify potential risk areas and be able to suggest ways of detecting and avoiding incidences of fraud. Detection of fraud is rare and unlikely to be experienced by students, so you must concentrate in your project on how the systems in your place of work prevent fraud and can help in detecting fraud.

## Test your understanding answers

 **Test your understanding 1**

You should refuse to accept the £5,000 and report the actions of the safety inspector to the relevant authorities.

 **Test your understanding 2**

The ways of artificially inflating the value of stock include the following:

- Instead of being written off, obsolete or damaged stock may be shown at cost on the balance sheet.

- Records can be falsified at the stock count, i.e. generating stock that does not actually exist.

- Returns to suppliers may not be recorded or suppressed until after the year end stock count.

- Similarly with deliveries to customers – the reduction in stock may not be recorded or suppressed until after the year end stock count.

 **Test your understanding 3**

This list could be really long, but here are a few to start you off:

- You can claim for a meal that you did not have.

- You could take someone with you on business and both stay at the hotel at the company's expense.

- You could use the free 'park and ride' service but charge for parking the car in the city centre.

- You could travel in a group and share petrol costs but claim individually for mileage allowance.

- You could claim for tips that you did not give.

**Test your understanding 4**

There may be a variety of reasons, including:

- envy and resentment of the success of other employees
- frustrations that their own high expectations of rewards or recognition have not been achieved
- greed and selfishness (some employees consider this form of extra earning capacity as a perk)
- the intellectual challenge of beating the system or of having fun.

 **Test your understanding 5**

The top ones include – FRED (because it is easy to type in), SECRET, PASSWORD, naughty words and people's names.

**Test your understanding 6**

|  | Yes/No |
|---|---|
| The matching of all orders to goods received notes. | Y |
| A year-end inventory count. | N |
| The use of sequentially numbered orders. | Y |
| The use of sequentially numbered goods received notes. | Y |
| The matching of goods received notes to invoices. | Y |
| The use of sequentially numbered invoices. | N |
| A sequence check on all orders and goods received notes. | Y |

Cut-off testing should pick this transaction up whether an invoice is available or not.

All paperwork issued should be sequentially numbered. An order will be raised initially which should be matched to the GRN when the goods arrive. These two documents should be matched to the invoice when it arrives, but if it doesn't arrive before the year-end (hidden in Steve's desk) then the estimated cost of the goods (stated on the order or a quote, etc) should be used to account.

Glue is not recorded in the year-end inventory count.

Sequentially numbered invoices would not help as invoices received from suppliers will have their own numbering and not be in sequence according to Sciss.

---

### Test your understanding 7

| | |
|---|---|
| The department's reported profits should be independently scrutinized. | Y |
| The reported profit should be recalculated. | N |
| NL should be supervised by at least one other Board member with foreign exchange experience. | Y |
| Reviewing other bank's foreign exchange profits to see if they too are generally rising each year. | Y |
| Verifying that NL is a qualified accountant and able to produce financial statements. | N |

Option 2 – Recalculating the reported profits probably wouldn't help since simply adding up the profits would not ensure that the profit was actually realised.

Option 5 – NL is a qualified accountant and he has worked for B Bank for three years. He is probably quite capable of producing accurate financial statements, and also capable of manipulating them if he wanted to. This activity would not help to control the potential problem.

## Test your understanding 8

1   Window dressing is a type of false accounting. Management may occasionally wish to 'window dress' their balance sheet (i.e. present either a better or worse picture than that which can be fairly presented) by a variety of devices such as keeping the cashbook open for some days after the year-end so that money received after the year-end is included in the cashbook balance or entering cheques paid before the year-end but not sending them to creditors until after the year-end. This gives an incorrect impression of the company's credit worthiness to a reader of the accounts.

2   The information systems security is based on three elements. The people, the data/information elements and the physical elements, which acknowledge that the operation of computer equipment can be severely impaired where it is subject to events such as fire, flooding and improper environmental conditions, e.g. heat.

3   Examples of false accounting include:

- Obtaining external financing by falsely improving the results.

- Raising the share price by false means to aid acquisitions or to help a new issue of shares.

- Obtaining more business by appearing more successful or less indebted.

- Obtaining performance bonuses for managers by inflating profits.

- Covering up internal theft by altering, adding, falsifying or deleting bank/stock/purchase or other records. A fictitious customer can be created. Orders can be sent, goods despatched on credit and the 'customer' can neglect to pay their bill. The debt is written off.

- Hiding losses in the hopes that fortunes may reverse.

- Preventing or delaying intervention by a regulator.

**KAPLAN** PUBLISHING

4   Collusion is a common element in frauds whereby individuals pool their resources to achieve their aims – specialist skills might not be available to the individual acting independently. Employees can collude with customers, with other employees or with friends.

Examples are:

- The price, quantity or quality of goods sold to a customer can be manipulated to defraud the company.

- An employee could write off a debt or issue a credit note and get something in return.

- An employee could arrange for a supplier to falsify their invoice and show more goods or services than were received. Fictitious supply of goods or services.

5   Computer frauds include:

- Hacking/unauthorised access to bank accounts to transfer funds or to steal or manipulate information.

- Setting up as a legitimate Internet business and obtaining payment for goods that are either never delivered or are of lower quality than advertised.

- Theft of intellectual property.

- Publishing malicious claims about the company on anonymous bulletin boards, thus affecting the company's reputation.

- Disguising the true nature of a transaction by manipulation of date records and programs held on a computer.

6   Uncovering fraud means performing regular control checks, e.g. stocktaking and cash counts, being aware that fraud might be occurring and looking out for signs that there may be a problem e.g. late payments, work backlogs, incomplete audit trails, people with an extravagant life-style, people who are 'experts', confused decision making, multiple interlocking companies or deals, strange payments to countries with strict privacy laws, large transfers before public holidays.

7 Risks can be handled in a number of different ways. You can ignore the risks and do nothing – appropriate where the effect of the risk is small and the chances of it occurring remote. You can purchase insurance against the risk. Alternatively, you can transfer the risk – e.g. arranging for third parties to complete the riskier parts of the project or protect against the risk – arrange for additional staff to be available at critical parts of the project to minimise the possibility of the project overrunning.

8 There are three prerequisites for fraud to occur: dishonesty, opportunity and motive.

9 The areas covered in a fraud policy statement could include an allocation of responsibilities for the overall management of fraud, such that all those concerned are fully aware of their individual responsibilities, and so that accountability can be ensured. It could also include a manual of formal procedures to which staff must adhere if a fraud is discovered. This is required so that continuity of action results, and so that the actions of staff in such a situation are planned and well thought out, rather than ad hoc and ill conceived. It necessarily follows that where a manual of formal procedures exists, staff must be adequately trained to identify fraud or, better still, work to prevent it.

# Improving the accounting system

**7**

## Introduction

This chapter will cover all of the areas within an organisation that you might investigate when looking for ways of improving the effectiveness of an accounting system.

We have already made recommendations to deal with control weaknesses in chapter 3. Here we address the change process in more detail.

There are three main aspects in the syllabus:

1    What changes are needed and why

2    What are the implications of a change

3    What might be the effect on users of a change.

New methods might involve a new department structure, changes in planning and internal control systems, and recommending computerisation of some activities, changing the equipment or changing the methods of working or documents used.

| PERFORMANCE CRITERIA | CONTENTS |
|---|---|
| 4.1  Identify changes to the accounting system | 1    Identifying changes |
| 4.2  Analyse the implications of changes to the accounting system | 2    General reasons for change |
| | 3    Cost benefit analysis and cost control |
| 4.3  Consider the effects of recommended changes on the users of the system | 4    Implementing changes – dealing with resistance |
| 4.4  Justify recommended changes to the accounting system | 5    Implementing changes – approaches |
| | 6    Training |

# 1 Identifying changes

## 1.1 Methods for identifying the need for change

Identifying the need for change will have an obvious start point in that the existing system will need to be recorded and reviewed.

A useful tool for this process is to produce a flow of information diagram. The diagram below is an overview of an accounts department and the typical information flows involved:

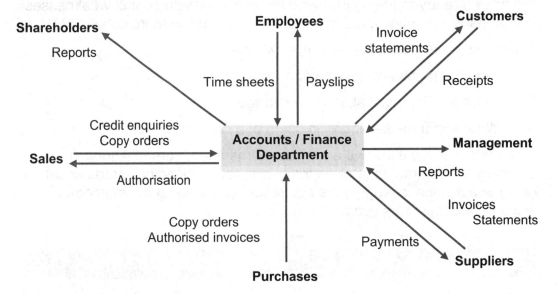

This can then be reviewed for potential change issues.

Another analysis tool is to consider the office procedures manual. Ideally these should be a documented form and show what is supposed to happen at the moment.

Any changes implemented should then be used to update standard procedures manuals.

Standard procedures are useful for organisations in that:

- Procedures should prescribe the most efficient way of getting a job done.

- There is no need to exercise discretion in routine tasks.

- Staff will find jobs easier to do when they are familiar with established procedures.

- Prescribed procedures ensure that a task of a certain type will be done in the same way throughout the organisation.

- The work will be done in the same way even when a different person starts in a job or takes over from the previous holder.

- A written record can be kept in a procedures manual so that people unfamiliar with how a job should be done can learn quickly and easily by referring to it.

- Procedures reduce the likelihood of departmental friction because disputes between departments about who should do what and when, should be avoided.

- They can be reviewed for weaknesses and areas for improvement.

 **Test your understanding 1**

X Ltd is a small retailer that has seen considerable growth. Having suffered various problems with the purchasing function, the Chief Accountant has decided to introduce new internal controls.

**Which TWO of the following controls in a purchase cycle could be implemented to reduce the risk of payment of goods not received?**

| | |
|---|---|
| Sequentially pre-numbered purchase requisitions and sequence check. | |
| Matching of goods received note with purchase invoice. | |
| Goods are inspected for condition and quantity and agreed to purchase order before acceptance. | |
| Daily update of inventory system. | |

**Which TWO of the following controls in the purchase cycle could be implemented to reduce the risk of procurement of unnecessary goods and services?**

| | |
|---|---|
| Centralised purchasing department. | |
| Sequentially pre-numbered purchase requisitions and sequence check. | |
| Orders can only be placed with suppliers from the approved suppliers list. | |
| All purchase requisitions are signed as authorised by an appropriate manager. | |

## 2 General reasons for change

### 2.1 General reasons for change

There are many reasons for an accounting system to have to change.

You need to understand all of these and be able to pick them out of the synoptic information.

| Reason for change | Example |
|---|---|
| **Regulation**:<br><br>Regulation changes often and the accounting system must by law reflect the current rules. | If the VAT rules change, rendering a new product VAT exempt, then the accounting system would need to ensure that any invoice raised for it would not add VAT. This may require programming changes and staff training. |
| **Growth**:<br><br>Some system work well on the existing volume of transactions. However, if the business grows then the existing system can become cumbersome or unworkable. | Growth can strain the resources of a business. It could be that the old system that each sales invoice is independently checked by a supervisor. However if the volume of transaction doubled (say) then this control could become too time consuming. |
| **New information flow**:<br><br>In the diagram above the typical information flows. If another flow emerges then the accounting system would need to reflect that. | The government could introduce new report requirements. For example following the June 2016 Brexit vote the UK government was anxious to see what effect that might have on the level of trade. Reporting requirements changed, with more detailed and more frequent reporting needed. |

| Reason for change | Example |
|---|---|
| **Resources:**<br><br>All systems require resources of people or machines. Short-term capacity issues can result in a need to change the accounting system. | A PC failure might mean that in the short term transaction recording might have to take place using a different system. |
| **Identified weakness:**<br><br>Past errors can reveal weaknesses in the accounting systems (see chapter 3). It is the duty of the directors to maintain effective control and so it is usual that the accounting system would have to change. | A sales invoice might have contained a pricing error. As a result the management decided to introduce an authorisation requirement on all sales invoices. This changed the information and document flow. |
| **Changes in the environment:**<br><br>The business environment influences the design and structure of the accounting system. A **PEST** model could be used as a checklist of ideas to consider – this considers political, economic, social and technological drivers of change. | Increasingly consumers in our society (social factors) are considering the impact an organisation has with regard to pollution as important.<br><br>The accounting function will need to gather data on this in order to prove the position of the business. |
| **New products:**<br><br>Clearly this will change the accounting system. | A business introduced a new product this has meant the creation of new general ledger accounts and a change to the overhead accounting. |

Having a clear idea regarding the need for change provides the basis for a subsequent **justification** of that change.

You may be asked to justify a change being suggested in your assessment.

# 3 Cost-benefit analysis and cost control

## 3.1 Financial evaluation of information systems change projects

In order to convince managers to accept that proposed changes to an accounting system are worthwhile, it is necessary to demonstrate that the project is 'cost-beneficial'. This means that the benefits of the changes outweigh their expected costs.

Cost-benefit analysis focuses on the balance between expected costs and benefits of a proposed system. Although non-financial benefits can be considered, economic feasibility should assess costs and benefits in financial terms.

## 3.2 Costs of information system changes

Tangible costs associated with developing and running information systems can be classified into one-off costs (e.g. development, buying new equipment) and on-going costs (e.g. maintenance, replaceable items). Tangible costs are easy to quantify and can be related directly to development and operation of a system.

However, information systems often incur intangible costs that are much harder to quantify or to relate back to specific systems. Examples of intangible costs include:

- staff dissatisfaction if systems are poorly specified or implemented

- the cost of increased staff mistakes and reduced performance during the learning period after a new system is implemented

- opportunity costs. Whenever money is invested in one area of the company, the opportunity to invest in another area is foregone

- lock-in costs. Purchasing a particular solution can bind a company to a particular supplier, reducing its ability to take advantage of future developments from other providers.

## 3.3 Benefits of information system changes

Benefits can be classified into tangible and intangible benefits. A selection of the benefits in each category is given below.

**Tangible benefits:**

- Savings resulting from an old system no longer operating. These include savings in staff salaries, maintenance costs and consumables.

- Greater efficiency. A new system should process data more efficiently and reduce response times.

- Business benefits gained through improved management information e.g. reduced stock levels due to improved inventory control.

- Gaining competitive advantage. A fully integrated ordering and delivery system, for example, could reduce costs, generating the ability to price competitively.

**Intangible benefits:**

- More informed or quicker decision-making.

- Improved customer service, resulting in increased customer satisfaction.

- Freedom from routine decisions and activities, resulting in more time being available for strategic planning and innovation.

- Better understanding of customer needs through improved analysis of data.

 **Test your understanding 2**

CHO Limited is considering converting its sales cycle from a manual system to a simple on-line computer system. This has been prompted by a growth in the number of transactions which needed processing each month.

**Which one of the following is a probable result associated with conversion to the computer system that can be incorporated into a cost-benefit analysis?**

| | |
|---|---|
| Increased number of processing errors. | |
| Fraud risk is reduced. | |
| Processing time is increased. | |
| Less segregated duties. | |

## 3.4 Cost-benefit analysis

Once information on project costs and benefits is available it becomes possible to carry out a cost-benefit analysis. Results should be interpreted with care, however, as analysis is based on estimates of future cash flows, and on assumptions regarding likely costs and benefits. Two possible methods of performing such an analysis should be familiar to you from previous studies, namely Payback, and Net Present Value.

## 3.5 Payback

Payback calculates the time taken for project cash inflows to equal project cash outflows. The decision rule is to accept the project that pays back most quickly. Whilst projects that payback quickly may be inherently less risky, the overall return on a project is not considered, as cash flows occurring after payback are ignored.

Payback is often used as initial project selection tool, to exclude projects that payback too slowly to be acceptable. The remaining projects are then appraised using more sophisticated tools.

**Payback example**

|  | Project 1 | Project 2 |
|---|---|---|
| Cost | (£100,000) | (£100,000) |
| Net savings |  |  |
| Year |  |  |
| 1 | £50,000 | £30,000 |
| 2 | £50,000 | £38,000 |
| 3 | £25,000 | £45,000 |
| 4 | £0 | £37,000 |
| 5 | £0 | £29,000 |

Project 1 has paid back by the end of year two.

Project 2, however, does not recover its investment until towards the end of Year 3.

Using payback, Project 1 would be selected, even though total return is greater for Project 2.

## 3.6 Net present value (NPV)

This method calculates the net present value of all the project cash flows. If NPV is equal to, or greater than, zero the project should be considered, as its return is at least equal to the discount rate used.

To perform an NPV calculation we do the following:

**Step 1:** Identify future incremental cash flows.

**Step 2:** Discount the cash flows so they are in today's terms (present values).

**Step 3:** The present values can be added up and netted off to give a net present value or NPV.

**Step 4:** If the NPV is positive, then it means that the cash inflows are worth more than the outflows and the project should be accepted.

### Example

(uses cash flows from project 2 above, and a 10% discount rate):

| Time | Cash flow £000 | Discount factor @ 10% | Present Value £000 |
|---|---|---|---|
| t = 0 | (100) | 1 | (100) |
| t = 1 | 30 | 0.909 | 27.3 |
| t = 2 | 38 | 0.826 | 31.4 |
| t = 3 | 45 | 0.751 | 33.8 |
| t = 4 | 37 | 0.683 | 25.3 |
| t = 5 | 29 | 0.621 | 18.0 |
| Net Present Value | | 35.8 | |

## 3.7 Cost estimation

Some costs might be difficult to calculate and some estimation will be needed.

Cost estimation invariably involves some judgement. For example, an estimation of labour time relies on the individuals in each section to give an opinion as to the time it would take to do a job. These estimates are more likely to be understated than overstated and the lack of consistency causes many problems.

The supervisor can improve the accuracy of estimates by:

- learning from previous mistakes

- having sufficient design information

- obtaining a detailed specification, and

- breaking the project down into smaller jobs and detailing each constituent part.

There are different classifications to denote the accuracy of cost estimates:

- **Definitive estimates** aim to be accurate to within 5% and are produced after the design work is done.

- **Feasibility estimates** are accurate to within 10%. These are made in the early design stage.

- **Comparative estimates** are made when the project under review is similar to a previous one. The accuracy of this estimate depends on the similarity and the prevailing economic conditions.

- **Ball-park estimates** are a rough guide to the project costs and are often made before a project starts. They may be accurate to within 25%.

### 3.8 The supervisor's contribution to cost control

Cost control for a supervisor means that staff are working well and properly supervised and all work procedures are carried out as they should be. Good supervision ensures that costs are kept under control.

As a supervisor your role in cost control derives from your responsibility for resources – people or machines for example. You are in charge of activities that incur costs and have therefore a cost responsibility. You have the job of controlling costs within specified parameters or against clear cost standards. You may even be charged with reducing or eliminating costs. This is true of all systems including the accounting system. Accounting departments can easily be over staffed or inefficient.

The typical costs of an accounts department include the wages of permanent and temporary staff, the costs of equipment and software, stationery and overheads.

However, you will only be able to control costs if you are given realistic standards to work to and reliable information about performance, especially about any variance or deviation that occurs. The standards should be derived from a thorough analysis of the job, the methods used and the efficiency of performance.

### 3.9 Cost reduction

Cost reduction means reducing the current or planned unit cost of goods or services without impairing their suitability for the use intended. As far as an accounting system is concerned cost reduction will mean a lower cost per transaction or report. The main areas that will be considered will be reducing staff levels, reducing expenditure on new equipment, changing operations to make them cheaper and using cheaper suppliers.

### 3.10 SWOT analysis

Another method to assess the worthiness of a new system is to carry out a SWOT analysis.

This is a structured approach which considers:

**Strengths**: Does the new system add to the strengths of the business and its reporting? For example will the new system produce better or quicker information?

**Weaknesses**: Will the new system reduce the existing weaknesses in the business? For example if could be that the existing system was prone to invoicing errors or costing inconsistencies and the new system might reduce those errors.

**Opportunities**: The new system may have external implications giving the business opportunities to succeed. For example the new system may mean the tender pricing is more reliable or accurate leading to more successful tenders.

**Threats**: New systems can be temperamental. Breakdowns can be costly and give competitors and edge and this threat needs to be recognised.

# 4 Implementing changes – dealing with resistance

### 4.1 Introduction

The existing system will be embedded and so any new system will be disruptive to the process. Change is time consuming and some delay is almost inevitable. This needs to be minimised through proper planning.

### 4.2 Identifying resistance to proposed changes

Resistance is 'any attitude or behaviour that reflects a person's unwillingness to make or support a desired change'.

Resistance to change is the action taken by individuals and groups when they perceive that a change that is occurring is a threat to them.

Resistance can be classified in to three general categories:

**Job factors**

These generally revolve around fear – fear of new technology, fear of change or fear of demotion or levels of pay.

**Social factors**

The people affected may dislike the potential new social dynamic (or like the existing social scene and not want that to change).

Equally there could be a dislike of the person attempting the change and the people affected would resist any change suggested by them.

Another factor here is that people like to be consulted and if that hasn't happened then they don't feel inclined to support any proposal at all.

**Personal factors**

These, by definition, are more varied as each person may react differently to a particular change.

There could be an individual that feels undervalued as a result of the change or may refuse to re-locate due to a personal preference.

Resistance may take many forms, including active or passive, overt or covert, individual or organised, aggressive or timid. For each source of resistance, management need to provide an appropriate response (see later).

### 4.3 Dealing with resistance to change

Above was a discussion of the various factors that might cause resistance to a change of accounting (or other) system. It is important to respond to these threats to a successful changeover.

| Source of resistance | Possible response |
|---|---|
| • The need for security and the familiar | • Provide information and encouragement, invite involvement |
| • Having the opinion that no change is needed | • Clarify the purpose of the change and how it will be made |
| • Trying to protect vested interests | • Demonstrate the problem or the opportunity that makes changes desirable |
| • Dislike the social upheaval | • Organise social team building events |

## 4.4 Increase the forces for change

Lewin identified that in most situations of change that there will some forces for change. The stronger these forces the more difficult it will be to resist the change.

Drivers for change were covered at the start of this chapter.

To increase the force for change, various tactics can be used:

- Allow participation in the decisions surround the change. Staff will buy in much more readily if they have been involved in the change decisions.

- Educate and communicate the reason for the change to staff. Staff are much more likely to accept change if they understand the reasons for it.

- Negotiate with the staff. The new system might involve more work for the staff. It is sometimes justifiable to consider rewarding staff in some way to give something to get something.

- Remove the support infrastructure for the old system making it impossible to use.

- Adopt a zero tolerance policy regarding the use of the old system.

## 4.5 Change agents

Many organisations employ 'change agents' to encourage and facilitate change. They can play a major role in helping deal with resistance to change.

Usually change agents are figures who are familiar and non-threatening to other people.

The quality of the relationship between the change agent and key decision makers is very important, so the choice of change agent is critical.

**Test your understanding 3**

M publishes several major magazines in country a. M's best-selling title is a fashion magazine – mean – although it also produces magazines on other topics, such as sport and technology.

The majority of M's shares are held by members of the founding family, who have traditionally occupied all of the senior positions within management, although most key decisions are made in consultation with the staff.

M currently employs around 2,500 staff in one large office building in country A's capital city.

The family has always been concerned with maintaining the family name and have focused on the quality of the magazines. Unfortunately, in recent years this has not prevented a significant reduction in M's profitability leading to M's first ever loss being made in the last financial year.

This has led M to hire a Finance Director (FD) who is not a member of the owning family for the first time in its history. After a careful review of M's expenditure he has discovered a large amount of unnecessary expenditure.

He has therefore proposed centralising a number of key functions, such as accounting, printing and proof-reading which are currently duplicated in each magazine. This will lead to around 300 job losses.

In addition he has suggested that the magazines should be produced using cheaper paper and inks, that the large expense accounts offered to senior managers should be cut and that M should start making use of intranets and groupware to allow staff to share ideas quickly and easily.

The FD's proposals have been met with significant resistance from M employees, as well as a number of members of the owning family. He is unsure as to why this is the case and has asked for your help.

**Task**

Write an email to the FD discussing the reasons that his proposals are likely to have met with resistance.

# 5 Implementing changes – approaches

## 5.1 Introduction

Changing accounting procedures are fraught with difficulty. Transactions or records can be lost or duplicated and so an organised process is recommended.

## 5.2 Testing

There are various forms of testing to be carried out before implementation can begin. The idea is that bugs or inefficiencies can be removed in advance of such implementation.

Testing methods include the following:

- **Realistic data testing** – the new system is tested against normal transactions to ensure it operates as expected.

- **Contrived testing** – the new system is presented with unusual data to see how it reacts e.g. negative sales invoices.

- **Volume testing** – a common problem with systems is that they fail to cope when volumes increase, so this is tested in advance. Systems may crash or slow down excessively.

- **Use acceptance testing** – systems are often designed by IT experts but then used by people with much less IT skill.
  The system can be cumbersome or difficult to use and so it is important to make sure that the users are happy in advance.

## 5.3 Changeover method

If new systems are being introduced, then it is critically important that the changeover is managed effectively.

There are four options here although sometimes one method is the only method that would realistically work. This idea is explained below.

### Direct

The old system ceases and the new system takes over on the same day. This may be risky if the new system fails, as there might not be a backup. As mentioned above this can be the only option in some circumstances.

For example a real time airline booking system is a system that cannot be run in combination with a second system. A passenger has booked and that is it!

### Parallel

In this system both the old and new systems are run at the same time. This enables a comparison of result and so increased confidence of the result.

On the other hand it (presumably) doubles the workload and this can stress the staff. It is often accused of being expensive, as more resource will be needed.

**Pilot**

The new system is piloted in a particular location. In this way operational bugs can be identified and removed before wider implementation takes place.

**Phased**

This is similar to a pilot, but it is the phrase used when the system is introduced in stages or in one sub system at a time.

For example an accounting system is made up of different sub systems (payroll, accounts receivable and so on, so a phased introduction would be to implement only payroll at first and then go from there.

Introducing new systems is very disruptive so phasing is sometimes a less stressful, more relaxed approach. Clearly it takes more time and the interaction between old and new sub systems can be problematic.

---

### Test your understanding 4

Which of the following statements relating to parallel information systems changeover is correct?

| | |
|---|---|
| It is cheaper than the direct changeover method | |
| It is mainly used for critical systems | |
| It is less likely to identify errors in the new system than the direct changeover method | |
| It involves gradual implementation of the new system, one sub-system at a time | |

# 6 Training

## 6.1 Introduction

New systems will clearly affect the operating users in many ways. It is important that these users are provided with appropriate levels of support if the new system introduction is to be successful.

## 6.2 Training

Few people would argue against the importance of training as a major influence on the success of an organisation. Training is necessary to ensure an adequate supply of staff that are technically and socially competent and capable of career advancement into specialist departments or management positions. It increases the level of individual and organisational competence and helps to reconcile the gap between what should happen and what is happening – between desired targets and actual levels of work performance.

In particular, when accounting system change then it is vital that the accounting staff are given the training they need.

## 6.3 Training model

The training model below takes account of all the major steps:

**Stage 1 –** Identification of training need: examining what skills and attributes are necessary for the job to be undertaken, the skills and attributes of the job-holder and the extent of the gap.

**Stage 2 –** Design, preparation and delivery of training.

**Stage 3 –** Discovering the trainee's attitude to training (reaction) and whether the training has been learnt (learning).
Reaction involves the participant's feelings towards the training content, the trainer and the training methods used. Learning is the extent to which the trainee has actually absorbed the content of the learning event.

**Stage 4 –** Discovering whether the lessons learnt during training have been transferred to the job and are being used effectively in doing the job. After the training needs have been met, work activities could be rescheduled, for example, to optimise the use and time of the available accounts department personnel.

**Stage 5 –** Evaluating the effects of the training on the organisation. This is the area in which there is perhaps most confusion, and subsequently little real action in the workplace.

**Stage 6** – Reinforcement of positive behaviour. It is optimal that any positive outcomes are maintained for as long as possible. It is not a rare event for changes in behaviour to be temporary, with a gentle slide back to previous ways of working.

## 6.4 Identifying training needs

Job training analysis is the 'process of identifying the purpose of a job and its component parts and specifying what must be learnt in order for there to be effective work performance'.

A training 'gap' or need is any shortfall in terms of employee knowledge, understanding, skill or attitudes against what is required by the job or the demands of organisational change.

There are four main methods for determining the training needs of individuals.

(i) **Performance appraisal** – each employee's work is measured against the performance standards or objectives established for their job. The current performance is assessed in terms of specific and measurable parts of the employee's job and potential performance is also considered.

(ii) **Analysis of job requirements** – uses data concerning jobs and activities e.g. job descriptions, personnel specifications, on the one hand, and leadership and communication activities on the other. The skills and knowledge specified in the appropriate job description are examined. Those employees without the necessary skills or knowledge become candidates for training.

(iii) **Organisational analysis** – uses data about the organisation as a whole e.g. its structure, markets, products or services, human resources requirements, etc. The key success factors are identified and analysed into Human Resources (HR) activities.

(iv) **Departments and/or individuals not performing up to standard will require additional training.**

Surveys of human resources use data about individuals e.g. appraisal records, personal training records, test results, notes made at counselling interviews and results of attitude surveys. Individuals are surveyed to establish any problems they are experiencing in their work and what actions they believe need to be taken to solve them.

## 6.5 Who gets trained?

This covers the whole spectrum of employees:

- New starters who require induction training.
- Operatives who require skills training on any new system.
- Supervisors who require supervisory training.

# 7 Additional 'Test your understanding' questions

 **Test your understanding 5**

1 In a training business consider one example of a technological factor that could cause a change in the accounting function of the business.

2 A person is upset that a change to the accounting function organisation will mean that she will not be able to sit near to one of her friends. Outline which type of resistance this is and suggest one way of overcoming that resistance.

3 A debit entry was attempted when a credit entry is more normal. Which type of testing is this?

4 Briefly explain what you understand as intangible benefits of a system change.

# 8 Summary

In this chapter we have considered the need for a change to an accounting system. Systems need constant monitoring to ensure they meet the business need. If a system does change then it is important that you recognise and can respond to the implications of that change.

## Test your understanding answers

### Test your understanding 1

**Which TWO of the following controls in a purchase cycle could be implemented to reduce the risk of payment of goods not received?**

| | |
|---|:---:|
| Sequentially pre-numbered purchase requisitions and sequence check. | |
| Matching of goods received note with purchase invoice. | ✓ |
| Goods are inspected for condition and quantity and agreed to purchase order before acceptance. | ✓ |
| Daily update of inventory system. | |

*Note:*

*1 prevents stock-outs/manufacturing delays.*

*4 prevents unnecessary goods being ordered.*

**Which TWO of the following controls in the purchase cycle could be implemented to reduce the risk of procurement of unnecessary goods and services?**

| | |
|---|:---:|
| Centralised purchasing department. | ✓ |
| Sequentially pre-numbered purchase requisitions and sequence check. | |
| Orders can only be placed with suppliers from the approved suppliers list. | |
| All purchase requisitions are signed as authorised by an appropriate manager. | ✓ |

*Note:*

*2 prevents stock-outs/manufacturing delays.*

*3 gives assurance about the quality of goods and reliability of supply.*

**Test your understanding 2**

| | |
|---|---|
| Increased number of processing errors. | |
| Fraud risk is reduced. | |
| Processing time is increased. | |
| Less segregated duties. | ✓ |

If the system is simple there shouldn't be an increased number of processing errors. Processing time is usually faster by a computer.

Fraud risk can be increased when using a computerised system with many transactions viewed by only a few employees.

When computerised tasks are automated fewer staff are usually needed and segregation of duties becomes more difficult.

 **Test your understanding 3**

**EMAIL**

**To: FD**

**Re: Resistance to change**

**Job factors**

Many employees may be resisting due to concerns about their jobs. For 300 employees, your proposals will mean unemployment, which means they are likely to be strongly resistant to them.

Many other employees will be affected by the plans to centralise key functions. Those members of staff who remain may be forced to take on a heavier workload to cover the roles of employees made redundant. This may also cause resistance.

Senior managers will be unhappy due to the reduction in their expense accounts as this will be perceived as a loss of their status within the business.

In addition, you are proposing increased use of intranets and groupware. Staff may well be unfamiliar with these systems and dislike the idea of having to learn how to use them. They may also have concerns over the impact they will have on their jobs.

## Personal factors

The changes you have suggested may well be seen as an implied criticism of the long-standing methods of the business. This may well cause resistance from not only the staff, but the owners who have been heavily involved in running the business.

Senior managers may feel less valued under the proposals due to the cuts to their expense accounts, leading to further resistance.

The owners of the company have traditionally focused on the quality of the magazines as they feel this reflects on their family name. The proposal to reduce the quality of the paper and ink is therefore likely to be poorly received by them.

## Social factors

The family has normally made key decisions within the company in full consultation with the employees. This does not seem to have been the case with your proposals, reducing the likelihood that employees will accept the changes.

You are also new in your role and, for the first time, not a member of the owning family. This may reduce his perceived authority, making it more likely that employees, managers and owners will feel that they do not have to follow your suggestions.

I hope you have found the above useful, please get in touch if you need any more information about this.

---

### Test your understanding 4

| | |
|---|---|
| It is cheaper than the direct changeover method | |
| It is mainly used for critical systems | ✓ |
| It is less likely to identify errors in the new system than the direct changeover method | |
| It involves gradual implementation of the new system, one sub-system at a time | |

Parallel changeover involves running the new and old system simultaneously. This is more expensive than a direct changeover, but provides assurance that the new system works properly – which is crucial for critical systems. Gradual implementation of sub-systems is part of a phased changeover.

**Test your understanding 5**

1   On-line booking for courses and programmes are increasingly common and indeed expected in the market. The accounting function will need to be able of capturing the order and taking payment. Many other answers are possible here.

2   This is an example of social factors resistance. Overcoming this is possible by the organisation of social events for the new team where new friendships can be formed.

3   This is an example of contrived testing.

4   An intangible benefit is a benefit that is difficult to quantify. Any of the items below are good examples of intangible benefits.

   - More informed or quicker decision-making.

   - Improved customer service, resulting in increased customer satisfaction.

   - Freedom from routine decisions and activities, resulting in more time being available for strategic planning and innovation.

   - Better understanding of customer needs through improved analysis of data.

# Ethics and sustainability

## Introduction

The accounting systems and control syllabus includes ethics and sustainability.

At first glance this might not seem significant but, amongst other aspects, honesty of recording of transactions, freedom from bias are integral to the proper functioning of the accounting systems.

| PERFORMANCE CRITERIA | |
| --- | --- |
| 1.1 | Discuss the purpose, structure and organisation of the accounting function |
| 1.2 | Discuss the purpose of key financial reports |
| 2.1 | Discuss how internal controls can support the organisation |
| 3.1 | Examine an organisation's accounting system and its effectiveness |
| 3.2 | Evaluate the underpinning procedures of an accounting system |
| 3.4 | Examine current and planned methods of operating |
| 4.2 | Analyse the implications of changes to the accounting system |

## CONTENTS

1   Ethical considerations

2   Sustainability

# 1 Ethical considerations

## 1.1 Introduction

Business ethics is the application of ethical values to business behaviour.

Whether an action is considered to be right or wrong normally depends on a number of different factors, including:

- the consequences – does the end justify the means?
- the motivation behind the action
- guiding principles – e.g. 'treat others as you would be treated'
- key values – such as the importance of human rights.

These principles must be applied to the accounting system as well as general business actions.

---

 **Example – Definition of business ethics**

You discover that a colleague at work has been stealing from the company. What do you do?

Do you report them to management which might lead to their dismissal and the loss of a friend?

Do you keep quiet and risk being punished yourself if your knowledge of the situation later becomes clear?

Do you urge the colleague to confess what they've done?

Does it depend on the size of the theft, e.g. a £1 pad of paper, or a £1,000 piece of machinery?

Does it depend on how friendly you are with the colleague?

You can see that ethical problems require moral judgements that can be extremely difficult and depend on many different factors.

---

## 1.2 Fundamental principles

You will be familiar with the principles from Professional Ethics, whether studied within the Advanced Diploma Synoptic Assessment, or the Professional ethics in accounting and finance/Professional Ethics units.

**Confidentiality** – Information obtained in a business relationship is not to be disclosed to third parties without specific authority being given to do so, unless there is a legal or professional reason to do so.

**KAPLAN** PUBLISHING

**Objectivity** – Business or professional judgement is not compromised because of bias or conflict of interest.

**Integrity** – This implies fair dealing and truthfulness.

**Professional Competence and Due Care** – The necessary professional knowledge and skills required to carry out work should be present.

**Professional Behaviour** – All relevant laws and regulations must be complied with and any actions that would bring the profession into disrepute avoided.

You can go back over your previous notes to re-familiarise yourself with how the principles affect your conduct as an accountant.

 **Test your understanding 1**

For each of the fundamental principles identify two ways that an organisation can adhere to them.

### 1.3 Why business ethics are important

Businesses are part of society. Society expects its individuals to behave properly and similarly expects companies to operate to certain standards. Business ethics is important to both the organisation and the individual.

| For the organisation | For the individual |
|---|---|
| • Good ethics should be seen as a driver of profitability rather than a burden on business. | • Consumer and employee expectations have evolved over recent years. |
| • An ethical framework is part of good corporate governance and suggests a well-run business. | • Consumers may choose to purchase ethical items (e.g. Fairtrade coffee and bananas), even if they are not the cheapest. |
| • Investors are reassured about the company's approach to risk management. | • Employees will not blindly accept orders to act in a manner that they personally believe to be unethical. |
| • Employees will be motivated in the knowledge that they operate in an environment of good ethical corporate behaviour. | |

## 1.4 Practical examples

Understanding the fundamental principles will enable you to see where the business may face issues which are not clear cut; there might not be a definitive right or wrong response. An ethical dilemma may be present.

An ethical dilemma involves a situation where a decision maker has to decide what is the 'right' or 'wrong' thing to do. Examples of ethical dilemmas can be found throughout all aspects of business operations.

> **The main area here is the impact that ethics has on the accounting system, so you should focus here!**

**Accounting issues**

- **Creative accounting** to boost or suppress reported profits. This can manifest itself in various ways. Transactions could be supressed if undesirable. The accounting treatment of a transaction could be manipulated (e.g. an understated provision). Transactions could be recorded in the wrong period (cut off error). This can influence (presumably) the view given by the key financial reports produced and so influence the view that users of those reports have. This is all unethical.

- **Directors' pay** arrangements – should directors continue to receive large pay packets even if the company is under performing? Is the level of pay justifiable?

- Should **bribes** be paid to facilitate contracts, especially in countries where such payments are commonplace? Bribes are generally forbidden in the UK. The view is that a bribe is used to benefit an individual at the expense of his organisation. This is viewed as unethical. Clearly the accounting department has a role in this as all cash transactions must be accounted for. Ask not how it should treated, more how it could be prevented!

- **Insider trading**, where for example directors may be tempted to buy shares in their company knowing that a favourable announcement about to be made should boost the share price. Again the accounting system may contain price sensitive information. This should be kept confidential from those that might benefit from it.

In chapter 3 of this text, the area of internal controls was discussed. The prevention of the above ethical issues is encouraged by a robust system of internal control.

## Production issues

- Should the company produce certain products at all, e.g. guns, pornography, tobacco, alcoholic drinks aimed at teenagers?

- Should the company be concerned about the effects on the environment of its production processes?

- Should the company test its products on animals?

## Sales and marketing issues

- Price fixing and anticompetitive behaviour may be overt and illegal or may be subtler.

- Is it ethical to target advertising at children, e.g. for fast food or for expensive toys at Christmas?

- Should products be advertised by junk mail or spam email?

## Personnel (HRM) issues

- Employees should not be favoured or discriminated against on the basis of gender, race, religion, age, disability, etc.

- The contract of employment must offer a fair balance of power between employee and employer.

- The workplace must be a safe and healthy place to operate in.

 **Stop! And research...**

The Fairtrade mark is a label on consumer products that guarantees that disadvantaged producers in the developing world are getting a fair deal.

For example, the majority of coffee around the world is grown by small farmers who sell their produce through a local cooperative. Fairtrade coffee guarantees to pay a price to a producer that covers the cost of sustainable production and also an extra premium that is invested in local development projects.

Consumers in the developed world may be willing to pay a premium price for Fairtrade products, knowing that the products are grown in an ethical and sustainable fashion.

Find out what other products are produced under the Fair Trade umbrella.

## 1.5 Corporate code of ethics

Most companies (especially if they are large) have approached the concept of business ethics by creating a set of internal policies and instructing employees to follow them. These policies can either be broad generalisations (a corporate ethics statement) or can contain specific rules (a corporate ethics code).

There is no standard list of content – it will vary between different organisations. Typically, however, it may contain guidelines on issues such as honesty, integrity and customer focus.

Many organisations appoint Ethics Officers (also known as Compliance Officers) to monitor the application of the policies and to be available to discuss ethical dilemmas with employees where needed.

---

 **Example – Tesco plc**

Tesco states that it is committed to conducting its business in an ethical manner, treating employees, customers, suppliers and shareholders in a fair and honest manner and ensuring that there are constant and open channels of communication.

Tesco has a code of ethics for its employees, including a policy on the receipt of gifts and a grievance procedure to cover employment issues.

Employees are able to ring a confidential telephone helpline to raise concerns about any failure to comply with legal obligations, health and safety issues, damage to the environment, etc.

---

## 1.6 Safeguards

Business organisations can also help to reduce the threat of ethical breaches by their employees by, amongst other things, having an effective internal complaints procedure that enables the reporting of unprofessional and unethical behaviour.

They can also create a culture that makes it as easy as possible for employees to follow their professional codes and behave ethically.

There are six values that organisations can apply in order to accomplish this. They can be easily remembered using the acronym HOTTER.

If these principles are part of an organisation's values, it will foster an ethical culture which will make breaches of the IFAC and AAT codes far less likely.

- **Honesty** – employees should be encouraged to be honest at all times – even when this may be seen as detrimental to the organisation itself.

  A salesperson should never overstate the benefits or features of the product they are selling.

- **Openness** – this means that the organisation should be willing to freely provide information, as needed, to stakeholders.

  This should make it easier for shareholders, for example, to decide whether to invest in the business or not.

- **Transparency** – this is similar to openness in many ways and indicates that a company makes it easy for key stakeholders to review its activities.

  This can be helped by regular audits and the production of detailed reports on business activities.

- **Trust** – organisations need to be trustworthy in their dealings with others and attempt to work in the best interests of as many stakeholders as possible.

  This could involve, for instance, not overcharging customers.

- **Empowerment** – this involves giving employees and other stakeholders more ability to make their own decisions.

  This will improve their self-image and their motivation.

- **Respect** – all employees and stakeholders should be treated with dignity by the organisation regardless of their age, gender, ethnicity, religion or sexuality.

  This could be embedded into the organisation by having a diversity policy in place.

# 2 Sustainability

## 2.1 What do we mean by 'sustainability'?

### 🔍 Definitions of sustainability

There are a number of different definitions of sustainability:

- Sustainable development is development that meets the needs of the **present** without compromising the ability of **future** generations to meet their own needs. *(The UN's Bruntland Report)*

- A sustainable business is a business that offers products and services that fulfil society's needs while placing an equal emphasis on people, planet and profits. *(The Sustainable Business Network)*

- Sustainable trading is a trading system that does not harm the environment or deteriorate social conditions while promoting economic growth. *(European Union (EU) website)*

Sustainability can thus be thought of as an attempt to provide the best outcomes for the human and natural environments both now and into the indefinite future.

One aspect of this is the ability of the business to continue to exist and conduct operations with no effects on the environment that cannot be offset or made good in some other way.

Importantly, it refers to both the inputs and outputs of any organisational process.

- Inputs (resources) must only be consumed at a rate at which they can be reproduced, offset or in some other way not irreplaceably depleted.

- Outputs (such as waste and products) must not pollute the environment at a rate greater than can be cleared or offset.

Recycling is one way to reduce the net impact of product impact on the environment.

Firms should use strategies to neutralise these impacts by engaging in environmental practices that will replenish the used resources and eliminate harmful effects of pollution.

**Example – Firms acting sustainably**

- Some logging companies plant a tree for every one they fell.

- Coca Cola is one of the companies that have taken a stand in writing a corporate water strategy where they aim to return as much water to nature and communities as they use in their drinks.

- Apple tries to make its products easy to recycle, helping to ensure that materials are reused rather than wasted.

However, it is important to note that sustainability is more than just looking at environmental concerns. It relates to environmental ('planet'), social ('people') and economic ('profit') aspects of human society.

 **Example – Unsustainable practices**

**Environmental**

- deforestation

- the use of non-renewable resources including oil, gas and coal

- long term damage from carbon dioxide and other greenhouse gases.

**Social**

- anything contributing to social injustice

- rich consuming countries and poorer manufacturing countries

- rich companies exploiting third world labour as cheap manufacturing.

**Economic**

- strategies for short term gain (e.g. cutting staff costs to increase reported profits)

- paying bribes (also unethical and often illegal)

- underpayment of taxes.

 **Test your understanding 2**

Why do you think the under-payment of taxes (by large businesses in particular) is considered to be an unsustainable practice?

## 2.2 Why businesses should act in a sustainable manner

Business sustainability is about ensuring that organisations implement strategies that contribute to long–term success.

Organisations that act in a sustainable manner not only help to maintain the well–being of the planet and people, they also create businesses that will survive and thrive in the long run.

In addition, it may be in the firm's **financial** interest to act sustainably.

---

 **Example – How sustainability can boost profits**

- Sustainability may help directly increase sales of products and services.

  For example, some customers may buy your product because a label on it says it has been manufactured using extra-safe working conditions for the labour force, or because it is Fair-trade.

- It may result in **cost savings**.

  For example, lower energy usage may reduce costs and increase profit.

- It may create **positive PR** and thus contribute to business in the long run.

  While sustainability may not enhance product sales right away, if it enhances the image of a company which in turn contributes to better business in the long-term, then it's worth it.

- Avoiding **fines** for pollution.

  The Deepwater Horizon oil spill in 2006 resulted in BP being fined $4.5 billion by the US Department of Justice. However, it is estimated that the total cost to date is in excess of $42 billion in terms of criminal and civil settlements and payments to a trust fund.

---

Directors have a duty to try to increase the wealth of their shareholders and some would see sustainability as conflicting with this objective.

However, many would argue that sustainability should result in better business performance in the long run.

**Example – Sustainability and business success**

A recent working paper from Harvard Business School, '*The Impact Of A Corporate Culture Of Sustainability On Corporate Behaviour And Performance*', compared a sample of 180 US-based companies.

Over an 18-year period, those classified as high-sustainability companies dramatically outperformed the low-sustainability ones in terms of both stock market (i.e. share prices) and accounting measures (such as profit).

## 2.3 Sustainability and the accounting system

In this particular unit it is sustainability in the accounting system that is in question.

The areas, therefore, that you should focus your mind on are:

**The accountancy department**

- The paperless office – how much of the paper use in the accounting department is justified?

- The energy usage for lights, the machines and for heating.

- The use of sustainable materials for the office furniture.

- The level of carbon dioxide produced (if any).

**'What gets measured gets done'**

- The accountancy function can help champion sustainability by suggesting environmental performance measures and measuring these KPIs.

 **Test your understanding 3**

List three different actions an accounting department in a manufacturing company could do to improve the effect it has on society.

**Test your understanding 4**

Jacob is a professional accountant working for Hoggs Furniture Ltd ('Hoggs'), a furniture manufacturer that supplies many high street retailers.

At the last management meeting it was announced that a major client of the company was threatening to terminate their contract with Hoggs unless it could demonstrate a clear commitment to sustainability.

The team were unclear what this meant for Hoggs and asked Jacob to investigate further.

**Required:**

Explain FOUR areas that Hoggs should appraise in order to answer the client's concerns.

List THREE other ways Jacob can contribute to sustainability through his role as an accountant.

## 2.4　The future

At the moment, there are no laws as to the level of sustainability an organisation achieves; however; there are plans afoot to make it a compulsory requirement. Any organisation that therefore adopts a sound policy ahead of this legislation will find themselves ahead of the competition and be able to implement measures at their own speed.

It isn't going to be easy so senior management have to show that they embrace the ethos and lead by example. There is much to be done if we, of this generation, are to leave a bountiful legacy for the next.

Human beings, whether as individuals or organisations, cannot afford to use up all of the earth's resources and leave nothing for future generations but, by the same token, we must exist, prosper, consume. The key is balance.

Resources should be renewed in at least the same proportion as they are being consumed; quality of life, for everyone, should be aimed for whilst renewing the environment and resources; raising the standards of living in a community where all elements of resource be they human, natural or economic, live in harmony.

## Test your understanding 5

You work in the finance team of a well-known chain of fast food restaurants. There has been a lot of negative press recently about the responsibilities of such companies towards society.

Name five things you could suggest which would help to improve their image.

## Stop! And research...

Find out what the FTSE4GOOD is and what the criteria is against which they measure organisations.

# 3   Summary

In this chapter we have explored the ethical and sustainability issues surrounding the accounting function of businesses.

## Test your understanding answers

###  Test your understanding 1

The following are suggestions rather than an exhaustive list:

**Confidentiality**

- Confidential footer on emails.
- Restricted access to sensitive information.
- Passwords for every computer with a requirement to change it every so often.
- Door codes and locks.
- Bag searches.
- The use of removable discs is prohibited.
- A whistle blowing policy with anonymous phone line.
- Confidential information is dealt with on a 'need to know' basis.
- Files and customer information is not allowed off the premises.
- Privacy screens on computers where payroll information is being processed.

**Objectivity**

- A transparent tender/order process.
- Open-door promotions.
- The Board of Directors not being under the control of one forceful character.

**Integrity**

- Equal pay for men and women.
- Evidence of a diversity policy.
- Transparent discount schemes for customers based on order quantities.

**Professional competence and due care**

- Realistic targets, goals and deadlines.
- Training for all staff, relevant to their job role.
- Refresher courses for production personnel or those in H&S.
- CPD for all members of the professional bodies.
- Quality supervision.

**Professional behaviour**

- Staff uniforms.
- H&S, DPA and accounting standards all being up to date.
- Management lead by example and foster a professional attitude.
- No gifts, bribes or other incentives allowed.

---

 **Test your understanding 2**

Underpayment of tax is considered to be unsustainable as the organisations concerned are not contributing to maintaining the country's infrastructure (schools, roads, etc.).

---

 **Test your understanding 3**

(a) **Manufacturing company accounting department**

- Set measurements to assist reducing its inputs and waste to more acceptable levels. This should be monitored year on year.
- Authorise only the use of recyclable packaging wherever possible.
- Assist in sourcing raw materials to more environmentally friendly ones where possible.
- Implement TQM policies.
- Review machinery and equipment regularly to ensure efficiency.
- Monitor pollution and emissions and aim to reduce them year on year.

**Test your understanding 4**

(a) Areas that Hoggs should appraise in order to answer the client's concerns include the following:

- Whether non-renewable hard woods are used in manufacture.

 The client would want reassurance that all materials are form renewable sources.

- The energy efficiency and level of emission of greenhouse gases due to the operation of the factory.

 While these cannot be eliminated altogether, the client would want to see evidence that Hoggs has taken steps to improve energy efficiency (e.g. thermal insulation, double glazing, installation of solar panels, etc) or uses carbon offset schemes.

- Treatment of staff

 Sustainability is not just about environmental issues but also incorporates social (people) aspects. The client may want to know what Hoggs' record is concerning accidents, staff development, diversity, etc.

- Tax

 Economic sustainability includes factors such as whether the company is paying tax and so contributing to the local/national community.

(b) Other ways Jacob can contribute to sustainability through his role as an accountant include the following:

- Helping create an ethics-based culture in Hoggs.

- By championing and promoting sustainability.

- By highlighting the risks of not acting sustainably and draw attention to reputational and other ethical risks.

- By incorporating targets and performance measures consistent with a sustainability approach.

**Test your understanding 5**

The fast food restaurant could:

- Use fresh, wholesome ingredients which are sourced ethically.

- Introduce healthier food onto the menu.

- Publicise the dietary information to allow the consumers to make their own choice.

- Fully train and develop staff so that they understand the significance of the product's, and the company's, impact on society.

- Develop strong ties with the community by holding fund raising days, donating to local charities, etc.

- Monitor waste and reduce levels year on year.

- Ensure that the supply chain is vetted and transparent.

- Review the logistics policy and see whether more efficient delivery methods could be used.

# SAMPLE ASSESSMENT

# 1 Sample Assessment 1 Questions

## Introduction

This chapter contains the revised sample assessment 1 issued by the AAT in 2017.

You should work through this assessment both to familiarise yourself with the format and structure, but also as a practice exam, before looking at the walkthrough in the next chapter.

## ADVANCED PRE-RELEASE INFORMATION

This material is designed to contextualise the tasks you will receive in your sample assessments. Studying this material will encourage you to think about the assessment topics in an integrated way, which is necessary for performing well in the synoptic assessment.

You have access to this material through pop-up windows in the live assessment, should you need to refer to it.

### Company background and history

SL Products Ltd (SLP) is a market-leading manufacturing business supplying advanced technological electronics to a number of companies around the world.

The company operates through a manufacturing division and a sales division. The manufacturing division supplies electronics to the sales division, which sells both its own manufactured products and other complementary products that it buys in from third parties.

SLP has its head office on an industrial estate in Manchester, where its management team and accounts department are both based. Its main manufacturing plant is also on this site, as is the sales division's offices and large central warehouse.

SLP was established 10 years ago by three of its four controlling shareholders, Shaun Murphy, Colin Smith and Cynthia Moss. Six years ago they sold most of their shareholding in the business, and now do not have a controlling interest.

Louise Harding was brought into the company and joined the board as Finance Director just over 18 months ago when the other directors and main shareholders realised the company's urgent need to have more high-level professional accounting expertise.

Over the past 10 years, the company has grown rapidly and in the year ended 31 December 20X1 it had a turnover of £20 million. It also now employs around 400 full-time equivalent employees. However, profits from operations have fallen in recent years.

In an attempt to improve profitability, SLP has recently acquired a controlling interest in Merville Ltd, a small manufacturing business that offers unique, patented products that are complementary to those manufactured by SLP. Merville Ltd has prepared initial accounts for its first year of trading under the control of SLP. A management bonus is linked to these results but it has not yet been authorised for payment by SLP's remuneration committee.

## SLP's mission statement

We aim to be a market-focused business that specialises in the research, manufacture and distribution of passive electronic components.

Our priority is providing great service and a product range at the cutting-edge of technology. We offer our customers cost-effective products of the highest quality.

We aim to develop long-term relationships with all our stakeholders and deal with suppliers, customers and our staff with the highest levels of integrity.

## Developments in the electronics market

During the past few years, the company has been feeling the effects of a recession. Intense competition from overseas manufacturers, made worse by the strength of the pound, has led to a progressive lowering of market prices within the areas in which SLP operates.

It is also becoming increasingly difficult for small companies like SLP to compete with the research and development (R&D) budgets available to larger businesses. As the pace of technological change in electronics has accelerated, the company's product range has gradually lost the lead it once had in cutting-edge technology.

The directors have now reluctantly decided that they may be forced to downsize some parts of the business that they spent the past 10 years building up. On the other hand, as they are unable to outspend their bigger competitors on R&D, they are looking to acquire stakes in companies like Merville Ltd to fill the resulting gaps in their product range.

## SLP's strategic planning and control

When Louise Harding joined SLP, she suggested that they need to view the business from different perspectives rather than just focus on its financial results. The directors and the controlling shareholders agreed to develop measures, collect data and judge the company's performance relative to each of these perspectives. These measures have now been in place for a full year and have just been reviewed.

## Perspective 1

The first perspective involves employee training and having corporate cultural attitudes that relate to both individual and corporate self-improvement. In an organisation, such as SLP that relies on problem solving and creative thinking its people are an important resource. In a market characterised by rapid technological change, it is necessary for staff to be in a continuous learning mode.

Measures were put into place to focus training and development funds where they could help the most.

This perspective, which recognises that "learning" is more than "training"; also considers aspects like the effectiveness of mentoring within the organisation, as well as the ease of communication among workers that allows them to get help with a problem easily, when needed.

In general, the first year's results show that the company has performed well in relation to this perspective.

## Perspective 2

The second perspective refers to internal business processes. Measures based on this perspective allow the directors to see how well their business is running, and whether its products and services conform to customer requirements (as per its mission statement).

Those who know these processes most intimately, namely the various line managers within SLP, carefully designed these measures.

In general, the first year's results show that the company has performed poorly in relation to this perspective. This is because the business is gradually losing its technological lead in several of its products.

## Perspective 3

The third perspective relates to how SLP's customers view the business. Cynthia Moss has stressed the importance of customer focus and customer satisfaction. She has emphasised that these are leading indicators; if customers are not satisfied, they will eventually find other suppliers that will meet their needs better. Poor performance on this perspective is therefore a key indicator of future decline, even though the current financial results may still look reasonable.

In order to develop measures for customer satisfaction, SLP examined its customers both in terms of the kinds of customers they are, and the kinds of products that they are buying from SLP.

The first year's results indicate that customers were generally satisfied with the customer care and service, but were less satisfied with some of the older products in the product range that were overdue for replacement.

Interestingly, customers were generally more satisfied with the bought-in products being sold by the sales division than those manufactured in-house by SLP itself. There was considerable interest in the new products manufactured by Merville Ltd.

## Perspective 4

The fourth and final perspective is the traditional outlook using financial data. Louise Harding instigated the use of more accurate and timely monthly management accounts immediately after she was appointed.

She argued that the previous focus on only financial data had led to an "unbalanced" situation with no attention having been paid to the real drivers of business performance.

The financial results continue to show falling profits which the other three perspectives help to explain.

## Strategy-mapping

SLP has used the first year's results to carry out a strategy-mapping exercise (strategy maps are communication tools used to tell a story of how value is created for the organisation. They show a logical, step-by-step connection between strategic objectives in the form of causes and effects).

Generally speaking, improving performance in the objectives from the first of SLP's perspectives will enable it to improve its internal processes. This will enable it to improve its results for customer satisfaction and eventually its financial performance.

This implies that SLP needs to reallocate resources towards increasing its R&D spend; which will, in turn, redirect its internal processes towards new product development. This should result in improved customer satisfaction and retention, with the final outcome being increased profitability.

Some of the directors, however, believe that the root cause of SLP's problems lies in exactly the matters that are under the Finance Director's direct control – i.e. the problems are due to poor internal controls and systemic weaknesses. The directors also point out that they will struggle to finance any increased R&D.

At this point in time, the board is divided and uncertain how best to proceed.

## Staff

SLP's key personnel are as follows:

| | |
|---|---|
| Managing Director | Shaun Murphy |
| Finance Director | Louise Harding |
| Production Director | Colin Smith |
| Sales Director | Cynthia Moss |
| Chief Accountant | Sue Hughes |
| Purchasing Manager | Tony Clark |
| Warehouse Manager | Robert Utley |
| Credit Controller | Ray Massey |
| Accounts Payable Clerk | Liz Hall |
| Accounts Receivable Clerk | Matthew Tunnock |
| General Accounts Clerk and Cashier | Hina Khan |
| Payroll Clerk | Jane Patel |

**SLP's financial statements**

The financial statements for SLP for the year ended 31 December 20X1 show that the company had a turnover of £20 million, and made a profit after tax of £960,000. These accounts do not include the results of Merville Ltd, which was acquired on 1 January 20X2.

**SL Products Ltd — Group statement of profit or loss for the year ended 31 December 20X1**

| Continuing operations | £000 |
| --- | ---: |
| **Revenue** | 20,000 |
| Cost of sales | (14,322) |
| | |
| Gross profit | 5,678 |
| Operating expenses | (4,413) |
| | |
| **Profit from operations** | 1,265 |
| Finance costs | (47) |
| | |
| **Profit before tax** | 1,218 |
| Tax | (258) |
| | |
| **Profit for the period from continuing operations** | **90** |

**SL Products Ltd — Statement of financial position as at 31 December 20X1**

|  | £000 |
|---|---|
| **ASSETS** | |
| **Non-current assets** | |
| Property, plant and equipment | 4,330 |
| | 4,330 |
| **Current assets** | |
| Inventories | 3,614 |
| Trade receivables | 2,976 |
| Cash and cash equivalents | 8 |
| | 6,598 |
| **Total assets** | **10,928** |
| **EQUITY AND LIABILITIES** | |
| **Equity** | |
| Ordinary share capital (£1 shares) | 800 |
| Share premium | 1,160 |
| Retained earnings | 4,065 |
| **Total equity** | 6,025 |
| **Non-current liabilities** | |
| Bank loans | 1,200 |
| | 1,200 |
| **Current liabilities** | |
| Trade payables | 3,360 |
| Bank overdraft | 124 |
| Tax liabilities | 219 |
| | 3,703 |
| **Total liabilities** | 4,903 |
| **Total equity and liabilities** | **10,928** |

## ASSESSMENT

### Task 1.1 (20 marks)

Louise Harding, the Finance Director of SL products Ltd, has asked you to analyse the published accounts of a competitor business. Until recently you were employed by that business. Therefore, you have a detailed understanding of its financial position.

**(a)   Answer the following questions**                          **(4 marks)**

Which of your fundamental principles is threatened by this offer?

| | |
|---|---|
| Confidentiality | |
| Objectivity | |
| Professional competence and due care | |

What action should you take?

| | |
|---|---|
| Obtain the competitor's agreement | |
| Base your analysis entirely on the published results | |
| Refuse to do the analysis | |

Hina Khan, the Cashier of SL Products Ltd, is preparing a cash flow forecast. She asks which of the following are cash flow items.

**(b)   Show whether each of the following should be included in a cash flow forecast**                          **(8 marks)**

| | Include in cash flow | Do not include |
|---|---|---|
| Revaluation of premises | | |
| Bonus issue of shares in SL Products Ltd | | |
| Payment of dividend on ordinary shares | | |
| Write off of obsolete inventory | | |

**(c)   Liz Hall, Accounts Payable Clerk, asks you for advice. She wants to know whether the following errors and discrepancies would be detected by reconciling the accounts payable ledger to its control account.**                          **(5 marks)**

∇ Drop down list for task 1.1 (c):

| |
|---|
| Would be detected |
| Would not be detected |

| A supplier has been paid for an invoice twice | ▽ |
|---|---|
| A supplier invoice has been posted to the wrong supplier account | ▽ |
| A cheque payment has been debited to the accounts receivable control account | ▽ |
| VAT on some purchases has been omitted from the VAT Return | ▽ |
| A purchase invoice has been debited to the account of a supplier | ▽ |

Liz Hall maintains the accounts payable ledger. Her duties include ensuring that the accounts payable ledger agrees to its control account.

**(d)** **What sort of access should Liz have to the accounts payable control account?** **(1 mark)**

| No access | |
|---|---|
| Read-only access | |
| Full access, including data entry | |

An inventory count is to take place as SL Products Ltd's financial year end. Sue Hughes, Chief Accountant, is concerned that the inventory value will appear to be too high. She suggests that all inventory receipts in the final week of December should be dated 1 January and that those items should be excluded from the count. The relevant purchase invoices would be posted in the new accounting period.

This would slightly reduce the reported value of inventory.

**(e)** **Which of the following statements describes this suggestion?**

**(2 marks)**

| Acceptable commercial practice | |
|---|---|
| Unethical 'window dressing' | |
| Fraud | |
| Beach of the control environment | |

**(Total: 20 marks)**

## Task 1.2

SL Products Ltd acquire a controlling interest in a small manufacturing business caller Merville Ltd on 1 January 20X2.

Unaudited accounts for Merville Ltd's financial year ended 31 December 20X2 have been prepared and an operating budget has been drafted for approval by the directors of SL Products Ltd.

The administration costs for 20X2 include a provision of £21,000 for a profit related management bonus, payable to the directors of Merville Ltd.

**You have been asked to review the budget proposal and supporting submission.**

**Budget submission:**

The directors of Merville Ltd are pleased to present a budget proposal for 20X3. Actual (unaudited) results for 20X2 are provided for comparison. Your approval of the budget is requested.

Substantial sales growth was achieved in 20X2. We introduced more than a dozen innovative new products. The key features of these products are patented and therefore protected from direct competition. Merville Ltd has a solid customer base.

In 20X3, Merville Ltd will retain its own identity in the market place. In addition, we plan to develop a sales channel through SL Products Ltd and to be promoted in that company's catalogue.

We have 50 products in our catalogue at all stages of the product life cycle. More exciting new products are being planned. We do not feel that it is realistic to try to calculate sales revenue and costs at product level. However, we are confident that we will achieve the budgeted 10% volume growth.

We have not assumed any increase in selling prices because this is difficult to achieve with high-tech products.

In addition to the 10% volume growth, we have allowed 2.5% for the cost increases in line with expected inflation.

| Operating budget for year ended 31 December 20X3 | Unaudited results 20X2 | Draft budget 20X3 |
|---|---|---|
| Sales volume | 7,950 | 8,745 |
| | £ | £ |
| Sales revenue | 1,128,900 | 1,241,790 |
| Costs: | | |
| Materials | 246,450 | 277,256 |
| Labour | 409,425 | 460,603 |
| Production overheads | 144,690 | 162,776 |
| Depreciation | 46,800 | 52,650 |
| Marketing | 18,640 | 20,970 |
| Administration | 92,600 | 104,175 |
| Total | 958,605 | 1,078,430 |
| Operating profit | 170,295 | 163,360 |
| Operating profit % to sales | 15.1% | 13.2% |

(a) Examine the planning assumptions and calculations in the proposed budget and identify any weaknesses. **(5 marks)**

(b) Explain how costs and profitability should be managed in an organisation that manufactures multiple products. **(5 marks)**

(c) Give your opinion, with reasons, on how well the budget would motivate managers to create sustainable, profitable growth.

**(5 marks)**

**(Total: 15 marks)**

## Task 1.3

You have been asked to review the adequacy of the controls in SL Products Ltd's purchasing procedures. Your review has established the following information.

The company operates an integrated accounting system which includes a purchase accounting module. Tony Clark, the Purchasing Manager, is responsible for managing purchasing activities.

### Ordering and receipt:

- All purchases, except petty cash items, must be documented on an official purchase order. The order should state the agreed price, if known.

- All departments are provided with books of pre-numbered order forms. These books can be obtained from the stationery store.

- Orders for production materials and items for resale must be signed by Robert Utley, the Warehouse Manager.

- Capital expenditure orders must be signed by Louise Harding, the Finance Director.

- There is no cash limit for purchase orders provided that they are within the approved budget.

- Other orders must be signed by the relevant budget holders.

- Four copies of the order form are printed. Once signed, the original is sent to the supplier. A copy printed on yellow paper is sent to Liz Hall, the Accounts Payable Clerk. Two further copies, printed on pink and green paper, are retained by the individual who raised the order.

- When the goods or service(s) are received, the individual who raise the order signs the green copy and sends it to Liz Hall. This individual retains the pink copy for their files.

### New suppliers:

- New suppliers are contacted by Tony Clark. He provides a trade reference and banking details and requests credit terms.

- He usually requests payment terms as either of the following:

    - Two months from the end of the month in which delivery takes place.

    - With a 5% discount for payment within 21 days of delivery.

However, terms are subject to negotiation.

- He enters the agreed supplier details and payment terms into the supplier file in the accounting system.

### Accounting:

- All purchase invoices are checked by Lis Hall. She checks the calculations, matches the invoices to appropriate yellow and green copy orders and clears the invoices for payment.

- Liz posts the cleared invoices to the computerised accounting system.

- Liz takes up queries with suppliers, requesting credit notes when appropriate.

- Invoices are automatically paid as they fail due through the Bankers Automated Clearing System (BACS). Liz authorises one payment run every week.

(a) **Complete you review as follows, using the provided answer spaces below:**

   - **Identify five systemic weaknesses in the company's internal controls for handling purchases on credit.**

   - **Explain how each weakness that you have identified could create a problem for the company.**

   **Note: You are NOT required to make recommendations to change the procedures.** **(15 marks)**

| First weakness | Potential problem for the company |
|---|---|
|  |  |

| Second weakness | Potential problem for the company |
|---|---|
|  |  |

| Third weakness | Potential problem for the company |
|---|---|
|  |  |

| Fourth weakness | Potential problem for the company |
|---|---|
|  |  |

| Fifth weakness | Potential problem for the company |
|---|---|
|  |  |

**(Total: 15 marks)**

## Task 1.4

### Review of product pricing

The latest annual results of SL Products Ltd have confirmed the trend of decline in the gross profit margin. The board of directors has asked Cynthia Miss (Sales Director) and Louise Harding (Finance Director) to review the situation and report back with an agreed proposal.

The company operates in a very competitive, high-tech market. It is necessary to create a stream of innovative new products that are as good as, or better than, those marketed by competitors. Meanwhile, older products rapidly go into decline. It is almost impossible to increase the price of a product after it is launched.

Louise proposes that all new products should be priced to give a 30% mark-up over cost. She says "We only get one chance to get the price right. Production costs are always rising but we cannot increase our prices. If we launch the product with a 30% mark-up, they will be profitable for a few years."

Sue Hughes, the Chief Accountant, has created a simple spreadsheet model to determine the selling prices for new products.

She has used this model to calculate the selling price of two new products that are ready for launch.

## Pricing spreadsheet

Sue explains that this is a full overhead recovery pricing model.

The variable element of production overheads is equal to 15% of the direct costs. (The direct costs are all variable.) Marketing and administration costs are fixed.

| Prices for new products | £ per unit | |
| --- | --- | --- |
| | NP1 | NP2 |
| Direct cost | 18.00 | 42.00 |
| Production overhead | 3.60 | 8.40 |
| Marketing & administration | 5.40 | 12.60 |
| 30% mark-up | 8.10 | 18.90 |
| Selling price | 35.10 | 81.90 |

## Sales Director's response

Cynthia says that the spreadsheet prices are not competitive.

She knows that the business will suffer if she cannot refresh the product range with new products at attractive prices. She has compared each of the two products (NP1 and NP2) with competitors' products and has estimated the sales potential at three price levels.

| Price levels and estimated annual volumes | NP1 | | NP2 | |
| --- | --- | --- | --- | --- |
| | £ each | Volume | £ each | Volume |
| To undercut competition | 21.00 | 250 | 52.00 | 600 |
| Market price | 28.00 | 150 | 60.00 | 400 |
| Spreadsheet price | 35.10 | 50 | 81.90 | 150 |

Cynthia asks you to calculate which prices would be most profitable.

(a)  For each product calculate the marginal cost per unit and the annual contribution that would be earned at each of the three prices that Cynthia has considered.         **(12 marks)**

| Calculation of contribution | NP1 | NP2 |
|---|---|---|
| | £ | £ |
| Marginal cost per unit (to the nearest penny) | | |
| **Annual contribution** | £ | £ |
| To undercut the competition | | |
| Market price | | |
| Spreadsheet price | | |

(b)  Select the price that would give the highest contribution to profit for each of the three products.         **(3 marks)**

∇ Drop down list for task 1.4 (b):

| To undercut the competition |
|---|
| Market price |
| Spreadsheet price |

| Product | Best price | |
|---|---|---|
| NP1 | | ∇ |
| NP2 | | ∇ |

(c)  Discuss the potential impact of Louise Harding's proposed policy on the business         **(5 marks)**

## Task 1.5

Louise Harding, the Finance Director, is preparing a presentation for the board of directors. She has asked you to complete and comparative 'score card' of key financial ratios which she will use as part of her presentation.

Relevant data has been extracted from the last two years' accounts.

These extracts do not include the results of Merville Ltd.

| Extracts from accounts of SL Products Ltd | Y/E 31/12/20X1 £000 | Y/E 31/12/20X2 £000 |
|---|---|---|
| Sales revenue | 20,000 | 20,900 |
| Cost of sales | 14,322 | 15,144 |
| Profit from operations | 1,265 | 470 |
| | | |
| **Assets** | | |
| Non-current assets | 4,330 | 4,234 |
| Inventories | 3,614 | 3,908 |
| Trade receivables | 2,976 | 3,032 |
| Cash and equivalents | 8 | 6 |
| **Total** | **10,928** | **11,180** |
| **Equities and liabilities** | | |
| Equity | 6,025 | 5,550 |
| Non-current liabilities | 1,200 | 1,400 |
| Trade payables | 3,360 | 3,730 |
| Bank overdraft | 124 | 260 |
| Tax liabilities | 219 | 240 |
| **Total** | **10,928** | **11,180** |

(a) **Complete the scorecard by calculating the missing ratios.**

(10 marks)

| SL Products Ltd Scorecard | Year ended 31 December 20X1 | Year ended 31 December 20X2 |
|---|---|---|
| **Profitability and gearing (correct to 1dp):** | | |
| Gross profit % | 28.4% | % |
| Operating profit % | 6.3% | 2.2% |
| Return on capital employed | 17.5% | % |
| Gearing | 16.6% | 20.1% |
| **Liquidity ratios (correct to 1dp):** | | |
| Current ratio | 1.8:1 | :1 |
| Acid test/Quick ratio | 0.8:1 | :1 |
| **Working capital days (correct to nearest day)** | | |
| Inventory holding period | 92 days | 94 days |
| Trade receivables collection period | 54 days | 53 days |
| Trade payables payment period | 86 days | 90 days |
| Working capital cycle | 60 days | days |

(b) **Select the ONE correct observation about each aspect of business performance below.** (10 marks)

**Profitability**

| | |
|---|---|
| This has been a year of steady, if unspectacular, progress. Although profitability has dipped, the return on capital employed has been kept under control. | |
| The profitability ratios give cause for concern. The small increase in sales revenue has not improved the gross profit percentage. Operating expenses have increased, reducing operating profit and return on capital employed. | |
| The ratios give mixed messages. Some have improved and some have deteriorated. Further investigation is required. | |

### Gearing

| | |
|---|---|
| The increased gearing ratio is entirely due to the increase in non-current liabilities. | |
| It is likely that the interest cover ratio has increased. | |
| The increased gearing ratio shows that the company has become more risky. | |

### Liquidity

| | |
|---|---|
| Both ratios have deteriorated which indicated that the company is less solvent. | |
| Both ratios remain too high, indicating that working capital is not being used effectively. | |
| Some profitability ratios have improved and some have deteriorated. Further investigation is required to understand where profitability is improving. | |

### Working capital

| | |
|---|---|
| The working capital cycle has worsened. The inventory holding period has improved but the other ratios indicate a lack of financial control. | |
| There is a welcome improvement in the working capital cycle, mainly due to the change in the payment period for payables. | |
| The working capital cycle is worse than a year ago because of the increased cost of sales. | |

### Overall performance

| | |
|---|---|
| Profitability has declined in 20X2, mainly due to competitive pressures. However, the gearing and liquidity measures show an improving financial position. | |
| 20X2 has been a bad year. Profitability has declines and finances are coming under pressure. | |
| Steady progress has been made in 20X2. The ratios show that the company is being better managed. | |

**(Total: 20 marks)**

## Task 1.6

You have been asked to carry out a review of SL Products Ltd's sales order processing procedures and make recommendations for improvement.

You have interviewed the Sales Director, (Cynthia Moss), Credit Controller (Ray Massey) and Accounts Receivable Clerk (Matthew Tunnock). Your findings are below.

### Catalogue

The 85-page illustrated catalogue is updates and posted to customers in the spring and autumn of each year. The print run is 5,000 copies. An online version is put on the company's website.

Orders can be placed by post, telephone or online if the customer has been granted credit terms. Otherwise, orders will only be placed by post and must be paid for in advance by cheque (in British pounds). These cheques are cleared before despatch is allowed.

Accounts that are dormant for 18 months are closed. These customers are removed from the catalogue distribution list.

### Customer base

80% of sales are made to just 20% of the credit customers.

Most of these sales are repeat orders for some long-established items in the catalogue.

95% of sales, by value, are to credit account customers.

There are 4,210 customers with credit accounts: 4,000 in the UK; 150 in other European Union countries and 60 elsewhere around the world. Over the last year, 129 customers have been granted credit accounts. 608 inactive accounts have been closed.

Sales to customer outside the UK have declined over the last five years and now make up only 7% of total sales.

### Credit accounts

Account application forma are sent to new customers by Matthew Tunnock, Trade and bank references are required. When the form and references are returned, Matthew checks them and drafts a confirmation letter which Ray Massey authorises.

Matthew sends the confirmation letter, a copy of the company's terms of trade and a catalogue to the new credit customer. There is no formal credit limit at this stage. Credit limits are placed on regular late payers.

Most customers settle their accounts within the agreed periods or very soon after. There are very few bad debts.

You are required to identify four features of these procedures: one strength; one weakness; one threat and one opportunity. Do not use the same feature more than one.

(a)  Identify one strength in these procedures. Explain how the business benefits from this.  **(3 marks)**

(b)  Identify one weakness in these procedures. Explain how this damages the business and suggest a remedy.  **(4 marks)**

(c)  Identify an opportunity to improve the procedures. Explain how the procedure should be changed and how the business could benefit.  **(4 marks)**

(d)   Identify one threat to the effectiveness of these procedures. Explain how this could damage the business and suggest an action that would reduce the risk.                    (4 marks)

(Total: 15 marks)

# 2 Sample Assessment 1 – Walkthrough and answers

## Introduction

This chapter contains a detailed walkthrough of the revised sample assessment 1 issued by the AAT in 2017.

## ADVANCED PRE-RELEASE INFORMATION

This material is designed to contextualise the tasks you will receive in your sample assessments. Studying this material will encourage you to think about the assessment topics in an integrated way, which is necessary for performing well in the synoptic assessment.

The question arises, however, how best to assess the pre-release information.

The simplest approach is to read through each section and ask yourself what this is telling you about the company, focussing on control issues and the effectiveness of its systems and processes.

Let us take each section in turn:

### Company background and history

Key aspects from this section are that SLP has grown considerably but is now experiencing falling profits.

- High growth can often lead to control problems – for example, credit control staff may struggle to manage the extra customers resulting in worsening receivables days and problems with cash flow. Eventually extra staff will be recruited but there may be an interim period where problems develop.

- Falling profit may mean that it is now even more important to control costs and quality.

A more subtle point you could consider here is what the different control issues will be between making products in-house and buying some in from external suppliers. For example, with external suppliers there may be a need for a service level agreement to manage risks.

Finally we are told that SLP has recently acquired a controlling interest in Merville Ltd. This could pose the following issues:

- There may be problems integrating the two accounting and reporting systems.

- Errors may arise as it is the first year of consolidated accounts.

- The management bonus (being linked to results) may result in window dressing of results to boost the bonus.

### SLP's mission statement

Controls are required to ensure organisations achieve their objectives, so it is worth asking what those objectives might be.

Given we have shareholders, then one answer is to boost shareholder value.

An alternative is to look at the mission statement, which states that SLP aims to provide great service and a product range at the cutting-edge of technology, offering our customers cost-effective products of the highest quality.

Thus any scenario could be discussed by reference to the impact of problems and control issues on technology development, cost effectiveness and quality.

### Developments in the electronics market

A recession and competition from overseas manufacturers mean that the directors have now reluctantly decided that they may be forced to downsize some parts of the business.

Control issues here could include managers distorting results to ensure that their part of the business does not get 'downsized' or to prevent them losing their jobs.

### SLP's strategic planning and control

This section adopts a balanced scorecard approach (from MADCL – see appendix 3) for evaluating and monitoring performance.

| Perspective | Focus | Specific details |
|---|---|---|
| 1  Innovation and learning | How can we continue to improve and create future value? | Performed well. Investing in training and development. |
| 2  Internal business processes | What processes must we excel at to achieve our financial and customer objectives? | Performed poorly. SLP is gradually losing its technological lead in several of its products. |
| 3  Customer | What is it about us that customers value? | Problems with older products. Problems with products manufactured in-house by SLP itself (compared to those bought in). |
| 4  Financial | How do we create value for our shareholders? | Falling profits. |

Each of the problem areas could result in control issues.

## Strategy-mapping

Strategy maps are often used to translate the results of a balanced scorecard exercise into action points - what needs to be done in terms of (1) learning and innovation to help (2) improve internal processes that result in (3) improved customer satisfaction and (4) higher profit?

This implies that SLP needs to reallocate resources towards increasing its R&D spend; which will, in turn, redirect its internal processes towards new product development. This should result in improved customer satisfaction and retention, with the final outcome being increased profitability.

You may want to consider what KPIs would be required to monitor this, or what particular control issues increasing R&D would generate.

Some directors believe that the problems are due to poor internal controls and systemic weaknesses. Expect to see these brought out in tasks.

## Staff

A list of key staff help you see how the organisation is structured and also if there are obvious control issues relating to responsibilities – for example, having a separate Accounts Payable Clerk and Accounts Receivable Clerk may mean better segregation of duty.

## SLP's financial statements

You could calculate ratios to see if any key problems are highlighted:

| | (Working) | Ratio |
|---|---|---|
| Gross Margin (%) | 5,678/20,000 | 28.4% |
| Operational Margin (%) | 1,265/20,000 | 6.3% |
| ROCE (%) | 1,265/(6,025 + 1,200) | 17.5% |
| Current ratio | 6,598/3,703 | 1.8× |
| Quick ratio | (6,598-3,614)/3,703 | 0.8× |
| Inventory days | (3,614/14,322) × 365 | 92 days |
| Receivables days | (2,976/20,000) × 365 | 54 days |
| Payables days | (3,360/14,322) × 365 | 86 days |
| Operating cycle | 92 + 54 – 86 | 60 days |
| Gearing (Debt/Equity) | 1,200/6,025 | 0.2× |

The effectiveness of such an exercise is limited by the fact that we only have one year of results so have no basis of comparison to evaluate figures.

Despite this, we can make the following comments:

- Profit margins seem low, probably as a result of intense competition.

- However, ROCE seems healthy.

- Possible concern that the quick ratio is less than 1 – this could indicate short term liquidity risk.

- Inventory days seem very high, especially given the danger that products may become obsolete.

- We would need to know industry norms and SLP's credit terms to evaluate whether receivables days of 54 days is excessive.

- Payables days seems high – is there a danger that we are upsetting suppliers, which could result in delays in delivery or poor quality?

- Financial gearing is low, so there may be scope to raise finance for new projects.

**What next?**

You do not need to learn any of the above analysis – the aim is to help you feel comfortable with the company and what it does and to think about the assessment topics in an integrated way.

In some respects the main reason for looking at the pre-release material is to feel comfortable with the scenario and to know what is there so you can refer back to it if necessary.

- In sample assessment 1 all relevant information was given to you within the tasks, so there was little need to refer back to the pre-release material in order to answer them.

- However, in sample assessment 2 you needed to refer back to the financial statements in order to calculate ratios.

## THE SAMPLE ASSESSMENT

## TASK 1.1

### Introduction

In the sample assessment, task 1.1 correlates with assessment objective 1:

| Assessment objective 1 | Demonstrate an understanding of the roles and responsibilities of the accounting function within an organisation and examine ways of preventing and detecting fraud and systemic weaknesses. |
|---|---|

Task 1.1 is, therefore, primarily about accounting systems and control, although it relies on a good understanding of bookkeeping from level 3 of your earlier studies.

### Task 1.1(a)

Part (a) considers an **ethical** dilemma and how best to respond.

**Key considerations**

- Make sure you can remember the five ethical principles!

- Detailed knowledge of the competitor's financial position clearly came from a privileged position (i.e. working there), so must be considered confidential.

- This does not prevent you from working with the competitor's information but does restrict you only to using what would be in the public domain

The correct answer is thus

Which of your fundamental principles is threatened by this offer?

| Confidentiality | ✓ |
|---|---|
| Objectivity | |
| Professional competence and due care | |

What action should you take?

| Obtain the competitor's agreement | |
|---|---|
| Base your analysis entirely on the published results | ✓ |
| Refuse to do the analysis | |

## Task 1.1(b)

Part (b) looks at identifying whether accounting items also have a cash flow implication.

### Key considerations

- Not all accounting entries involve cash. If you are unsure, then it may be a good idea to consider what the double entry for each item would involve

- Revaluation DR Asset account CR Revaluation reserve

- Bonus shares DR P&L reserve CR Share capital

- Payment of dividend DR P&L reserve CD Cash

- Write off DR Closing inventory (P&L) CR Closing Inventory (SOFP)

The correct answer is thus

|  | Include in cash flow | Do not include |
|---|---|---|
| Revaluation of premises |  | ✓ |
| Bonus issue of shares in SL Products Ltd |  | ✓ |
| Payment of dividend on ordinary shares | ✓ |  |
| Write off of obsolete inventory |  | ✓ |

## Task 1.1(c)

Part (c) looks at a common **accounting control** – performing a control account reconciliation. This topic was covered in your level 3 studies as part of advanced bookkeeping.

### Key considerations

- The accounts payable ledger will receive postings from individual invoices in the purchases day book and individual payments in the cash book.

- Individual items in these books of prime entry are added up and monthly totals posted to the accounts payable control account as part of the double entry.

- For each error you thus need to consider whether and how each total (accounts payable ledger and accounts payable control account) will be affected. If both totals would be affected the same way, then the figures will still agree with each other and the error go undetected.

The correct answer is thus

|  | **Comment** |  |
| --- | --- | --- |
| A supplier has been paid for an invoice twice | Both totals wrong, so still agree | Would not be detected |
| A supplier invoice has been posted to the wrong supplier account | Both totals still correct so agree | Would not be detected |
| A cheque payment has been debited to the accounts receivable control account | Only accounts payable control account wrong | Would be detected |
| VAT on some purchases has been omitted from the VAT Return | Neither affected | Would not be detected |
| A purchase invoice has been debited to the account of a supplier | Only accounts payable ledger wrong | Would be detected |

## Task 1.1(d)

Part (d) looks at the level of access required.

### Key considerations

- The key issue here is segregation of duties. Should Liz, who controls the payables ledger, also have access to the control account?

- Full access would allow her to hide errors or fraud that the control account reconciliation would normally detect

The correct answer is thus

| No access |  |
| --- | --- |
| Read-only access | ✓ |
| Full access, including data entry |  |

## Task 1.1(e)

Part (e) considers a proposal to alter the period end inventory count.

### Key considerations

- This is clearly not normal practice. The main problem is knowing how best to identify the type of issue.

- Moving transactions from one period to another to improve the look of a business is known as 'window dressing'.

The correct answer is thus:

| | |
|---|---|
| Acceptable commercial practice | |
| Unethical 'window dressing' | ✓ |
| Fraud | |
| Beach of the control environment | |

## TASK 1.2

### Introduction

In the sample assessment, task 1.2 correlates with assessment objective 2:

| Assessment objective 2 | Evaluate budgetary reporting; its effectiveness in controlling and improving organisational performance. |
|---|---|

Task 1.2 is, therefore, primarily about the role and use of budgets and variances in controlling the organisation. As such it will draw heavily on underlying knowledge from the management accounting units at this level.

In this task you are given a **budgetary report** plus accompanying narrative outlining the basis of preparation, future plans and assumptions.

### Task 1.2(a)

In this task you are given a budget plus accompanying narrative outlining the basis of preparation, future plans and assumptions.

Part (a) asks you to examine the planning assumptions and calculations in the proposed budget and identify any weaknesses. This was covered in chapter 2, where it was stressed that you should use the information given in the specific scenario as much as possible.

**Key considerations**

To start with you should make sure you know what figures have been used:

- Sales volume – 10% growth
- Sales revenue – 10% growth
- Costs – 12.5% growth = 10% volume + 2.5% inflation

Then you can see if these figures can be justified.

- Sales volume – 10% growth.

    High sales growth was achieved in 20X2 but will this continue in 20X3?

We are not old that any more products will be introduced within Merville but that there is a plan to develop a sales channel through SLP. Will this be enough to justify 10% growth in volume?

We can also challenge the assertion that "We do not feel that it is realistic to try to calculate sales revenue and costs at product level". They have 50 products not 5000, so estimating sales by product should be feasible.

- Sales revenue – 10% growth

Given sales volume growth of 10%, this assumes no increase in price levels. The reason for this we are told is "because this is difficult to achieve with high-tech products."

However, companies often charge a premium for new high-tech products with innovative features, especially if protected by patents.

- Costs – 12.5% growth = 10% volume + 2.5% inflation

Assuming the 10% volume factor can be incorporated into all cost increases, along with inflation, assumes that all costs are variable in nature.

While this may be true for direct materials and even direct labour, it is unlikely to be valid for administration costs, say.

In addition we are told that administration costs for 20X2 include a provision of £21,000 for a bonus. Has this been included again in 20X3, even though such a bonus would not yet have been agreed?

Given all of this, the main problem is getting all your ideas down in the time available.

## Model answer

> The draft budget is based on the assumption of 10% growth in sales volume. No justification is offered for this round figure assumption. I suggest that we need to review recent trends in Merville Ltd's products; look at the potential for the anticipated new products and estimate the likely additional business generated from our own customers. With only 50 current products, this should not be difficult.
>
> The assumption that sales revenue will only grow relative to sales volume is probably pessimistic. Although we are told prices can never be raised, new products should command a healthy margin when launched, particularly as they are patent protected.
>
> All costs have been increased by 12.5% in the draft budget (2.5% for inflation and 10% for growth). There is no reason why fixed costs should increase by more than an appropriate rate for inflation. Each line of costs needs to be considered carefully according to its cost type (variable, fixed, etc.) and its own cost pressures.

In particular, agreement is required about the management bonus. This has been accrued at £21,000 for 20X2 and, in effect, budgeted at £23,625 for 20X3. This has not yet been approved.

### Task 1.2(b)

Part (b) asks you to explain how costs and profitability should be managed in an organisation that manufactures multiple products.

**Key considerations**

There are a number of different ways you could answer this, relying on your management accounting knowledge, for example:

- You could argue that standard costing to facilitate better management control through the use of variances, for example.

- Alternatively, you could argue that the use of activity based costing (ABC) would result in more realistic costs and hence better pricing decisions and cost control.

- At a more basic level you could argue that a formal costing system that allowed review and planning for individual products was essential to allow managers to make better decisions regarding individual products.

**Model answer**

In a multi-product manufacturing organisation, it is essential that costs and profitability are reviewed by product. Therefore, a costing system needs to be in place.

A standard costing system has particular advantages in that it is based on calculations of what the costs should be - called standard costs. This is useful for control as variances from these standards can be reported and investigated.

The standard cost of each product can be compared with its selling price to identify profitability.

Standard costs can be calculated for planned new products to inform price setting.

## Task 1.2(c)

Task (c) then asked you to give your opinion, with reasons, on how well the budget would motivate managers to create sustainable, profitable growth.

This looks at the way budgets can be used to motivate managers.

### Key considerations

- Budgetary targets will motivate managers if targets are seen as fair, are stretching but achievable, only relate to factors under managers' control and are matched to managers' responsibilities.

- The budgets were prepared by the directors of Merville Ltd, the very same people who would benefit from a profit related management bonus.

- Participation in target setting can result in more realistic targets and better ownership of them BUT may result in budget padding/slack.

- It is possible that the directors have set themselves easy targets through a very cautious budget to increase the chance of gaining a bonus.

- This could explain why fixed costs have been increased as if they were variable.

- You could also argue that the budget will cause managers to focus only on the next year and so could encourage short-termism, such as cutting marketing costs. This could result in the planned sales increase not being achieved.

### Model answer

> Budgetary control can be a powerful tool to encourage managers and staff to create sustainable, profitable growth.
>
> To do this, budgets need to be stretching but achievable.
>
> The proposed Merville Ltd budget has been prepared by its own directors who have a vested interest, in the form of the management bonus, in ensuring that it is easy to achieve.
>
> They have not provided sufficient supporting data to enable us to verify that the sales volume and pricing assumptions are stretching.
>
> Increasing all costs, fixed and variable, by 12.5% cannot be justified and created significant budgetary slack.
>
> I do not believe that this draft budget would motivate Merville Ltd to create sustainable, profitable growth.

## TASK 1.3

### Introduction

In the sample assessment, task 1.3 correlates with assessment objective 3:

| | |
|---|---|
| Assessment objective 3 | Evaluate an organisation's accounting control systems and procedures. |

Task 1.3 is, therefore, primarily about the detail of control systems, covered in some depth in chapter 3.

### Task 1.3(a)

The focus here is on the purchases cycle. You are required to identify five systemic weaknesses in the company's internal controls for handling purchases on credit and explain how each weakness that you have identified could create a problem for the company.

**Key considerations**

- You have a considerable amount of information to deal with, so you cannot afford to keep reading and re-reading it. Instead you need to be able to identify weaknesses as you go along.

- You may recall that chapter 3 contained a number of internal control questionnaires (ICQs), including one on the purchases cycle, to help you identify control weaknesses.

- Either you can learn such checklists and use them to evaluate the information given, or (better) you now know what to look for and can critically assess each step or process you are given.

- Try to imagine what could go wrong, whether through mistakes that are not detected, or through deliberate fraud – could someone in the scenario steal funds without detection?

- Whenever told that person X does a particular task, ask yourself whether they should be doing it or would it be better if someone else (more senior?) did it instead.

- Some weaknesses may be more subtle to spot – especially those relating to a lack of segregation of duties.

- The model answer gives 11 possible weaknesses – you were only asked for five, so be encouraged that you don't have to spot them all!

- You are not asked for recommendations.

## Model answer

| No | Weakness | Potential problem |
|---|---|---|
| 1 | The Purchasing Manager appears to have very little involvement in day to day purchasing, apart from negotiating terms with new suppliers. | Failures in the system and system abuses could go unnoticed. |
| 2 | No apparent security for order stationery. | Potential for anyone to commit fraud by making purchases for their own use in the company's name. |
| 3 | Budget holders and the warehouse manager can raise orders and sign that the good or services have been received. | There is a potential for fraud as there does not appear to be any check that these purchases are necessary, or eve, for business use. |
| 4 | The procedures do not include any mention of checking that goods and services of the correct standard have been received. | If this is not happening the company could be paying for unsatisfactory supplies. |
| 5 | There is no cash limit to purchase orders provided that they are within the approved budget. | Without a second signature on large purchases, there is scope for errors, poor judgement or fraud to be very costly. |
| 6 | Orders can be placed without agreeing a price. | The company is in a weak position to negotiate price after the good or services have been received. |
| 7 | Lack of authorisation of new accounts. | There should be a policy for choosing new suppliers. Potential for fraud through collusion with suppliers. |
| 8 | The terms agreed by Tony Clark are not countersigned. | Potential for fraud through collusion with suppliers. |
| 9 | Only one signature is required on purchase orders. | Potential for fraud through collusion with suppliers. |

| No | Weakness | Potential problem |
|----|----------|-------------------|
| 10 | Liz Hall checks, clears and arranges payment of invoices. | Potential for fraud through collusion with suppliers. |
| 11 | Tony Clark and Liz Hall control all aspects of purchase accounting. | Potential for fraud through collusion. |

Note: the weakness is a statement of fact from the scenario – the justification of that weakness as a problem is where you need to ensure you write enough detail.

## TASK 1.4

### Introduction

In the sample assessment, task 1.4 correlates with assessment objective 4:

| Assessment objective 4 | Analyse an organisation's decision making and control using management accounting tools. |
|---|---|

Task 1.4 is, therefore, primarily about decision making, topics covered in detail in the underlying Management Accounting: Decision and Control unit, the key aspects of which are summarised in appendix 3. As well as performing the relevant analysis, you may also be asked to consider whether the best technique has been used, whether "right" decision has been made, potential problems that may arise and what could be done differently.

In the sample assessment 1 this task focusses on a pricing decision and gives you detailed information concerning costs and demand levels.

You are given three prices – cost plus, market rate and a price to undercut the competition and have to discuss which should be used.

### Task 1.4(a)

This simply asks you to calculate marginal costs and contribution levels under different scenarios.

**Key considerations**

- You are told how different costs behave so use this when identifying which costs are variable to determine marginal cost.

  For example, for NP1: MC = 18 × 115% = £20.70

- Contribution = selling price – all variable costs.

  For example, NP1 priced to undercut the competition, total contribution = 250 × (21 – 20.70) = 75

### Model answer

| Calculation of contribution | NP1 | NP2 |
|---|---|---|
| | £ | £ |
| Marginal cost per unit (to the nearest penny) | 20.70 | 48.30 |

| Annual contribution | £ | £ |
|---|---|---|
| To undercut the competition | 75 | 2220 |
| Market price | 1095 | 4680 |
| Spreadsheet price | 720 | 5040 |

### Task 1.4(b)

Here you simply interpret the results of part (a):

| Product | Best price |
|---|---|
| NP1 | Market price ▽ |
| NP2 | Spreadsheet price ▽ |

### Task 1.4(c)

Task (c) asks you to discuss the potential impact of the policy on the business. If you are unsure where to begin, then you could consider whether Louise Harding's proposed policy ensures that all new products are profitable as this is mentioned in the question. Secondly, you could explain how Louise Harding's proposed policy could be damaging to the business.

### Key considerations

### Profitability

- Check which price is being considered here – this is the cost plus one.

- To discuss profitability you need to refer to both contribution **and** fixed costs.

- On a basic level, given cost plus pricing has been used with full cost, the price must cover the apportioned fixed costs.

- However, you do need to be careful about volumes – as long as the volume used to calculate the fixed cost per unit and the selling volume are the same, cost plus pricing should result in a profit. If not, then the sales volume may be insufficient to recover all fixed costs (effectively they are under-absorbed).

## Potential damage

This requires you to consider what could go wrong with cost-plus pricing and/or why the alternatives might be better.

- You could argue that using cost-plus discourages cost control and hence could undermine the company's long term competitiveness.

- Alternatively you could discuss the fact that cost-plus pricing effectively ignores what price customers are willing to pay. This could result in lower sales volumes, fixed costs not being recovered and losses.

- Similarly the approach does not reflect the behaviour of competitors, again leaving SLP vulnerable to being priced out of the market.

### Model answer

Proposed policy would ensure that all new products are profitable:
- o Any price that is higher than marginal cost will contribute
- o and therefore increase profits
- o The policy generates prices which are greater than total unit cost, including an apportionment of fixed costs
- o Therefore, all products should be profitable at any volume of sale

Despite being profitable, the new policy could be damaging to the business:

- o The pricing policy does not allow the sales director to respond to market conditions and find the combination of profit and volume
- o that will optimise contribution
- o SLP is in a price competitive business
- o If new products are not priced competitively they will only sell in small volumes.
- o As ageing products decline they must be replaced by innovative new ones.
- o The business will go into decline if the product range is not refreshed

## TASK 1.5

### Introduction

In the sample assessment, task 1.5 correlates with assessment objective 5:

| Assessment objective 5 | Analyse an organisation's decision making and control using ratio analysis. |
|---|---|

Task 1.5 is, therefore, primarily about ratio analysis, either 'normal' ratio analysis or using specific key performance indicators. You have met this many times in other units, such as 'Financial Statements of Limited Companies'. It was also recapped in detail in chapter 5 of this text.

The emphasis within the 'Accounting Systems and Controls' aspect is on using ratios to identify control weaknesses.

However, in the synoptic assessment you may also be asked to use ratios as part of performance appraisal. Make sure you read the question carefully!

### Task 1.5(a)

Part (a) asks you to calculate missing ratios. This should be very straightforward:

**Model answer**

| SL Products Ltd – Scorecard | 20X1 | 20X2 |
|---|---|---|
| **Profitability and gearing** | | |
| Gross profit % | 28.4% | **27.5%** |
| Operating profit % | 6.3% | 2.2% |
| Return on capital employed | 17.5% | **6.8%** |
| Gearing | 16.6% | 20.1% |
| **Liquidity ratios** | | |
| Current ratio | 1.8:1 | **1.6:1** |
| Acid test/Quick ratio | 0.8:1 | **0.7:1** |
| **Working capital days** | | |
| Inventory holding period | 92 days | 94 days |
| Trade receivables collection period | 54 days | 53 days |
| Trade payables payment period | 86 days | 90 days |
| Working capital cycle | 60 days | **57 days** |

### Task 1.5(b)

Part (b) then asks you to identify which statements best reflect the ratios calculated. In previous units you may have had to suggest a narrative but here you just need to ick the ones that make the most sense.

**Model answer**

**Profitability**

| | |
|---|---|
| This has been a year of steady, if unspectacular, progress. Although profitability has dipped, the return on capital employed has been kept under control. | |
| The profitability ratios give cause for concern. The small increase in sales revenue has not improved the gross profit percentage. Operating expenses have increased, reducing operating profit and return on capital employed. | ✓ |
| The ratios give mixed messages. Some have improved and some have deteriorated. Further investigation is required. | |

**Gearing**

| | |
|---|---|
| The increased gearing ratio is entirely due to the increase in non-current liabilities. | |
| It is likely that the interest cover ratio has increased. | |
| The increased gearing ratio shows that the company has become more risky. | ✓ |

**Liquidity**

| | |
|---|---|
| Both ratios have deteriorated which indicated that the company is less solvent. | ✓ |
| Both ratios remain too high, indicating that working capital is not being used effectively. | |
| Some profitability ratios have improved and some have deteriorated. Further investigation is required to understand where profitability is improving. | |

## Working capital

| | |
|---|---|
| The working capital cycle has worsened. The inventory holding period has improved but the other ratios indicate a lack of financial control. | |
| There is a welcome improvement in the working capital cycle, mainly due to the change in the payment period for payables. | ✓ |
| The working capital cycle is worse than a year ago because of the increased cost of sales. | |

## Overall performance

| | |
|---|---|
| Profitability has declined in 20X2, mainly due to competitive pressures. However, the gearing and liquidity measures show an improving financial position. | |
| 20X2 has been a bad year. Profitability has declines and finances are coming under pressure. | ✓ |
| Steady progress has been made in 20X2. The ratios show that the company is being better managed. | |

## TASK 1.6

### Introduction

In the sample assessment, task 1.6 correlates with assessment objective 6:

| Assessment objective 6 | Analyse the internal controls of an organisation and make recommendations. |
|---|---|

In many respects this task is similar to task 1.3. The main differences are that

- You may need to identify not just weaknesses but strengths, weaknesses, opportunities and threats.

- You may need to make recommendations.

In the sample assessment this task focusses on the sales cycle. You may recall that chapter 3 contained a number of internal control questionnaires (ICQs), including one on the sales cycle, to help you identify control weaknesses.

## Task 1.6(a)

Part (a) asks you to identify one strength and explain how the business benefits from this.

### Key considerations

- Students normally find it easier to identify weaknesses than strengths. If you can find any aspects in the scenario that are working as they should, then that can be a strength.

- Make sure you explain clearly both the control and the benefits of doing this.

### Model answer

> Effective credit control is in place.
>
> New applicants are credit checked and there is routine credit control.
>
> This minimises bad debt and assists cash flow.

## Task 1.6(b)

Part (b) asks you to identify one weakness, explain how this damages the business and suggest a remedy.

### Key considerations

- Make sure you explain in sufficient detail each of the weakness, the potential damage and a remedy.

### Model answer

> It is not easy for new customers to place orders, particularly from overseas.
>
> The requirement to apply for credit terms or to send a cheque through the post is an obstacle to trade and is probably sending potential customers elsewhere.
>
> Only 5% of sales are made against cleared cheques.
>
> The account opening procedure needs to be performed electronically.
>
> Customers should be able to apply online for a small initial credit limit which can be immediately checked with a credit reference agency.
>
> Alternatively, a facility to pay online by credit or debit card when placing an order would be attractive to small businesses and those with a poor credit record.

## Task 1.6(c)

Part (c) asks you to identify an opportunity to improve the procedures, explaining how the procedure should be changed and how the business could benefit.

### Key considerations

* The easiest way to identify an opportunity is to find another weakness as there will then be an opportunity to rectify it. The benefit will be the threat avoided.

* Make sure you explain in sufficient detail each of the opportunity, the change required and the benefit.

### Model answer

There appears to be an opportunity to improve relations with customers.

Printed catalogues are expensive to produce and distribute and not as effective as targeted electronic communications.

Customers could be sent daily electronic mail shots tailored to their own buying records and browsing history. The catalogue could be updated daily.

This could save money and should boost sales.

## Task 1.6(d)

Part (d) asks you to identify a threat, explaining the potential damage and give an action point.

### Key considerations

* The easiest way to identify a threat is to find another weakness as weaknesses result in threats.

* Make sure you explain in sufficient detail each of the threat, the damage and the action required.

### Model answer

We operate in a competitive environment. 80% of our sales are made to just 840, or so, customers and consist mainly of repeat orders for established products.

We are vulnerable if our competitors offer new or cheaper products to these customers.

We must protect this business by ensuring that we develop or buy the best available products at competitive prices.

# 3 Sample Assessment 2 Questions

## Introduction

This chapter contains the revised sample assessment 2 issued by the AAT in 2017.

This assessment is based on the same pre-release scenario, SL Products Ltd, as sample assessment 1.

## ASSESSMENT

### Task 1 (20 marks)

(a) **Who has the statutory duty to prepare accounts for SL Products Ltd?** (2 marks)

| | |
|---|---|
| The company auditors. | |
| The directors of the company. | |
| Sue Hughes, the Chief Accountant. | |
| Companies House. | |

At SL Products Ltd, the duties of sales invoicing, sales ledger and credit control are separated from each other. Ray Massey, Credit Controller, discovers that a sales invoice has been duplicated. The invoice and the duplicate invoice have been posted to the sales ledger.

(b) **What is the correct action for Ray Massey to take?** (2 marks)

| | |
|---|---|
| Prepare a credit note and send it to the customer. | |
| Advise the sales ledger clerk to reverse the duplicate entry. | |
| Advise the invoicing team of the error. | |
| All of the above. | |

SL Products Ltd's turnover is growing rapidly. Its business model is to pay out all its annual profits as dividends each year, rather than retaining some as reserves.

(c) **Which of these is a valid criticism of SL Product Ltd's business model?** (2 marks)

| | |
|---|---|
| It is illegal | |
| It is unethical. | |
| It is unprofitable | |
| It is unsustainable | |

(d) **Liz Hall, Accounts Payable Clerk, has asked you to show where the following errors would be detected by reconciling the accounts payable ledger to the accounts payable control account.** (6 marks)

∇ Drop down list for task 1.1 (c):

| |
|---|
| Would be detected |
| Would not be detected |

| A purchase invoice posted to the wrong supplier account | ▽ |
| A pricing error in a purchase invoice | ▽ |
| A purchase invoice debited to the supplier's account | ▽ |
| Batch of sales invoices posted to accounts payable control account | ▽ |
| VAT in a purchase invoice posted to stationery instead of VAT control | ▽ |
| Wrong percentage of quantity discount calculated on invoice | ▽ |

You have been asked to set up a 10-character password for SL Products Ltds' accounting system.

**(e) Which of the following would be the most secure?** (2 marks)

| 13june1946 | |
| TwoxFour=8 | |
| mypassword | |
| 1234567890 | |

Your duties at SL Products Ltd include the preparation of a monthly commentary on the results of its subsidiary, Merville Ltd. The Chief Accountant of Merville Ltd has written you an email to thank you for your support. Included in the email is the following paragraph:

"As you know, Merville Ltd has a VIP box at Bellchester Wanderers' football club. I know you are a fan of this team, so please accept a pass for the upcoming season which you can use to attend all games and join us for a mean and a drink."

**(f) Answer the following questions** (4 marks)

Which of your fundamental principles is threatened by this offer?

| Confidentiality | |
| Objectivity | |
| Professional competence and due care | |

What action should you take?

| You can accept but must advise the auditors | |
| You can accept but must advise your manager | |
| You must decline | |

**(g)** **Which internal control procedure over sales and subsequent receipts is most likely to be effective for SL Products Ltd in reducing the risk of fraud?** **(2 marks)**

| | |
|---|---|
| Matthew Tunnock, the Accounts Receivable clerk, accounts for the sales transactions and receives customers' cheque payments | |
| Matthew Tunnock, the Accounts Receivable clerk, accounts for the sales transactions; and Hina Khan, the Cashier, receives customers' cheque payments | |
| Hina Khan, the Cashier, accounts for the sales transactions and receives customers' cheque payments | |
| Hina Khan, the Cashier, accounts for the sales transactions and the appropriate Sales Manager receives customers' cheque payments | |

**(Total: 20 marks)**

## Task 2 (15 marks)

You are provided with the following information regarding the 20X2 budgetary and actual trading position of Merville Ltd (a small manufacturing business, which SL Products Ltd acquired a controlling interest in on 01/01/20X2).

Merville Ltd has a long term spanning five years. 20X2 was year three of this five-year plan. To date, all three years' budgets are as per the five-year plan, and none has been flexed for changes in activity.

---

**Commentary from Merville Ltd's management regarding the past financial year**

We are pleased to present the results for the third year of our five-year plan.

Sales volume exceeded budget by 20%. Our range of innovative products continues to be well-received by the market. Demand was once again strong throughout 20X2.

To meet our sales targets, we discounted prices across our product range once again. As a result, turnover exceeded our budgeted target. This along represented a 15% growth over that achieved last year.

Operating costs, however, inevitable rose in line with the substantial increase in the volume of units sold.

Direct materials costs were well controlled and only increased by just over 5% in total compared to the 20X2 budget.

---

During the year, the company experienced some difficulty in employing enough skilled labour to cope with the increased volume. As in 20X1, a substantial amount of paid overtime work was required to meet demand. As variable production overhead is recovered on the basis of direct labour hours, this caused adverse variances in both the direct labour cost and production overhead.

Selling and distributions costs were well-controlled, and only exceeded budget by just over 6%. Similarly, fixed costs were kept very close to the budgeted level. Despite the inevitable cost overruns, we still achieved a creditable level of profit.

| Operating statement for year ended 31 December 20X2 | Budget | Actual | Variance |
|---|---|---|---|
| Sales volume (units) | 12,600 | 15,120 | 2,520 |
| | £000 | £000 | £000 |
| Turnover | 1,575.0 | 1,587.6 | 12.6 |
| Variable costs: | | | |
| Direct materials | 378.0 | 397.0 | –19.0 |
| Direct labour | 236.3 | 312.3 | –76.0 |
| Production overheads | 315.0 | 402.4 | –87.4 |
| Selling and distribution | 157.5 | 167.3 | –9.8 |
| Fixed costs: | | | |
| Production, administration, selling and distribution | 73.8 | 76.8 | –3.0 |
| Total costs | 1,160.6 | 1,355.8 | –195.2 |
| Operating profit | 414.4 | 231.8 | –182.6 |

Louise Harding, the Finance Director of SL Products Ltd, has asked you to comment on the effectiveness of Merville Ltd's long term planning, budgetary and control procedures.

**Evaluate and make recommendations for improving the following:**

**(a)   The long term planning procedure.**

**(b)   The 20X2 budgetary procedure.**

**(c)   The internal controls used to try and achieve the 20X2 budget.**

**(a)   The long term planning procedure**                    (5 marks)

**(b)   The 20X3 budgetary procedure**                         (5 marks)

**(c)** **The internal controls used to try and achieve the 20X2 budget**

**(5 marks)**

[blank answer box]

## Task 3 (15 marks)

You have been provided with the following information about SL Products Ltd's payroll procedures:

**Payroll and payments**

The company operates two separate payrolls using specially-written payroll software.

- One payroll is for weekly-paid employees.

- Another is for the monthly paid office, sales and management staff.

Jane Patel, the payroll clerk, runs the weekly payroll every Thursday morning to pay the hourly-paid employees. Most have their pay paid into their bank account, by BACS. However 28% are still paid in cash.

Jane advises Hina Khan, who is in charge of the cashbook, of the cash to be withdrawn from the bank for the weekly-paid employees paid in cash. Hina collects this from the bank every Thursday afternoon and locks it in the office safe overnight. Jane then assembles the pay packets each Friday morning.

At 4pm every Friday, the employees paid in cash queue outside of Jane's office and collect their pay packets. SL Products Ltd's stated procedure is that each employee must collect their own pay packet in person. In reality, employees often ask a colleague to collect their pay. Jane allows this because it makes the process quicker, both for her and for the employees.

For those of the weekly-paid employees who are paid by BACS, their pay is credit to their bank accounts each Friday. The payroll for the monthly-paid staff is run three days before the month end, and all of these staff are paid by BACS.

Jane has to notify HMRC as soon as payments are made using the RTI (real time information) system. She therefore makes four or five notifications a month for weekly-paid staff, and another one for monthly-paid staff. Each submission takes a couple of hours to complete.

During the last two days of each week, a part time member of staff is employed to help with the cash payment procedures.

**Payroll software and data back-up**

SL Products Ltd has been using its specially-written payroll software for the past six years. The software is not capable of being integrated with the main financial accounting systems. Jane, therefore, posts the payroll information to the general ledger each month using journal entries. However, the software is otherwise effective, and Jane is reluctant to change it as she is very familiar with using it. The cost of replacing it with an updated equivalent version would be about the same as buying off-the-shelf standard software.

Jane backs up the data after each payroll run, and saves a copy on a memory stick which is then locked in the office safe for security.

**Use the answers spaces below as follows.**

- **Identify and discuss five systemic weaknesses with the company's procedures, including its internal controls, that underpin its payroll practices and systems.**

- **For each weakness BRIEFLY explain how it may cause the company problems.** **(15 marks)**

**Note: You are NOT required to make recommendations about changing the above.**

| First weakness | Potential problem for the company |
|---|---|
| | |

| Second weakness | Potential problem for the company |
|---|---|
|  |  |
| **Third weakness** | **Potential problem for the company** |
|  |  |
| **Fourth weakness** | **Potential problem for the company** |
|  |  |
| **Fifth weakness** | **Potential problem for the company** |
|  |  |

## Task 4 (15 marks)

SL Poducts Ltd (SLP) is reviewing its product range. Following the acquisition of Merville Ltd (ML), SLP has identified that in addition to the unique patented products which ML sells, there are two products which are similar to products already sold by SLP.

### Product information

SLP's product SL65 is similar to ML's product M65. Likewise, SLP's product SL66 is similar to ML's product M66. The total sales volumes are the same for both pairings of similar products (i.e. 11,250 units in total for SL65/M65, and 12,000 units in total for SL66/M66.

The table provided shows the sales and profitability of these four products. SLP recovers its variable production overhead based on labour hours, whereas ML uses a machine hour basis. Both companies allocated their fixed production and non-production costs to individual products on traditional, and quite arbitrary, bases. All four products use material KC9, which is sometimes in short supply.

### Sales and profitability data

| Product | SL65 | M65 | SL66 | M66 |
|---|---|---|---|---|
| Sales volume (units) | 6,250 | 5,000 | 8,000 | 4,000 |
| | £ | £ | £ | £ |
| Sales revenue | 500,000 | 720,000 | 900,000 | 465,000 |
| Variable production costs: | | | | |
| Direct materials | 60,000 | 83,000 | 75,000 | 58,000 |
| Direct labour | 80,000 | 107,000 | 115,000 | 72,000 |
| Production overhead | 160,000 | 350,000 | 230,000 | 235,000 |
| Total variable production costs | 300,000 | 540,000 | 420,000 | 365,000 |
| Contribution | 200,000 | 180,000 | 480,000 | 100,000 |
| Fixed production costs | 120,000 | 40,000 | 160,000 | 30,000 |
| Fixed non-production costs | 90,000 | 50,000 | 80,000 | 40,000 |
| Operating profit | (10,000) | 90,000 | 240,000 | 30,000 |
| Contribution per unit | 32 | 36 | 60 | 25 |
| Use of scarce resource KC9 (kg) | 250 | 180 | 1,200 | 200 |

### Directors' discussion and final decision

At a board meeting, the directors of DSLP gave their views as to which of the four products to discontinue. Louise Harding, the Finance Director, was out of the country and not contactable during this period.

Shaun Murphy, the Managing Director, argued that, based on operating profits, SL65 should be dropped in favour of M65, and M66 should be dropped in favour of SL66. His argument was that the allocated fixed overhead had to be taken into account as, however arbitrarily it might be spread, it was still a cost to the business.

Cynthia Moss, the Sales Director, disagreed. Her opinion was that the allocated fixed costs were irrelevant and that they should just look at the total contributions. Therefore, she favoured dropping M65 and continuing with SL65. However, she did agree with Shaun about dropping M66 and continuing with SL66.

Colin Smith, the Production Director, recalled similar discussion he'd had with Louise in the past. He thought the correct approach was to look at the contribution per unit, rather than the total contribution. So he recommended discontinuing SL65 and continuing with M65. He agreed with the other two directors that SL66 should be continued with and M66 should be dropped.

Eventually, the decision was made to discontinue SL65 in favour of M65, and to continue with SL66 and discontinue M66. Note: As material KC9 was not in short supply at the time of the meeting, it was not considered in the board's discussions.

(a)   **BRIEFLY discuss the validity of each of the three directors' views on how the final decision should be made as to which products to discontinue.**                                    **(9 marks)**

You are now required to consider what effect material KC9 should have in making the decision.

**(b) BRIEFLY explain, with reasons, which of the substitute products should be continued and which should be discontinued if KG9 is in short supply. Provide any supporting calculations.**

**(6 marks)**

## Task 5 (20 marks)

Louise Harding, the Finance Director of SL Products Ltd (SLP), has asked you to investigate the recent financial performance of the company. The markets in which SLP operate are becoming increasingly competitive, and she wishes to identify any areas of the business that the company needs to improve upon in order to survive in the industry and remain profitable.

Louise has asked you to use SLP's 20X1 financial statements to calculate the five Key Performance indicators (KPIs) and then use these, together with SLP's equivalent past KPIs and industry averages to analyse what has been going wrong in the company.

SL Products Ltd's pas figures and current industry averages are shown below. You are also provided with the 20X1 Statement of Profit or Loss and Statement of Financial Position for SLP in the pre-release material which you should use this to calculate the Key Performance Indicators set out below.

**(a)** Calculate SL Products Ltd's five KPIs shown below for 20X1, using the financial statements in the pre-release material.

Round all your calculations to one decimal place.  **(5 marks)**

| Ker performance indicator | SL Products Ltd 20W9 | SL Products Ltd 20X0 | Industry average 20X1 | SL Products Ltd 20X1 |
|---|---|---|---|---|
| Gross profit % | 20.6% | 29.2% | 27.7% | ☐ % |
| Operating profit % | 9.5% | 7.4% | 8.8% | ☐ % |
| Current ratio | 2.2:1 | 1.9:1 | 1.7:1 | ☐ :1 |
| Trade receivables collection period (days) | 47.2 days | 51.6 days | 46.6 days | ☐ days |
| Asset turnover (Non-current assets) | 6.6 times | 5.1 times | 5.8 times | ☐ times |

**(b)** Based on the three year trend of SL Products Ltd's KPIs, including the year you have made calculations for, complete the following statements.  **(5 marks)**

**The gross profit percentage is…**

| | |
|---|---|
| improving and is better than the industry average | ☐ |
| improving but is worse than the industry average | ☐ |
| deteriorating but is better than the industry average | ☐ |
| deteriorating and is worse than the industry average | ☐ |

**The operating profit percentage is…**

| | |
|---|---|
| improving and is better than the industry average | ☐ |
| deteriorating but is worse than the industry average | ☐ |
| improving but is worse than the industry average | ☐ |
| deteriorating and is better than the industry average | ☐ |

**The current ratio is…**

| | |
|---|---|
| improving and is better than the industry average | |
| deteriorating but is better than the industry average | |
| improving but is worse than the industry average | |
| deteriorating and is worse than the industry average | |

**The trade receivables collection period is…**

| | |
|---|---|
| getting steadily better and is shorter than the industry average | |
| getting steadily better but is longer than the industry average | |
| getting steadily worse but is shorter than the industry average | |
| getting steadily worse and is longer than the industry average | |

**The asset turnover (non-current assets) ratio is…**

| | |
|---|---|
| rapidly improving and is much better than the industry average | |
| rapidly improving but is much worse than the industry average | |
| rapidly deteriorating bus is much better than the industry average | |
| rapidly deteriorating and is much worse than the industry average | |

**(c)** **If you now assume that ALL the Key Performance Indicators are deteriorating, which of the following factors could have caused each of them to get worse?** **(10 marks)**

Gross profit %

Operating profit %

Current ratio

Trade receivables collection period

Asset turnover (non-current assets)

∇ Drop down list for task 5 (c):

| |
|---|
| Increased overheads |
| Increased non-current assets |
| Ineffective credit control procedures |
| Inventories have decreased |
| Inventories have increased |
| Reduced creditor payment terms agreed |
| Reduced overheads |
| Reduced non-current assets |
| Reduced selling prices |

## Task 6 (15 marks)

You have been provided with the following information about SL Products Ltd's purchasing procedures:

### The Purchasing Manager

Tony Clark, the Purchasing Manager of SL Products Ltd (SLP), is responsible for:

- identifying, approving and liaising with suppliers
- negotiating all contracts and prices with them
- agreeing any price revisions
- agreeing changes in payment terms.

Tony has been in his position for the past six years, but is due to retire in early 20X3. Ruth Holmes, who Tony recruited after joining SLP, assists him. Ruth worked for Tony at a previous company.

Tony uses a small number of suppliers who he has long-standing close relationships with. He believes he gets a better level of service this way, as well as lower prices due to quantity discounts. Normally, he buys at lower than SLP's budgeted standard prices, and regularly has favourable buying variances. Senior management has accordingly given him complete freedom in purchasing arrangements, without involving more senior staff.

### Buying-in prices and terms

Over the past year, the buying-in prices of several components have unusually been well over budget. SLP only calculates a total material price variance each month. As this is always favourable, the adverse variances within it were not apparent.

This only came to SLP's attention via Emily Jones, the Sales Director of Danter Electronics, a supplier to SLP. Emily complained to Shaun Murphy, SLP's Managing Director, that her company had bid an extremely competitive price to SLP but had failed to win the particular contract. She claimed that her tender price was not much greater than marginal cost, and could not understand how the winning supplier, Loebid Ltd, could possibly have undercut her.

Shaun investigated and found that Loebid Ltd had provided the most competitive tender, and so won the contract. However, six months later, Tony Clark had agreed a 15% price increase with them. Tony explained he agreed this because there had been changes in the technical specifications of Loebid Ltd's supplies. Their credit payment terms had also been reduced from 45 to 30 days.

### General procedures

In the past, whenever a new supplier was identified, they were checked for financial stability by Liz Hall, the Accounts Payable Clerk. The procedure was changed last year on Tony Clark's recommendation. Ruth Holmes now runs a check using a large credit reference agency.

Almost all purchases are negotiated to be on 30–day credit terms from end of month of purchase.

When Tony or Ruth raises a purchase order, they immediately enter the details in the company's inventory system. The goods inwards warehouse staff then check that the correct quantities are received in the warehouse. The accompanying goods received notes (GRNs) are checked against the purchase order details on the inventory system. Any discrepancies are noted and investigated by Tony or Ruth.

Suppliers' invoices are sent directly to Ruth. Either she or Tony checks these against the GRNs and the purchase orders. Once invoices are approved they add them to an approved for payment pre-list, on a spreadsheet. This is emailed at the end of each week to Liz Hall, who posts the details in the accounts payable and general ledgers.

Liz produces a monthly age trade payables listing, identifying suppliers due to payment. Sue Hughes, the Chief Accountant, then reviews the company's cash position and either approves all due payments, or delays some if there is a shortage of cash.

Once Sue has decided upon the final approved payments, Hina Khan, who is in charge of the cash book, produces the Bank Automated Clearing System (BACS) transfer authority and cheques. Around a quarter of SL Products Ltd's suppliers are paid by cheque.

**(a)** **Identify TWO weaknesses in the company's systems, practices and internal controls in respect of each of the following procedures:** **(6 marks)**

- **Purchasing**

- **Accounts payable**

- **Internal reporting.**

**(b)** **For each of the three procedures listed above, make a recommendation to improve ONE of the weaknesses you have identified.** **(3 marks)**

Any improvements involve some financial outlay.

**(c)** **Identify and BRIEFLY discuss the analytical method of evaluating whether it would be worthwhile to improve the internal controls in this area.** **(6 marks)**

# 4 Sample Assessment 2 Answers

## Introduction

This chapter contains the model answers to sample assessment 2 issued by the AAT in 2017.

## SAMPLE ASSESSMENT 2

### Task 1(a)

| | |
|---|---|
| The company auditors. | |
| The directors of the company. | ✓ |
| Sue Hughes, the Chief Accountant. | |
| Companies House. | |

### Task 1(b)

| | |
|---|---|
| Prepare a credit note and send it to the customer. | |
| Advise the sales ledger clerk to reverse the duplicate entry. | |
| Advise the invoicing team of the error. | ✓ |
| All of the above. | |

### Task 1(c)

| | |
|---|---|
| It is illegal | |
| It is unethical. | |
| It is unprofitable | |
| It is unsustainable | ✓ |

### Task 1(d)

| | | Comment |
|---|---|---|
| A purchase invoice posted to the wrong supplier account | Would not be detected | Both totals still correct, so agree |
| A pricing error in a purchase invoice | Would not be detected | Wrong figure posted to both so still agree |
| A purchase invoice debited to the supplier's account | Would be detected | Only accounts payable ledger wrong |
| Batch of sales invoices posted to accounts payable control account | Would be detected | Only control account wrong |
| VAT in a purchase invoice posted to stationery instead of VAT control | Would not be detected | Neither affected |

## Task 1(e)

| | |
|---|---|
| 13june1946 | |
| TwoxFour=8 | ✓ |
| mypassword | |
| 1234567890 | |

## Task 1(f)

| | |
|---|---|
| Confidentiality | |
| Objectivity | ✓ |
| Professional competence and due care | |

| | |
|---|---|
| You can accept but must advise the auditors | |
| You can accept but must advise your manager | |
| You must decline | ✓ |

## Task 1(g)

| | |
|---|---|
| Matthew Tunnock, the Accounts Receivable clerk, accounts for the sales transactions and receives customers' cheque payments | |
| Matthew Tunnock, the Accounts Receivable clerk, accounts for the sales transactions; and Hina Khan, the Cashier, receives customers' cheque payments | ✓ |
| Hina Khan, the Cashier, accounts for the sales transactions and receives customers' cheque payments | |
| Hina Khan, the Cashier, accounts for the sales transactions and the appropriate Sales Manager receives customers' cheque payments | |

## Task 2 (15 marks)

**(a)** **The long term planning procedure** (5 marks)

**Indicative content:**

- Length of the plan (5 years) is realistic and is in line with typical commercial practices
- Long term plan is fixed – has not been changed to reflect large increase in sales volume in all three of the first years of the plan
- Fixed plan may have required less effort and therefore less costly to produce
- Fixed plan has led to the sales volume budgets for 20X1 and 20X2 being unrealistic
- Rolling 5-year plan would be better (particularly when major changes occur)
    - Would mean that at end of each year, a new 5th year plan would be added in
    - Reflects changes in the business environment
    - Advantage of rolling plans - encourage forward-looking management; keep the plan in line with current conditions
    - Disadvantage of rolling plans – may take up disproportionate amount of management time

**Marking guidance**

| Marks | |
|---|---|
| 0 | No response worthy of credit |
| 1 – 2 | Limited evaluation of Merville Ltd's long term planning procedure; limited relevant points made with minimal use of data or supporting evidence. Response may include simplistic comments relating to the long-term plan with no further explanation. |
| 3 – 4 | To achieve marks in the second band, the response will present a balanced evaluation of Merville Ltd's long term planning procedure; relevant points will be well-supported by evidence. To achieve higher marks in the band, the response will make a recommendation for improvement (i.e. a 5-year rolling plan) with some explanation. |
| 5 | To achieve full marks, the response will include a recommendation with a full explanation of the impact, positive and negative, that this alternative method would have. Response demonstrates a solid understanding of long term planning procedures. |

**(b)   The 20X3 budgetary procedure**                    **(5 marks)**

**Indicative content:**

- Fixed budget – has not been flexed for the 20% increase in activity
- A fixed budget means that variable costs are not changed in line with changes in activity
- A flexible budget means that the turnover and variable costs are changed in line with changes in activity – so in this case they would be increased by 20%; fixed costs remain unchanged from original budget
- Advantages of fixed budgeting, for example, takes less time, therefore less costly
- Disadvantages of fixed budgeting, for example variances are less meaningful, therefore control is reduced
- Advantages and disadvantages of flexible budgeting are the opposite of this
- Flexible budget calculations, for example:
  - Turnover 1,890.0; direct materials 453.6; direct labour 283.6; production overhead 378.0; selling and distribution costs 189.0; (fixed costs 73.8 (unchanged); total costs 1378.0; operating profit 512.0)
- Budgeted cost figures derived just as a % of budgeted turnover, for example:
  - Direct materials 24%
  - Direct labour 15%
  - Production overheads 20%
  - Selling and distribution costs 10%
- This is a top-down approach – has advantage of improved communication of plans and coordination of activities; disadvantage of reduced commitment and motivation of lower management
- Cost figures more accurate if budget bottom-up by lower management building up the relevant costs

**Marking guidance**

| Marks | |
|---|---|
| 0 | No response worthy of credit |
| 1 – 2 | Limited evaluation of Merville Ltd's budgetary procedure; limited relevant points made with minimal use of data or supporting evidence. Response may specify budgetary procedures used, i.e. fixed budget, with minimal explanation with no further evaluation of the impact for Merville Products Ltd. |

| 3 – 4 | Good evaluation of the budgetary procedures, extending beyond a simple identification of the budgetary procedure used and consider benefits and drawbacks of current procedures. Points made are relevant both from a technical point of view, but also linked to the scenario. Some use of calculations to support answer. To achieve the higher marks in the band, an alternative recommendation will be included, although perhaps not fully explained. |
|---|---|
| 5 | To achieve full marks, the response will include a thorough evaluation, linked to the scenario, with a justified recommendation for improvement (i.e. bottom - up). Positive and negative impact of the alternative method would be included. Response demonstrates a solid understanding of budgeting procedures with use of calculations to support answer. |

(c)   **The internal controls used to try and achieve the 20X2 budget**
**(5 marks)**

**Indicative content:**
- Company is using variance analysis
  - Variance analysis involves comparing budgeted and actual costs and revenues to produce the differences (variances)
  - Turnover less than budget or costs higher than budget which would lead to adverse variances
  - Adverse variances should be investigated, corrective action taken
  - In the opposite situation, favourable variances arise – these should also be investigated for causes
- Variances are meaningless in this situation as they are produced against fixed budget – budget should be flexed for a more valid comparison
- Identification of variances
  - Merville Ltd's management using unflexed budget to disguise poor control over direct labour – would still be adverse even if budget was flexed
  - Management claiming that direct material has been well controlled as there is a favourable variance against flexed budget – same for selling and distribution costs
- Direct labour has been poorly controlled evidenced by adverse variance against a flexed budget – which has also resulted in an adverse variance for production overheads

**KAPLAN** PUBLISHING

**Marking guidance**

| Marks | |
|---|---|
| 0 | No response worthy of credit |
| 1 – 2 | Limited evaluation of internal controls used by Merville Ltd although response does correctly identify internal controls being used. Limited further explanation made with minimal use of data and supporting evidence. |
| 3 – 4 | Good evaluation of Merville Ltd's internal controls; range of relevant points made, supported by evidence. Explanations go beyond a simple identification of the internal controls being used and explore the benefits and drawbacks on the current controls. To achieve the higher marks in the band, the response will also include an alternative recommendation, although perhaps not fully explained. |
| 5 | To achieve full marks, the response will also include a fully explained and well justified recommendation for improvements to Merville Ltd's internal control processes. Overall demonstration of solid understanding of internal controls. |

### Task 3 (15 marks)

1 x mark for identification; 2 marks for explanation (maximum 3 marks per weakness).Note: There are more suggested answers shown below than are required to be given in the task.

**Weakness 1:** The company is operating with two payrolls **(1)**. This increases costs by effectively doubling the amount of work involved both in running both payrolls **(1)**; and by increasing the time taken to make extra RTI submissions to HMRC **(1)**.

**Weakness 2:** Use of non-standard payroll software **(1)**. This does not link to the main accounting systems, so causing the General Ledger entries to have to be posted using journal entries **(1)** – taking time and incurring additional costs and adding to the risk of errors occurring **(1)**.

**Or,**

Using non-standard software could also result in operational difficulties **(1)** if the payroll clerk were absent, as other members of staff may be unable to use it **(1)**.

**Weakness 3:** Paying some employees in cash could be a major weakness **(1)**. This involves time to organise and collect from the bank; time to produce manual pay packets and will these with cash **(1)**; and then there is the risk of theft as the cash is brought back from the bank, and kept in the safe overnight **(1)**.

**Or,**

In addition there is the (avoidable) cost of employing a part time member of staff **(1)** to help deal with the cash payment procedures **(1)**.

**Weakness 4:** Employees are permitted to collect other colleagues' pay packets **(1)**. This puts the company at risk of compensation claims **(1)** if pay does not actually reach the employee **(1)**.

**Weakness 5:** Backing the payroll up weekly only **(1)**. Although the payrolls are only run weekly they will be regularly updated during the interim for changes in employees' details (such as tax codes and addresses) **(1)**. This information could be lost (before the system is next backed up) **(1)**.

**Weakness 6:** Backing up data on a memory stick **(1)**. Alternative method of backing up data should be used, for example, use of cloud computing **(1)** as the memory stick could be lost or become corrupted **(1)**.

**Weakness 7:** There is a lack of segregation of duties **(1)**. Jane both runs the payroll, and makes up and distributes the pay packets **(1)** which could lead to missed errors and/or potential fraud **(1)**.

*Other suitable weaknesses may also be awarded marks.*

**Task 4 (20 marks)**

(a) **BRIEFLY discuss the validity of each of the three directors' views on how the final decision should be made as to which products to discontinue.** **(9 marks)**

> **Indicative content:**
> - The Managing Director is basing his decisions on the reported profits of each product.
>   - The reported operating profits include an arbitrary allocation of fixed costs that undermines their credibility. Fixed costs are irrelevant to the decision as they are unavoidable regardless of the decision
>   - This is misleading since the four products all have different sales volumes.
>   - A product such as SL66 which has twice the number of units sold as its competitor M66 will usually have a higher contribution and reported operating profit.
>   - The variable production overhead is recovered on a different basis in each company.

- – These costs are also much higher per unit for Merville Ltd than for SL Products Ltd.
- – This makes comparisons at the contribution level difficult
- The Sales Director is basing her decisions on the reported contributions of each product.
  - – This approach has the same weaknesses outlined in the last two points above.
  - – It does, however, avoid considering the arbitrary allocation of fixed costs.
  - – A better approach might be to use throughput, which measures the difference between output (ultimately sales) and material input into the product
- The Production Director is basing his decisions on the contribution per unit.
  - – This approach gets around the problem of different sales volumes.
  - – It also avoids the arbitrary allocation of fixed costs. But the variable production overhead is recovered on a different basis in each company.
  - – It is the correct approach if there are no limiting factors, such as KC9 sometimes being in short supply.

**Marking guidance**

| Marks | |
|-------|---|
| 0 | No response worthy of credit |
| 1 – 3 | Limited range of factors discussed; response only makes reference to one or two of the director's views with limited evidence to support decision on whether the products should be continued or discontinued |
| 4-6 | Range of factors discussed; response only makes reference to two or three of the director's views with some evidence to support decision on whether the products should be continued or discontinued. |
| 7-9 | Wide range of factors discussed; response makes reference to all three of the director's views with sound evidence to support decision on whether the products should be continued or discontinued |

(b) **BRIEFLY explain, with reasons which of the substitute products should be continued and which should be discontinued if KG9 is in short supply. Provide any supporting calculations.**

**(6 marks)**

---

**Indicative content:**

- Recognition of KC9 being a limiting factor - anything that constrains the output of the business
- Where there is a limiting factor the correct approach is to rank the four products in order of their contribution per unit of it i.e. per kg of KC9 used
- The decision to discontinue a product is long term and strategic – therefore even though KC9 is not currently in short supply; it may become so.
- Calculations to support explanation (contribution per kg of KC9):
  - SL65      £800
  - SL66      £400
  - M65       £1,000
  - M66       £500
- Therefore, M65 should be continued; SL65 discontinued (£1,000 is more than £800)
- Therefore, M66 should be continued; SL66 discontinued (£500 is more than £400)

**Marking guidance**

| Marks | |
|-------|---|
| 0 | No response worthy of credit |
| 1 – 2 | Limited range of factors considered with limited use of calculations to support explanation. Answer may not fully reflect which products should be continued and/or discontinued. |
| 3 – 4 | Range of factors considered which are supported by use of calculations. Reference made to KC9 being a limiting factor. Answer makes good reference to products which should be continued and/or discontinued. |
| 5 – 6 | Wide range of factors considered which are supported by use of calculations. Reference made to KC9 being a limiting factor; in addition to the decision of product supply being long term and strategic. Answer makes good reference to products which should be continued and/or discontinued. |

KAPLAN PUBLISHING

## Task 5 (20 marks)

(a) Calculate SL Products Ltd's five KPIs shown below for 20X1, using the financial statements in the pre-release material. Round all your calculations to one decimal place. **(5 marks)**

| KPI | SLP 20W9 | SLP 20X0 | Industry average 20X1 | SLP 20X1 |
|---|---|---|---|---|
| Gross profit % | 20.6% | 29.2% | 27.7% | 28.4 % |
| Operating profit % | 9.5% | 7.4% | 8.8% | 6.3 % |
| Current ratio | 2.2:1 | 1.9:1 | 1.7:1 | 1.8 1 |
| Trade receivables collection period | 47.2 days | 51.6 days | 46.6 days | 54.3 days |
| Asset turnover (Non-current assets) | 6.6 × | 5.1 × | 5.8 × | 4.6 × |

(b) Based on the three year trend of SL Products Ltd's KPIs, including the year you have made calculations for, complete the following statements. **(5 marks)**

**The gross profit percentage is...**

| | |
|---|---|
| improving and is better than the industry average | |
| improving but is worse than the industry average | |
| deteriorating but is better than the industry average | ✓ |
| deteriorating and is worse than the industry average | |

**The operating profit percentage is...**

| | |
|---|---|
| improving and is better than the industry average | |
| deteriorating but is worse than the industry average | ✓ |
| improving but is worse than the industry average | |
| deteriorating and is better than the industry average | |

**The current ratio is…**

| | |
|---|---|
| improving and is better than the industry average | |
| deteriorating but is better than the industry average | ✓ |
| improving but is worse than the industry average | |
| deteriorating and is worse than the industry average | |

**The trade receivables collection period is…**

| | |
|---|---|
| getting steadily better and is shorter than the industry average | |
| getting steadily better but is longer than the industry average | |
| getting steadily worse but is shorter than the industry average | |
| getting steadily worse and is longer than the industry average | ✓ |

**The asset turnover (non-current assets) ratio is…**

| | |
|---|---|
| rapidly improving and is much better than the industry average | |
| rapidly improving but is much worse than the industry average | |
| rapidly deteriorating bus is much better than the industry average | |
| rapidly deteriorating and is much worse than the industry average | ✓ |

**(c)** **If you now assume that ALL the Key Performance Indicators are deteriorating, which of the following factors could have caused each of them to get worse?** **(10 marks)**

| | |
|---|---|
| Gross profit % | Reduced selling prices ▽ |
| Operating profit % | Increased overhead ▽ |
| Current ratio | Inventories have decreased ▽ |
| Trade receivables collection period | Ineffective credit control procedures ▽ |
| Asset turnover (non-current assets) | Increased non-current assets ▽ |

## Task 6 (15 marks)

**(a)** **weaknesses in the company's systems, practices and internal controls:** **(6 marks)**

**Purchasing**

*1 x mark awarded for reference to any one of the following; maximum 2 marks.*

- There is no effective segregation of duties in the purchasing procedures.

- Purchasing Manager is, without any restrictions, able to identify and approve suppliers/negotiate new contracts/agree any subsequent price increases/agree any subsequent changes to payment terms.

- Risk that the Purchasing Manager may have developed a relationship that is too close with suppliers/has had a very close working relationship with Ruth Holmes for at least 6 years

- The potential for the Purchasing Department to collude with a supplier (such as Loebid Ltd) to award apparently fair contracts and then subsequently change their terms in return for a bribe.

**Accounts payable:**

*1 x mark awarded for reference to any one of the following; maximum 2 marks.*

- The weekly pre-list of approved supplier payments is unnecessary.
- Paying a quarter of suppliers by cheque, rather than by BACS, could be a weakness.
- Cheque processing is costly in terms of both the time involved and bank charges.
- It is also more prone to errors and cheques can be easily lost in the post and possibly misappropriated.
- The pre-list itself, using a spreadsheet, is a possible source of error due to staff making mistakes in entering data.

**Internal reporting:**

*1 x mark awarded for reference to any one of the following; maximum 2 marks.*

- The internal reporting of material price variance (MPV) is too limited. It only calculates the total MPV.
- This means that detailed price variances by supplier, and product line re not being reviewed.
- There may well be significant adverse variances that are not being investigated because they are netted off against other favourable variances in arriving at the total MPV. This is the case in this specific task.

**(b)** **Recommendations to improve ONE of the weaknesses identified.** **(3 marks)**

*Maximum of 3 marks to be awarded for reference to any one Weakness identified in part (a).*

**Purchasing:**

- Senior management should review and approve all contracts and orders over a certain value.

- Senior management should also approve any subsequent significant changes in prices or payment terms.

- Someone outside of the Purchasing Department should do the financial stability checks on suppliers

- There should be a defined central policy, probably set by the board, for the criteria to use in selecting suppliers.

- There should be an independent check that purchase prices and goods are as agreed. Tony and Ruth should not be the only individuals checking that invoices are as agreed.
  Another member of staff (probably the Accounts Payable clerk or Tony's boss) should sample check that the invoiced prices and goods are as agreed. Suppliers' invoices should be sent to the Accounts Payable clerk not the Purchasing Department. They can then be entered into the system before Tony is asked to approve them. This provides both a more secure audit trail and a better segregation of duties.

**Accounts payable:**

- Invoices should be passed for Accounts Payable posting on a daily basis as approved.

- All suppliers should, if possible, be paid by BACS.

- If the company decides to continue using a pre-list it should be derived electronically from the Accounts Payable ledger.

**Internal reporting:**

- Price variances should be calculated by supplier and product line.

- Accounts Department staff should then investigate all significant adverse variances to enable appropriate remedial action to be taken.

- Significant favourable variances should also be investigated so as to further exploit any opportunities this shows up.

**(c)** **The analytical method of evaluating whether it would be worthwhile to improve the internal controls in this area.(6 marks)**

**Indicative content:**

- The analytical method of evaluating whether it would be worthwhile to improve the internal controls in this area is a Cost Benefit analysis.

- This examines the costs incurred in making improvements, and the benefits arising from this cost outlay.

- Costs include those for changes to procedures, software, and staff roles and training.

- Benefits include more efficient controls, less risk of errors and reduced risk of fraud.

- Whilst most costs can be quantified the benefits are difficult to measure in monetary terms.

- However, some attempt should be made to do this.

- For the improvements to be worthwhile the benefits must outweigh the costs.

**Marking guidance**

| Marks | |
|-------|---|
| 0 | No response worthy of credit |
| 1 – 2 | Limited range of factors discussed. The response will |
| | Identify the analytical method to use is cost benefit analysis; however, will not be supported by much further reasoning to justify use of method. |
| 3 – 4 | Range of factors discussed. The response will |
| | Identify the analytical method to use is cost benefit analysis; which will be supported with some reasoning to justify use of method. |
| 5 – 6 | Wide range of factors discussed. The response will |
| | Identify the analytical method to use is cost benefit analysis; and will include sound understanding with supported reasoning to justify use of method. |

# MOCK ASSESSMENT

# 1 Mock Exam Questions

## Introduction

This mock is based on the same pre-release scenario used in the AAT Sample assessment 1 that was covered in the previous two chapters:

SL Products Ltd (SLP) is a market-leading manufacturing business supplying advanced technological electronics to a number of companies around the world.

## Task 1 (20 marks)

**(a)** **Which the following is NOT normally a feature of the statutory accounts of a company like SL Products Ltd?** **(2 marks)**

| | |
|---|---|
| The information is available to all shareholders | |
| The presentation is strictly governed by regulation | |
| They must be 100% accurate | |
| They must include a cash flow statement | |

Hina Khan, the general accounts clerk, has recently attempted to carry out a bank reconciliation for SL Products.

**(b)** **Which of the following errors could be revealed by such an exercise?** **(5 marks)**

| | |
|---|---|
| A cheque was filled out for the wrong amount | Yes/No |
| A direct debit was missing for the cash book | Yes/No |
| A payment was entered in the cash book near to the year-end but the cheque was not sent out to the supplier | Yes/No |
| A debtor made a payment on an invoice but deducted more discount than allowed and so paid less then needed | Yes/No |
| Interest charged on the account appeared only on the bank statement | Yes/No |

SL Products Limited has a firewall in place to protect its systems.

**(c)** **Which of the following statements are true?** **(2 marks)**

| | |
|---|---|
| A firewall assists in preventing the system from overheating | |
| A firewall will prevent employees inputting inaccurate data into the system | |
| A firewall prevents external people from accessing any part of the system | |
| A firewall prevents employees sharing copied data with unauthorised third parties | |

A close friend of yours has heard about the problems SL Products are having with their aging product lines. He happens to work at a rival company and has, himself, designed a new electronic product whilst working for them.

He has suggested that SL Products could benefit from the new design and has asked you to approach your managing director with an offer to buy the design from him.

**(d)** **Answer the following questions** **(4 marks)**

Which of your fundamental principles of ethical behaviour does this threaten?

| | |
|---|---|
| Confidentiality | |
| Professional integrity | |
| Professional competence and due care | |

What action should you take?

| | |
|---|---|
| Report your friend to the police immediately | |
| Decline the offer but say nothing to anyone else | |
| Decline the offer and report the incident to your line manager | |

Louise Harding (FD) is suspicious that the profit of the business is being overstated due the pressure being put on it by its environment.

She fears that some managers are resorting to 'creative accounting' to show better results than those actually being achieved.

**(e)** **Which of the following errors could overstate profit creatively?**
**(2 marks)**

| | |
|---|---|
| The useful economic lives of assets is being understated | |
| An improvement to an asset has been written off as repairs | |
| A doubtful debt has been ignored in the provision calculation and written off instead | |
| The provision for warranty repairs has been ignored in the accounts | |

SL Products Ltd controls its petty cash by the Imprest system.

**(f)** **At the end of each month, what equivalent amount should SL Products Ltd withdraw from the bank to maintain its Imprest balance?** **(2 marks)**

| | |
|---|---|
| The amount of the closing monthly cash in hand | |
| The amount of the opening monthly cash in hand | |
| The amount of the closing monthly total of petty cash vouchers | |
| The amount of the total Imprest petty cash float | |

**(g)** **Segregating the duties of SL Products Ltd's existing accounting staff, without changing staff numbers, would have which one of the following effects?** **(3 marks)**

| | |
|---|---|
| It would increase the chances of fraud | |
| It would reduce the chances of fraud | |
| It would increase the administration overhead cost | |
| It would reduce the administration overhead cost | |

## Task 2 (15 marks)

SL Products acquired a small business right at the end of 20X1 and is now trying to produce sensible budgets for 20X2.

Some past data is available and an **extract** follows:

| | Notes | 20X0 | 20X1 |
|---|---|---|---|
| Material costs | 1 | £288,000 | £336,000 |
| Lease rental | 2 | £50,000 | £50,000 |
| Production royalty | 3 | £21,800 | £23,300 |
| Production volume | | 36,000 units | 42,000 units |

**Notes:**

1    Material costs are thought to be a totally variable cost based on production volume.

2    Lease rental cost is for the businesses only building and is a fixed cost in the short term.

3    The production royalty is thought to be more complicated. The business has to pay a fixed amount regardless of volume in addition there is a variable extra payment based on production volume in the year.

In 20X2 it is expected that the business will produce 48,000 units as past growth continues.

(a) **Calculate the budget figures for the selected costs above to be included in the 20X2 budget for the newly acquired business (ignore inflation).** **(6 marks)**

|  | Budget 20X2 £ |
|---|---|
| Material costs |  |
| Lease rental |  |
| Production royalty |  |

**Prepare a brief report in three sections as follows:**

(b) **Briefly explain your treatment of the three costs above in your budget calculations.** **(3 marks)**

(c) Give two potential reasons why the lease rental figure might increase in future periods. **(2 marks)**

(d) Explain the motivational aspects that support the view that budgets need to be flexed to allow for actual production levels before the assessment of performance via the use of variances. **(4 marks)**

## Task 3 (15 marks)

SL Products' payroll clerk, Jane Patel, has documented the businesses payroll system as follows:

- SL Products operates from two sites. The main site contains the head office, accounts department and sales offices together with the main manufacturing plant. The second site is another manufacturing plant. It has over 400 employees, 320 of which are directly involved in manufacturing.

- All non-manufacturing employees are paid an annual salary on a monthly basis by bank transfer. All manufacturing employees are paid weekly based on hours worked. About 30% of the manufacturing employees are paid in cash, as this is an offered option, the rest are paid by bank transfer.

- Factory staff are each issued a sequentially numbered clock card, which details their employee number and name. Employees swipe their cards at the beginning and end of the eight-hour shift and this process is not supervised. During the shift, employees are entitled to a 30-minute paid break and employees do not need to clock out to access the dining area.

- Clock card data links into the payroll system, which automatically calculates gross and net pay along with any statutory deductions. The payroll clerk, for each payment run, checks on a sample basis some of these calculations to ensure the system is operating effectively.

- Most new appointments of staff are controlled by Jane, who checks the paperwork and enters the staff onto the appropriate system. However, some staff are appointed directly by Colin Smith the production director when there is an urgent need for temporary staff. These temporary staff are paid by Colin, who then collects the cash back through his expenses each month end.

- For employees paid by bank transfer, the payroll clerk reviews the list of the payments and agrees it to the payroll records prior to authorising the bank payment. If any changes are required, the payroll clerk amends the records. For employees paid in cash, the pay packets are prepared in the payroll department and the clerk distributes them to employees; as she knows most of these individuals she does not require proof of identity nor are these pay packets signed for.

(a) **You are required to document 5 weaknesses in the above system and for each weakness, describe the potential effect that the weakness could have on the business.** (15 marks)

| Weakness | Effect of Weakness |
|---|---|
| 1 | |
| 2 | |
| 3 | |
| 4 | |
| 5 | |

**KAPLAN** PUBLISHING

## Task 4 (15 marks)

One of SL Products potential new products is an electronic cigarette called E-Drag. This is seen as a great hope for the business as cigarette smoking is increasingly being seen as harmful and the e-cigarette could encourage many people to switch away from the more traditional cigarettes, which have been linked, to cancer and heart disease.

The product is going through the final design stage and the question of pricing has arisen.

Louise Harding (FD) has suggested that target costing could be a sensible approach and her team has produced some analysis to assist in the calculations.

| | |
|---|---|
| 1 | Similar e-cigarettes are already on the market |
| | • E-Puff has more features than E-Drag and sells for £20 |
| | • E-Smoke is a budget version and so is not as good as E-Drag and sells for £7 |
| | • E-Vap is similar to E-Drag and sells for £15 |
| | • The average of the above prices is £14. |
| 2 | Material for the sample E-Drag cost £4 but it is expected that discounts should be available in future of 10%. |
| 3 | The sample E-Drag took a long time to get right but, with practice and some mechanisation, SL Products feels that the product can be made in an average time of 6 minutes per unit. |
| | The skilled labour required costs £16 per hour. |
| 4 | Overheads are estimated to be £8 per unit. |
| 5 | The owners of the business have been consulted and are known to expect a margin on selling price of 15% at least to give them a reasonable return on their investment. |

Louise has asked that you help with the calculations and deal with some queries on the target costing process.

**(a)** **What is the most appropriate price to include in the target costing calculation?** **(2 marks)**

| | |
|---|---|
| £20 to match the E-Puff | |
| £7 to match the E-Smoke | |
| £15 to match the E-Vap | |
| £14 to match the industry average price | |

**(b)** **What is the total of material and labour cost for the new E-Drag?** **(2 marks)**

| | |
|---|---|
| £5.20 | |
| £5.60 | |
| £13.20 | |
| £13.60 | |

**(c)** **Assuming that a selling price of £15 is agreed, what is the 'cost gap' that might result?** **(4 marks)**

| | £ |
|---|---|
| Selling price | |
| Less: desired margin | |
| Target cost | |
| Actual cost expected | |
| Cost gap | |

**(d)** **Briefly explain what 'value engineering' is and suggest two ways in which any cost gap could be removed.** **(7 marks)**

## Task 5 (20 marks)

SL Products uses performance measures based on a balanced scorecard approach in four areas or perspectives.

These are shown in the pre-release background information but broadly are:

Perspective 1: Learning and training

Perspective 2: Internal business processes

Perspective 3: Customers

Perspective 4: Financial outlook

Data from the management information system is now provided as follows:

| | Notes | 20X1 | 20X2 |
|---|---|---|---|
| **Learning and training** | | | |
| Staff retention rate generally | | 92% | 88% |
| Staff retention in R&D department | | 100% | 100% |
| Staff wellbeing rating (out of 100) | 1 | 94 | 91 |
| Staff undertaking NVQ training | 2 | 45% | 46% |
| **Internal business processes** | | | |
| % Revenue derived from new products | 3 | 35% | 25% |
| Money spent on research | | £500,000 | £480,000 |
| Lead time to introduce new projects | 4 | 160 days | 265 days |
| **Customers** | | | |
| Satisfaction – Own manufactured goods | 5 | 56% | 48% |
| Satisfaction – Bought in goods | 5 | 85% | 92% |
| Brand recognition | 6 | 65% | 45% |
| **Financial outlook** | | | |
| Gross profit margin % | | 28.4% | 31% |
| Operating profit margin % | | 6.3% | 5.8% |
| Inventory holding period | | 92 days | 126 days |
| Gearing | 7 | 16.6% | 12% |
| Average wage rate | | £21,000 | £21,000 |

**Notes**

1   This is assessed using a confidential staff questionnaire.  The rating is a weighted index based on a variety of factors including the degree staff feel "supported" and "valued".

2   National vocational qualifications (NVQs) are available in many fields including the AAT.

3   Any product that was introduced within the last 2 years falls under this category.

4   This is the time taken from concept to delivery of a new product.

5   This is assessed by customer survey.

6   This is assessed by independent external survey.

7   Gearing is measured as debt/(debt + equity).

(a) **Select the ONE correct observation about each aspect of business performance below.** (10 marks)

**Learning and training**

| | |
|---|---|
| People are leaving because they are not being educated and trained | |
| 100% staff retention is always a good thing | |
| Poor wage rises is probably at the heart of the staff wellbeing issue | |

**Internal business processes**

| | |
|---|---|
| The money being invested in research is being well spent | |
| The experience of the research team is coming through | |
| The efficiency of the research department is worsening | |

**Customers**

| | |
|---|---|
| Customers are showing increased dissatisfaction with SL Products | |
| Brand recognition matters as this could lead to higher sales | |
| SL Products should increase the proportion of products it manufactures itself, as it's cheaper that way | |

**Financial**

| | |
|---|---|
| There is scope to borrow more debt to increase the spend on research | |
| With productivity down there is no justification to increasing wages | |
| Despite the problems the profitability is improving | |

**General**

| | |
|---|---|
| The extra revenue from new products could be increasing the gross profit margin (%) | |
| As long as SL Products can sell its inventory, holding more doesn't matter | |
| Overheads are well under control | |

The Directors are debating whether the existing research team is a strength or a weakness of the business.

**(b)   Briefly outline 5 factors to consider when evaluating the idea that SL Products should stick with its existing research team and give them a 15% pay rise.                    (10 marks)**

| |
|---|
| 1 |
| 2 |
| 3 |
| 4 |
| 5 |

## Task 6 (15 marks)

The sales and dispatch system for SL Products has been documented as follows by Robert Utley the Warehouse manager of SL Products.

- Sales orders are normally placed through the website although occasionally customers will telephone in with queries and that can lead to orders being placed at that time.

- Online orders are automatically checked for stock availability and the online customer is warned if the item they want is out of stock on screen. No alternative is offered and the system cannot estimate when stock will arrive in the future.

- For telephone orders the SL Products staff note down the order details on a two part internal order form a copy of which is scanned and sent to the customer by email after the call. One copy of the order is then sent to the warehouse for stock checking and processing, the other copy is retained by customer service in case of follow up calls. The internal order forms are not pre-numbered but are given a number by one of the customer service staff after the call.

- The warehouse manager at the start of each day prints a daily pick list which is used to determine which orders get satisfied each day. This list is used to generate a dispatch note, which accompanies the goods when sent to the customer.

- Sales invoices are raised from a copy of the dispatch note and sent to the customer by email.

(a) **You are required to identify 5 weaknesses in the accounting procedures above indicating the effect of that weakness and recommending a change that you feel is needed to improve the system.** **(15 marks)**

> 1

2

3

4

5

# 2 Mock Exam Answers

## Task 1 (20 marks)

**(a)**

| | |
|---|:---:|
| The information is available to all shareholders | |
| The presentation is strictly governed by regulation | |
| They must be 100% accurate | ✓ |
| They must include a cash flow statement | |

Note: Accounting statements do not need to be 100% accurate; all accounts include estimates, which must be reasonable.

**(b)**

| | |
|---|:---:|
| A cheque was filled out for the wrong amount | No |
| A direct debit was missing for the cash book | Yes |
| A payment was entered in the cash book near to the year-end but the cheque was not sent out to the supplier | No |
| A Debtor made a payment on an invoice but deducted more discount than allowed and so paid less then needed | No |
| Interest charged on the account appeared only on the bank statement | Yes |

**(c)**

| | |
|---|:---:|
| A firewall assists in preventing the system from overheating | |
| A firewall will prevent employees inputting inaccurate data into the system | |
| A firewall prevents external people from accessing any part of the system | ✓ |
| A firewall prevents employees sharing copied data with unauthorised third parties | |

Note: Those people (including employees) that are internal and hence inside the firewall are free to make errors or copy data (unless prevented from doing so by other controls).

**(d)**

| | |
|---|---|
| Confidentiality | |
| Professional integrity | ✓ |
| Professional competence and due care | |

| | |
|---|---|
| Report your friend to the police immediately | |
| Decline the offer but say nothing to anyone else | |
| Decline the offer and report the incident to your line manager | ✓ |

Note: Your professional integrity is being threatened here. Your friend is breaking confidentiality rules amongst other things but YOU are not. You should decline the offer and report the incident to your line manager. You have no obligation to go to the police.

**(e)**

| | |
|---|---|
| The useful economic lives of assets is being understated | |
| An improvement to an asset has been written off as repairs | |
| A doubtful debt has been ignored in the provision calculation and written off instead | |
| The provision for warranty repairs has been ignored in the accounts | ✓ |

Note: Ignoring a provision will increase the reported profits. Understating useful lives will decrease profit as will writing off an improvement as a repair. Writing off a doubtful debt rather than providing for it in full is profit neutral.

**(f)**

| | |
|---|---|
| The amount of the closing monthly cash in hand | |
| The amount of the opening monthly cash in hand | |
| The amount of the closing monthly total of petty cash vouchers | ✓ |
| The amount of the total Imprest petty cash float | |

**(g)**

| | |
|---|---|
| It would increase the chances of fraud | |
| It would reduce the chances of fraud | ✓ |
| It would increase the administration overhead cost | |
| It would reduce the administration overhead cost | |

## Task 2 (15 marks)

**(a) Budget 20X2**

|  | £ |
|---|---|
| Material costs (W1) | 384,000 |
| Lease rental (W2) | 50,000 |
| Production royalty (W3) | 24,800 |

**Workings**

**(W1) Material costs**

These are simply a variable cost.

Budget = 336,000 × 48,000/42,000 = £384,000

Or

Past VC per unit is £336,000/42,000 units = £8 per unit

Budget is thus 48,000 × £8 = £384,000

**(W2) Lease rental costs**

These appear to be a fixed cost, so budget is simply the £50,000.

**(W3) Production royalty costs**

These seem to be semi-variable and so some high/low analysis is needed:

|  | Cost (£) | Production volume (Units) |
|---|---|---|
| 20X0 | 21,800 | 36,000 |
| 20X1 | 23,300 | 42,000 |
| Difference | 1,500 | 6,000 |

Variable cost per unit is = £1,500/6,000 = £0.25 per unit

Total cost = Variable cost + fixed cost

£23,300 = (42,000 × 0.25) + fixed cost

So Fixed cost element = £12,800

Consequently the budget is = £12,800 + (48,000 × 0.25) = £24,800

**(b)   Explanation of treatment of costs**

The material costs appear to be wholly variable.  This means that as the production volume increases so should the cost.  Since the budget volume is higher than the earlier years volumes the budget cost needs to reflect that.  Consequently I have increased the actual figure for 20X1 to reflect the higher volume in 20X2.  As instructed I have ignore any inflationary elements.

The lease rental cost is a fixed cost.  This means that regardless of any increase in volume the cost will remain at £50,000 pa.

The production royalty cost has both fixed and variable elements. I have used high/low analysis to isolate each element.  The budget is then made up of a fixed element equal to the 20X1 cost and a variable element which reflects the increased volume as explained above under material costs.

The way high/low works is by taking the difference between two cost figures and assuming that any difference is solely caused by volume differences and hence is the variable cost.

**(c)   Reasons for the lease rental cost changing in the future**

The business could take on more space or exit part of the premises. This would change the cost.  More space would require an increased spend and the fixed cost would step up to a higher level.

Lease rental payments can be subject to rent review every few years. These are often upward only reviews so that for the same space the business will pay more rent.

**(d)   Motivational aspects**

For variable costs, the level of production determines the level of spend.  Consequently if the actual production level is different from that budgeted then there will be an inherent inconsistency.  This can have motivational issues.

If the budget is based on lower production levels than was actually achieved then the budget figure will be unfairly lower than it should be.  This can be demotivating for managers, as an adverse variance may appear to be inevitable and indeed, unjust.  They may simply give up trying to control cost here, as they know it will be very difficult to meet the budget in this case.

If the budget is based on higher production levels than was actually achieved then the budget (if not flexed) will be very easy to achieve. This isn't motivating either, as managers know that very little effort may be required to achieve their target.

**KAPLAN** PUBLISHING

## Task 3 (15 marks)

| | Weakness | Effect of Weakness |
|---|---|---|
| 1 | The process by which employees swipe their clock cards is not supervised. | Colleagues could swipe individual employees in when in fact they are not present. This could lead to overpayment for work not done or hours not worked. |
| 2 | Temporary staff fall outside the normal appointment process and consequently any normal checks might not be carried out. | Inappropriate employees could be employed leading to disruptive behaviour or poor standard of work.<br><br>Favouritism could result meaning that any equal opportunity objective might not be met. |
| 3 | Temporary staff are paid in cash by the production director. | The wrong amount could be paid, without proper accounting of deductions for tax and NIC.<br><br>Equally the rate of pay could be wrong meaning the company could pay too much for the level of work undertaken. |
| 4 | There is a general lack of segregation of duties in the system, which can undermine any controls in place. | Poor segregation of duties places too much responsibility and power in one person's hands. Abuse of that position is possible, which can result in a large range of errors, deliberate or otherwise.<br><br>For example fictitious employees can be created and paid. |
| 5 | The payroll clerk requires no proof of identity or signature of receipt for cash wages. | Wages could be given to the wrong people or retained by the payroll clerk falsely. |

## Task 4 (15 marks)

### (a) Price

| | |
|---|---|
| £20 to match the E-Puff | |
| £7 to match the E-Smoke | |
| £15 to match the E-Vap | ✓ |
| £14 to match the industry average price | |

Note: The correct price is £15 as target costing is based on a likely competitive product.

### (b) Prime cost

| | |
|---|---|
| £5.20 | ✓ |
| £5.60 | |
| £13.20 | |
| £13.60 | |

**Working:**

| | |
|---|---|
| Material cost (£4.00 less 10%) | £3.60 |
| Labour cost (6/60 × £16/hr) | £1.60 |
| | £5.20 |

### (c) Cost gap

| | £ |
|---|---|
| Selling price | 15.00 |
| Less: desired margin(15% × 15.00) | 2.25 |
| Target cost | 12.75 |
| Actual cost expected (3.60 + 1.60 + 8.00) | 13.20 |
| Cost gap | 0.45 |

### (d) Value engineering

Value engineering is a process by which the value added and non-value costs are first identified as part of a cost reduction exercise.

A value added cost is one which the end user or customer "values". For example in SL Products, an electronic product would probably need to be reliable and costs that contribute to that would be defined as value adding. This makes them poor targets for cost reduction as it risks reducing the value to the customer of the product.

Non-value adding costs (on the other hand) can be targeted for cost reduction more readily as the customer does not value them. This might include stock holding costs or staff welfare costs.

The cost gap could be removed by focussing on any non-value adding costs within materials, labour or overhead.

Within material it may be possible to find an alternate supplier that could provide equal quality for reduced cost.

Within labour, it might be possible to further speed up the process (speed of process is likely to be non-value added).

Overheads would need to be analysed to identify any non-value adding activity included. Property location is often non-value added and so some rent saving might be possible.

## Task 5 (20 marks)

### (a) Learning and training

| | |
|---|---|
| People are leaving because they are not being educated and trained | |
| 100% staff retention is always a good thing | |
| Poor wage rises is probably at the heart of the staff wellbeing issue | ✓ |

Note: The lack of wage rises is probably the most likely reason for poor wellbeing issue. Training proportions are up slightly and 100% staff retention means that departments are not being subjected to new ideas from new people and this is not always a good thing.

### Internal business processes

| | |
|---|---|
| The money being invested in research is being well spent | |
| The experience of the research team is coming through | |
| The efficiency of the research department is worsening | ✓ |

Note: The efficiency of the research department is indeed worsening with fewer new products and those are taking longer to come to market after concept. The money being spent on research has resulted in proportionately less revenue from new products, not more. There is no evidence that the experience of the research department is benefitting SL Products.

### Customers

| | |
|---|---|
| Customers are showing increased dissatisfaction with SL Products | |
| Brand recognition matters as this could lead to higher sales | ✓ |
| SL Products should increase the proportion of products it manufactures itself, as it's cheaper that way | |

Note: Brand recognition is important and could lead to more sales. Customer satisfaction data is giving a mixed message. There is no evidence that manufacturing in-house is cheaper (although it could be) and besides the customers do not appear to prefer SL's own manufactured products.

### Financial

| | |
|---|---|
| There is scope to borrow more debt to increase the spend on research | ✓ |
| With productivity down there is no justification to increasing wages | |
| Despite the problems the profitability is improving | |

Note: The debt ratio is down so there might be debt-borrowing capacity and research spending seems at least potentially justifiable. Increasing wages can be motivating and hence justified. Profitability is not improving as the operating profit margin is down.

### General

| | |
|---|---|
| The extra revenue from new products could be increasing the gross profit margin | ✓ |
| As long as SL Products can sell its inventory, holding more doesn't matter | |
| Overheads are well under control | |

Note: It is possible that the new products are being sold at higher margins as GP% is up. Holding more inventory results in holding costs (storage for example) and although products might be sellable, SL Products might have to reduce prices to do so in the technological market it operates in. Overheads are rising as indicated by the lowering of operating profit margin despite a rising gross profit margin.

### (b) Factors to consider

| | |
|---|---|
| 1 | The cost. 15% is a significant increase and SL Products should consider if it is affordable. |
| 2 | The effectiveness. The assumption is that increasing wages will increase output. This might not be the case. Research depends on having good ideas and just because someone is earning more money does not mean that they are more imaginative. |
| 3 | Effect on other staff. A large increase for one group without a corresponding increase for others can be divisive and de-motivational. |
| 4 | New staff might be needed to bring in fresh ideas. On the other hand, an increased wage level might attract good new people. |
| 5 | Research is important to SL Products and increasing the wages in this key area might be seen to be sensible. |

## Task 6 (15 marks)

| Weakness and effect | Recommendation |
|---|---|
| Inventory availability is not checked on telephone orders prior to acceptance.<br><br>This could lead to disappointed customers being subsequently informed that their order cannot be fulfilled on the originally intended schedule.<br><br>Customers may cancel their order and go elsewhere. | The inventory availability should be checked at the time of the customer's order.<br><br>If inventory is not available then it would be better if a due date could be given or alternative products be suggested. |
| Sales order forms are not pre-numbered.<br><br>Duplicate numbers could be created by accident leading to confusion on subsequent query.<br><br>Orders could also be lost. | Pre-numbered sales order forms should be acquired and used. This could be done electronically.<br><br>A sequential check could be carried out on a weekly basis to make sure there are no duplications or omissions. |
| The despatch note is generated from the pick list and not the stock actually picked.<br><br>It is possible that the wrong stock is picked or the stock is not available on the day of picking. | The despatch note should be derived from the stock actually picked.<br><br>This can be compared to the pick list to identify anomalies and the customer can then be contacted as necessary. |
| The sales invoices are generated from the pick list and not necessarily the stock that was actually picked.<br><br>This could lead to invoice errors, non-payment and upset customers. | The sales invoices should be raised to reflect the goods actually sent. |
| The customer does not sign for dispatched goods on delivery.<br><br>This can lead to disputes in relation to what was actually delivered (particularly given the problem above). | All despatch notes should be signed as agreed by the customer at the time of delivery.<br><br>Anomalies should be noted and followed up immediately. |

# Appendix 1: Financial Statements of Limited Companies

## Introduction

This chapter recaps the key aspects of the underlying Financial Statements of Limited Companies Unit.

| UNIT LEARNING OBJECTIVES STILL RELEVANT FOR THE SYNOPTIC ASSESSMENT | |
| --- | --- |
| LO1 | Demonstrate an understanding of the reporting frameworks and ethical principles that underpin financial reporting |
| LO5 | Interpret financial statements using ratio analysis |

## LO1 — Demonstrate an understanding of the reporting frameworks and ethical principles that underpin financial reporting

### Explain the regulatory framework that underpins financial reporting

#### Sources of regulation

- Legal regulation – The Companies Act 2006.
- The regulatory framework – The IFRS Foundation and supporting regulatory bodies.
- Others specific to types of NFP organisations – e.g. charities

#### IFRS Foundation

- The IFRS Foundation
- The International Accounting Standards Board
- The IFRS Interpretations Committee (IFRS IC)
- The IFRS Advisory Council (IFRS AC)

### Explain the International Accounting Standards Board (IASB) Conceptual Framework that underpins financial reporting

#### The objective of financial statements

- To provide information about position, performance and changes that is useful to a range of users.

#### Underlying assumptions

- Going concern
- Accruals

#### Qualitative characteristics

- Relevance
- Faithful representation
- Comparability
- Verifiability
- Timeliness
- Understandability

### The elements

- Assets, liabilities, equity, income and expenses.
- Recognition of the elements if criteria is met.
- Measurement of the elements using: historical cost, current cost, realisable value or present value.

### Discuss the ethical principles that underpin financial reporting in accordance with the AAT Code of Professional Ethics

- The five key principles are:
  - integrity
  - objectivity
  - professional competence and due care
  - confidentiality and
  - professional behaviour.
- The threats to accountant objectivity are:
  - self-interest
  - advocacy
  - familiarity
  - self-review and
  - intimidation.
- Safeguards can eliminate ethical threats or reduce them to an acceptable level.

## LO5 Interpret financial statements using ratio analysis

## Calculate ratios with regard to profitability, liquidity, efficient use of resources and financial position

### Profitability ratios

$$\text{Return on capital employed} = \frac{\text{Operating profit}}{\text{Total equity + non-current liabilities}} \times 100\%$$

$$\text{Return on shareholders' funds} = \frac{\text{Profit after tax}}{\text{Total equity}} \times 100\%$$

$$\text{Gross profit percentage} = \frac{\text{Gross profit}}{\text{Revenue}} \times 100\%$$

$$\text{Expense/revenue percentage} = \frac{\text{Specified expense}}{\text{Revenue}} \times 100\%$$

$$\text{Operating profit percentage} = \frac{\text{Profit from operations}}{\text{Revenue}} \times 100\%$$

### Liquidity ratios

$$\text{Current ratio} = \frac{\text{Current assets}}{\text{Current liabilities}} : 1$$

$$\text{Quick ratio or 'acid test' ratio} = \frac{\text{Current assets - inventories}}{\text{Current liabilities}} : 1$$

### Efficiency ratios

$$\text{Inventory turnover} = \frac{\text{Cost of sales}}{\text{Inventories}} = \text{X times}$$

$$\text{Inventory turnover (days)} = \frac{\text{Inventories}}{\text{Cost of sales}} \times 365 \text{ days}$$

$$\text{Receivables collection period} = \frac{\text{Trade receivables}}{\text{Revenue}} \times 365 \text{ days}$$

$$\text{Payables payment period} = \frac{\text{Trade payables}}{\text{Cost of sales}} \times 365 \text{ days}$$

Working capital cycle (days)
= Inventory days + receivables days – payables days

$$\text{Asset turnover (net assets)} = \frac{\text{Revenue}}{\text{Total assets - current liabilities}} = \text{X times}$$

### Financial position ratios

$$\text{Interest cover} = \frac{\text{Profit from operations}}{\text{Finance costs}} = \text{X times}$$

$$\text{Gearing} = \frac{\text{Non-current liabilities}}{\text{Equity + non-current liabilities}} \times 100$$

**Appraise the relationship between elements of the financial statements with regard to profitability, liquidity, efficient use of resources and financial position, by means of ratio analysis**

Points to consider:

- You need two ratios calculated on a consistent basis to make a comparison.

- One company can be compared over two time periods.

- Budget or forecast results can be compared with actual results.

- Financial performance and position of two companies can be compared.

- Has financial performance or position improved or deteriorated? (e.g. from the earlier year to the later year, or which company has the better ratio?).

- Try to consider **why** a specific ratio has improved or deteriorated.

- Perhaps use the ratio formula to give you guidance – think about the top part (numerator) and bottom part (denominator) of the ratio separately – why may each figure have increased or decreased?

- Does the task data give any clues? (e.g. does it tell you what has happened to the company or what it is doing? This may help to explain the ratios.

## Effectively present an analysis with recommendations

- Present key findings – which ratios are most important and why?

- Suggest how ratios could be improved and the potential consequences of doing so.

- Explain the limitations of ratio analysis
  - lack of suitable comparators
  - can be distorted – e.g. seasonal trade
  - calculation issues – e.g. getting required information.

A2:1

# Appendix 2: Management accounting: Budgeting

## Introduction

This chapter recaps the key aspects of the underlying Management Accounting: Budgeting Unit.

| UNIT LEARNING OBJECTIVES STILL RELEVANT FOR THE SYNOPTIC ASSESSMENT |
| --- |
| LO3 Demonstrate how budgeting can improve organisational performance |

## LO3 Demonstrate how budgeting can improve organisational performance

### Discuss how budgeting can promote effective, ethical and focused management

- Budgetary targets will motivate managers if
  - Targets are seen as fair
  - Targets are stretching but achievable
  - Targets only relate to factors under managers' control
  - Targets are matched to managers' responsibilities
  - Target setting is built on honesty and transparency.

- Targets need to be set to ensure goal congruence
  - Short term targets must be coordinated with each other and longer term goals
  - Excessive pressure to hit targets may result in short termism/ cutting corners/misreporting/etc.

- Participation in target setting can result in more realistic targets and better ownership of them BUT may result in budget padding/slack.

- Linking remuneration to results can boost motivation, provided
  - Targets are seen to be realistic and achievable
  - The extra remuneration is seen to be worth the effort.

- Financial targets are generally easier to manipulate.

### Discuss the use of budgeting for planning, coordinating, authorising and cost control

- **Planning** – budgeting forces management to look ahead, set targets, anticipate problems and give the organisation direction.

- **Co-ordination** – budgeting helps co-ordinate the different activities of the business and to ensure that they are in harmony with each other.

- **Authorisation** – budgets act as authority to spend.

- **Control** – the budget provides the plan against which actual results can be compared, for example using variances. This facilitates "management by exception".

## Break a budget down into control periods

- The time period for which a budget is prepared and used is called the budget period. It can be any length to suit management purposes but it is usually one year.

- Each budget period can be subdivided into control periods, of varying lengths, depending on the level of control which management wishes to exercise. The usual length of a control period is one month.

## Recommend appropriate performance measures to support budgetary control

- Using a mixture of financial and non-financial measures helps avoid many of the above problems relating to budgeting.

- The following table shows which measures would be suitable for each type of centre:

|  | Cost centre | Profit centre | Investment centre |
|---|---|---|---|
| Variance analysis | ✓ | ✓ | ✓ |
| Gross revenue |  | ✓ | ✓ |
| Contribution |  | ✓ | ✓ |
| Gross/Net margin |  | ✓ | ✓ |
| ROCE |  |  | ✓ |

- Non-financial measures are often grouped together into the broad headings of productivity or quality, for example measurements of resource utilisation or customer satisfaction.

## Integrate standard costing into budgetary control

- Key aspect of budgetary control is comparing actual v budget to identify areas for further investigation.

- Standard costs are often a vital element of budgeting – what should have happened.

- Standard costing facilitates splitting variances into further detail.

## Prepare and explain a flexed budget

- Variances should involve comparing actual v flexed budget.
- Budgets are flexed to actual volumes.
- May have to watch out for split between fixed and variable costs.

## Calculate variances between budget and actual income and expenditure

- RTQ to see if you need variances in absolute terms or %.
- Materials – price and usage.
- Labour – rate, efficiency (idle time).
- May have to do "backwards variances"

## Review and revise budgets to reflect changing circumstances

Budgets may be revised

- To reflect changes in operating conditions
- To correct errors in the original budget
- To use improved/updated standards
- To make targets easier/harder.

**KAPLAN** PUBLISHING

# Appendix 3: Management accounting: Decision and control

## Introduction

This chapter recaps the key aspects of the underlying Management Accounting: Decision and Control unit.

| UNIT LEARNING OBJECTIVES STILL RELEVANT FOR THE SYNOPTIC ASSESSMENT |
|---|
| LO1 Analyse a range of costing techniques to support the management accounting function of an organisation |
| LO2 Calculate and use standard costing to improve performance |
| LO4 Use appropriate financial and non-financial performance techniques to aid decision making |
| LO5 Evaluate a range of cost management techniques to enhance value and aid decision making |

## LO1 Analyse a range of costing techniques to support the management accounting function of an organisation

**Distinguish between different cost classifications and evaluate their use in a management accounting function**

| Purpose | Classification |
|---|---|
| Financial accounts | By function – Cost of sales, distribution costs, administrative expenses |
| Cost control | By element – materials, labour, other expenses |
| Cost accounting | By relationship to cost units – direct, indirect |
| Budgeting, decision making | By behaviour – fixed, variable |

**Discriminate between and use marginal costing and absorption costing techniques**

- **Key difference – inventory valuation**

| Absorption costing | Marginal costing |
|---|---|
| Inventory is valued at the full production cost (fixed and variable production costs) | Inventory is valued at the variable production cost only |

| Note: Differences in profit | |
|---|---|
| | £ |
| Absorption costing profit | X |
| Less: Change in inventory × OAR | +/–X |
| | |
| Marginal costing profit | X |

- **Format of income statement/profit and loss**

| Absorption costing | Marginal costing |
|---|---|
| Sales – cost of sales = gross profit | Sales – all variable costs = contribution |
| Costs are split based on function – production or non-production | Costs are split based on behaviour – variable or fixed |
| Non-production overheads are deducted after gross profit | Variable non-production overheads are excluded from the valuation of inventory but are deducted before contribution |
| Only non-production costs are period costs | All fixed costs are period costs |

- **Usefulness**

| Absorption costing | Marginal costing |
|---|---|
| Financial reporting | Decision making – focus on contribution |

# Recognise and calculate measures of profitability and contribution

## Relevant costing

- For any decision the relevant costs are future incremental cash flows

- In many questions, this is just

  Contribution = selling price – all variable costs

## CVP analysis

- Focus on contribution

- Breakeven point (units) = $\dfrac{\text{Fixed costs}}{\text{Contribution per unit}}$

- Margin of safety = (budgeted sales – BEP), usually given as a %

- Sales required to hit target profit (units) = $\dfrac{\text{Fixed costs + Target profit}}{\text{Contribution per unit}}$

- Profit/volume ratio = C/S ratio = $\dfrac{\text{Contribution}}{\text{Selling price}}$

- Breakeven point (£) = $\dfrac{\text{Fixed costs}}{\text{C/S ratio}}$

### Limiting factor analysis

1   Identify scarce resource

2   Calculate contribution per unit

3   Calculate contribution per scarce resource

4   Rank options and allocate scarce resource based on ranking.

5   Opportunity cost of scarce resource = normal cost + contribution

## LO2 Calculate and use standard costing to improve performance

### Discuss how standard costing can aid the planning and control of an organisation

### Advantages

*   Planning – predetermined standards make the preparation of forecasts and budgets much easier.

*   Control – Control is primarily exercised through the comparison of standard and actual results, and the isolation of variances.

*   Motivation – if the standards are perceived to be attainable, then they will serve to motivate the employees concerned.

*   Reporting – a standard costing bookkeeping system can be set up that will fulfil all requirements, for both internal and external reporting.

*   Cost accounting – recording of stock issues is simplified, as it is done at the standard price.

### Disadvantages

*   Costly to set up and maintain, and

*   Need to keep standards up to date.

### Types of standard

| Ideal | Based on perfect working conditions | Impossible to achieve, resulting in adverse variances |
|---|---|---|
| Basic | Unchanged over many years | May be out of date, so could be too hard or too easy? |
| Current | Based on current working conditions | Not challenging enough? |
| Attainable | Based on efficient (but not perfect) conditions | Provide realistic but challenging target |

## Calculate standard costing variances

### Materials variances

| | | |
|---|---|---|
| Actual quantity | × Actual rate | ⎫ Price variance |
| Actual quantity | × Standard rate | ⎬ |
| Standard quantity for actual production | × Standard rate | ⎭ Usage variance |

### Labour variances

| | | |
|---|---|---|
| Actual hours paid | × Actual rate | ⎫ Rate variance |
| Actual hours paid | × Standard rate | ⎬ Idle time variance |
| Actual hours worked | × Standard rate | ⎭ Efficiency variance |
| Standard hours for actual production | × Standard rate | |

### Variable OH variances

| | | |
|---|---|---|
| Actual hours worked | × Actual rate | ⎫ Expenditure variance |
| Actual hours worked | × Standard rate | ⎬ Efficiency variance |
| Standard hours for actual production | × Standard rate | ⎭ |

### Fixed OH variances (Absorption costing)

| | | |
|---|---|---|
| Actual expenditure | × Actual rate | ⎫ Expenditure variance |
| Budget expenditure | × Standard rate | ⎬ Volume variance |
| Standard hours for actual production | × Standard rate | ⎭ |

### Fixed OH variances (Marginal costing)

| | | |
|---|---|---|
| Actual cost | | ⎫ Expenditure variance |
| Budget cost | | ⎭ |

## Prepare and reconcile standard costing operating statements

Absorption costing:

| | | Adverse £ | Favourable £ | £ |
|---|---|---|---|---|
| Flexed budgeted/standard absorption cost of actual production (7,800 units × £272) | | | | 2,121,600 |
| **Cost variances** | | *Adverse* | *Favourable* | |
| Materials | price | | 45,000 | |
| | usage | 240,000 | | |
| Labour | rate of pay | 11,000 | | |
| | efficiency | 49,200 | | |
| Variable overheads | expenditure | | 43,500 | |
| | efficiency | 32,800 | | |
| Fixed overheads variance | expenditure | | 4,000 | |
| | volume | | 3,600 | |
| Total variances | | 333,000 | 96,100 | 236,900 A |
| Actual cost (per question) | | | | 2,358,500 |

Marginal costing:

| | | Adverse £ | Favourable £ | £ |
|---|---|---|---|---|
| Budgeted marginal cost (7,800 × £260) | | | | 2,028,000 |
| Add budgeted fixed overhead | | | | 90,000 |
| **Cost variances** | | *Adverse* | *Favourable* | |
| Materials | price | | 45,000 | |
| | usage | 240,000 | | |
| Labour | rate of pay | 11,000 | | |
| | efficiency | 49,200 | | |
| Variable overheads | expenditure | | 43,500 | |
| | efficiency | 32,800 | | |
| | | 333,000 | 88,500 | 244,500 |
| | | | | 2,362,500 |
| Fixed overheads variance | expenditure | | 4,000 | (4,000) |
| Actual cost (per question) | | | | 2,358,500 |

**Analyse and present effectively a report to management based on standard costing information**

Try to discuss

- Causes of variances using information in the scenario (e.g. learning)
- Who is responsible? Are variances controllable or uncontrollable?
- What action should be taken?

## LO4 — Use appropriate financial and non-financial performance techniques to aid decision making

**Identify and calculate key financial and non-financial performance indicators**

**Profitability ratios**

$$\text{Gross profit margin} = \frac{\text{Gross profit}}{\text{Turnover}} \times 100\%$$

$$\text{Operating profit margin} = \frac{\text{Operating profit}}{\text{Turnover}} \times 100\%$$

$$\text{Net profit margin} = \frac{\text{Net profit}}{\text{Turnover}} \times 100\%$$

$$\text{Return on capital employed} = \frac{\text{Operating profit (or profit before interest and tax)}}{\text{Capital employed}} \times 100\%$$

$$\text{Asset turnover} = \frac{\text{Turnover}}{\text{Capital employed}}$$

$$\text{Distribution costs as a \% of turnover} = \frac{\text{Distribution costs}}{\text{Turnover}} \times 100\%$$

$$\text{Administration costs as a \% of turnover} = \frac{\text{Administration costs}}{\text{Turnover}} \times 100\%$$

**Liquidity ratios**

$$\text{Current ratio} = \frac{\text{Current assets}}{\text{Current liabilities}}$$

$$\text{Quick ratio/Acid test} = \frac{\text{Current assets (excluding inventory)}}{\text{Current liabilities}}$$

$$\text{Inventory days} = \frac{\text{Inventory}}{\text{Cost of sales}} \times 365 \text{ (days) or 12 (months)}$$

$$\text{Receivable days} = \frac{\text{Receivables}}{\text{Turnover}} \times 365 \text{ (days) or 12 (months)}$$

$$\text{Payable days} = \frac{\text{Payables}}{\text{Purchases}} \times 365 \text{ (days) or 12 (months)}$$

**Investor ratios**

$$\text{Gearing} = \frac{\text{Debt}}{\text{Equity}} \times 100\% \text{ or } \frac{\text{Debt}}{\text{Debt + Equity}} \times 100\%$$

$$\text{Interest cover} = \frac{\text{Profit before interest}}{\text{Interest}}$$

**Non-financial performance indicators**

**The balanced scorecard**

A balanced scorecard for a company would be constructed by considering four perspectives:

- Financial – how do we create value for our shareholders?

- Customer – what is it about us that customers value?

- Internal – what processes must we excel at to achieve our financial and customer objectives?

- Innovation and learning – how can we continue to improve and create future value?

Within each of these categories a company should seek to identify a series of **critical success factors** and **key performance indicators**.

## Evaluate key financial and non-financial performance indicators

Consider the following:

- What the performance indicator means.

- How the various elements of the indicator affect its calculation.

- How some performance indicators interrelate with each other.

- How proposed actions may affect the indicator.

- What actions could be taken to improve the indicator.

- How lack of goal congruence can affect the overall business objectives when managers are attempting to maximise a given indicator.

- How ethical and commercial considerations can affect the behaviour of managers aiming to achieve a target indicator.

**KAPLAN** PUBLISHING

## Make recommendations using decision-making techniques

See "Recognise and calculate measures of profitability and contribution" above.

## Make recommendations and effectively communicate to management based on analysis

- Use the information in the question to show how analysis and calculations lead to recommendations.

- Use the analysis to make reasoned recommendations and communicate them effectively.

## LO5 Evaluate a range of cost management techniques to enhance value and aid decision making

## Use life cycle cost to aid decision making

### Idea

Lifecycle costing

- Is the profiling of cost over a product's life, including the pre-production stage.

- Tracks and accumulates the actual costs and revenues attributable to each product from inception to abandonment.

- Enables a product's true profitability to be determined at the end of its economic life.

### Calculation

- Calculation can be discounted or non-discounted.

### Interpretation

- If all costs cannot be recovered, it would not be wise to produce the product or service.

- Life-cycle costing allows an analysis of business function interrelationships, e.g. a decision towards lower R&D costs may lead to higher customer service costs in the future.

- Life-cycle costing reinforces the importance of tight control over locked-in costs, such as R&D in the development stage.

## Use target costing to aid decision making

- Target cost = expected selling price – target profit.
- Value analysis used to help achieve target cost.

## Calculate activity based costing (ABC) information

There are five steps to calculating an activity based cost.

1 Identify activities.

2 Estimate cost pools.

3 Identify cost drivers.

4 Calculate cost driver rate = The total in the cost pool divided by the total of the cost drivers.

5 Charge overheads to products via cost driver rates.

## Evaluate the commercial factors that underpin the life cycle of a product

**Typical lifecycle**

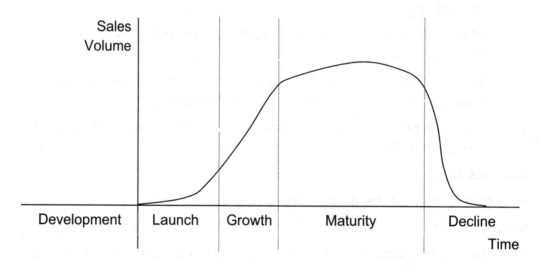

## Implications

- Scales of costs change throughout the product life cycle – production (e.g. economies of scale, mechanisation), R&D, marketing.
- Costs can switch between variable and fixed through the stages of the product life cycle.

## Take account of ethical considerations throughout the decision-making process

### Issues include

- How ethical considerations can be included in the design of a product and packaging in order to promote good corporate citizenship.

- How ethical considerations can be included in the value analysis/engineering of a product in order to promote good corporate citizenship.

- How ethical considerations can be included in the achievement of goal congruence of an organisation.

# INDEX